Success
as a Mediator
FOR
DUMMIES®

by Victoria Pynchon and Joe Kraynak

WILEY

John Wiley & Sons, Inc.

Success as a Mediator For Dummies®

Published by
John Wiley & Sons, Inc.
111 River St.
Hoboken, NJ 07030-5774
www.wiley.com

WILEY

About the Authors

Victoria Pynchon is a mediator, author, speaker, negotiation trainer, consultant, and attorney with 25 years of experience in commercial litigation practice. She's the co-founder of She Negotiates Training and Consulting with her business partner, Lisa Gates. A graduate of the University of California, San Diego, Victoria received her Juris Doctor degree from UC Davis School of Law (King Hall) and her Master of Laws degree in dispute resolution from the internationally acclaimed Straus Institute at the Pepperdine University School of Law.

Since earning her LL.M, she has served the mediation community as a member of the California State Bar's Standing Committee on Alternative Dispute Resolution, as a board member of the Southern California Mediation Association, as chair of the ADR Committee of the Women Lawyers Association of Los Angeles, and as chair of the Federal Bar Association's ADR Section.

Currently, she mediates and arbitrates complex commercial disputes with ADR Services, Inc., in Century City and the American Arbitration Association in downtown Los Angeles. She continues to serve as a Party Select Panel Mediator for the Los Angeles Superior Court and as a settlement officer with the U.S. District Court for the Central District of California. Victoria has taught deposition and trial practice for the National Institute of Trial Advocacy for more than a dozen years, business law to undergraduates at California State University at Northridge, and Employment ADR at the Straus Institute. She is a frequent speaker and lecturer at law firms, non-profit organizations, universities, and in-house legal departments.

Victoria is also a prolific writer and author of *The Grownups' ABCs of Conflict Resolution.* She writes the thrice-weekly *She Negotiates* blog at ForbesWoman and is a contributor to Forbes's *On the Docket* legal blog.

Joe Kraynak is a professional writer who specializes in teaming up with experts in various fields to produce top-notch trade publications. Joe has coauthored numerous *For Dummies* titles, including *Flipping Houses For Dummies, Bipolar Disorder For Dummies,* and *Food Allergies For Dummies.* For more about Joe, visit JoeKraynak.com.

Dedication

To my husband, Stephen N. Goldberg.

Authors' Acknowledgments

Thanks to our agent, Susan Lee Cohen of the Riverside Literary Agency, and to acquisitions editor Tracy Boggier and assistant editor David Lutton of Wiley, who ironed out all the preliminary details to make this book possible.

Heike Baird, our project editor, deserves a loud cheer for serving as a gifted and patient collaborator and editor — shuffling chapters back and forth, shepherding the text and graphics through production, making sure any technical issues were properly resolved, and serving as the unofficial quality control manager. Copy editor Todd Lothery earns the editor of the year award for ferreting out our typos, misspellings, grammatical errors, and other language foe paws (or is it faux pas?), in addition to assisting Heike as reader advocate. We also tip our hat to the production crew for doing such an outstanding job of transforming our text and graphics into such an attractive book.

This book could not have been written without the help of my many ADR teachers, mentors, and sponsors, most particularly attorney, mediator, author, and founder of Mediators Beyond Borders, Ken Cloke; University of Missouri School of Law Professor Richard Reuben; the co-directors of the Straus Institute, Peter Robinson and Tom Stipanowich; Pepperdine University School of Law Negotiation Professor Maureen Weston; and Straus Institute Adjunct Professor, Rev. Brian Cox, author of *Faith-Based Reconciliation: A Moral Vision That Transforms People and Societies*.

The mediation bloggers from whom I learned so much also deserve mention, particularly those who continue to inform my practice, most particularly Diane Levin of *The Mediation Channel*, Tammy Lenski of *Conflict Zen* and *Making Mediation Your Day Job*, John DeGroote of *Settlement Perspectives*, Stephanie West Allen of *Idealawg* and *Brains on Purpose*, and New York City detective and master mediator Jeff Thompson, who blogs at *Enjoy Mediation* and the *ADRHub*.

Others who have contributed directly and indirectly to the material contained in these pages include Lee Jay Berman, founder of the American Institute of Mediation; Jacob Ruytenbeek at PaperChace; Alexander Williams, III, Los Angeles Superior Court Judge (Ret.); Justice Victoria Chaney of the California Court of Appeals, Second District, and commercial arbitrator and mediator, Deborah Rothman who introduced me to the Fabulous Women Neutrals of Los Angeles who know who they are and how much they mean to my evolving practice.

I might have begun the writing of this book but I never would have finished it were it not for the writing skill, generosity, patience, quick wit, and organizational abilities of my co-author Joe Kraynak.

James Melamed, founder of Mediate.com; Kevin O'Keefe, founder of LexBlog; Caroline Howard and Kai Falkenberg at Forbes.com; my first publisher Ray Sobol, formerly of *Janis* and *Reason Press;* and the many hardworking people who manage to get the *Los Angeles Daily Journal* published every working day of the year, have all contributed to my still nascent writing career.

Lucie Barron, founder of ADR Services, Inc., deserves special praise not only for nurturing my career as a mediator by putting me on her esteemed panel of ADR providers but also for driving business my way whenever possible. Mike Powell of the American Arbitration Association has also been both mentor and sponsor for my work as an arbitrator to whom I owe more than he knows. Cathy Scott, true crime writer and lifelong friend, also deserves thanks for her undying support and inspiration.

Finally, I thank the friends and family who have given up hundreds of hours of my time that should have been devoted to nurturing those relationships. They certainly know who they are, but it would be thoughtless of me not to mention those nearest and dearest to me — my best friend and soul sister, Dr. Anne LaBorde, whose spirit and wisdom animates everything I do; my husband, attorney Stephen N. Goldberg, who continues laboring in the adversarial garden so that I can make what little contribution I can make to the consensual resolution of disputes; and my adult stepchildren, attorney Adam S. Goldberg and Julia Goldberg, Manager, Deloitte Consulting (Life Sciences and Health Care), both of whom have not only given me concrete reason to make the world a better place, but have also taught me how to lose gracefully at any board game ever invented.

Publisher's Acknowledgments

We're proud of this book; please send us your comments at http://dummies.custhelp.com. For other comments, please contact our Customer Care Department within the U.S. at 877-762-2974, outside the U.S. at 317-572-3993, or fax 317-572-4002.

Some of the people who helped bring this book to market include the following:

Acquisitions, Editorial, and Vertical Websites

Project Editor: Heike Baird

Acquisitions Editor: Tracy Boggier

Copy Editor: Todd Lothery

Assistant Editor: David Lutton

Editorial Program Coordinator: Joe Niesen

Technical Editor: Diane J. Levin

Senior Editorial Manager: Jennifer Ehrlich

Editorial Assistants: Rachelle S. Amick, Alexa Koschier

Art Coordinator: Alicia B. South

Cover Photos: © iStockphoto.com / Slavoljub Pantelic

Cartoons: Rich Tennant (www.the5thwave.com)

Composition Services

Project Coordinator: Sheree Montgomery

Layout and Graphics: Amy Hassos, Andrea Hornberger, Sennett Vaughan Johnson, Corrie Niehaus, Lavonne Roberts

Proofreaders: Lindsay Amones, Linda Seifert

Indexer: Cheryl Duksta

Publishing and Editorial for Consumer Dummies

Kathleen Nebenhaus, Vice President and Executive Publisher

Kristin Ferguson-Wagstaffe, Product Development Director

Ensley Eikenburg, Associate Publisher, Travel

Kelly Regan, Editorial Director, Travel

Publishing for Technology Dummies

Andy Cummings, Vice President and Publisher

Composition Services

Debbie Stailey, Director of Composition Services

Contents at a Glance

Table of Contents

Introduction

Welcome to the theory, practice, and business of mediation. Whether you've just taken your first 28-hour mediation course or completed your LL.M in dispute resolution, this book is your guide, reminder, resource, cheat sheet, and magic talisman to jump-start a new career or revive a flagging one.

If you, like me, have been foolhardy enough to launch yourself into a new career in an uncertain economic climate; if you don't care how flooded with mediators the market supposedly is; if you believe you've been called to this work by your better angels; and if you could use the companionship of like-minded people and advice from battle-scarred survivors who are flourishing in their practices, you've come to the right place.

Within these pages you'll find something I never did — easy-to-follow, comprehensive, field-tested principles and practices that set the standard all mediators should strive to meet. Because this profession is an accidental one, having grown out of informal neighborhood justice centers and formal courtroom practices, opinions about what "true" mediation practice really is are as plentiful as recipes for turkey stuffing.

I made my own way to mediation through the adversarial system, in which mediators focus on a single issue (usually money) and negotiate with each party in separate caucus, shuttling offers and counteroffers back and forth until the parties hammer out a deal. This approach remains the method of choice, at least in the Los Angeles market. Dissatisfied with the old settlement conference model in which judges lower everyone's expectations before coercing them into settlements that satisfy no one, I returned to school to learn as much as I possibly could about collaborative models, in which the mediator teams up with the parties to develop solutions (often beyond the confines of money) to satisfy each party's interests.

In short, I've studied and practiced all the approaches to mediation — directive, evaluative, facilitative, and transformative — and I know the strengths and weaknesses of each model. I'm also well-versed on the tools of the trade — the skills and techniques proven to be most effective in reopening the channels of communication, identifying issues and interests, engaging with the parties in collaborative problem-solving, and breaking through the parties' inevitable impasse. I fill you in on all these facets of mediation in this book.

In addition, I present everything you need to know to turn your passion into a good-paying profession. You discover when and how to launch your mediation business, how to market yourself and your services, and how to network with clients and colleagues to generate business.

As you begin your own journey to success as a mediator, never abandon hope that your clients can, with your assistance, find their own way to resolution. Always create for your clients a safe space in which to explore their dispute, no matter how hostile they may be and how bleak the outlook. Listen for the cry for help buried deep within every accusation. Know that accountability, recognition, apology, forgiveness, amends, and reconciliation are the natural processes of humankind. If it weren't so, competing needs would have doomed the human race to extinction long before humans started scratching numbers and letters on stone tablets.

Remember that *you* are the magic, that the entirety of your mindful experience is the technique, and that every conflict over which you preside presents you with the opportunity to bring peace into the world, or at least into your little corner of it.

About This Book

Achieving success as a mediator requires a two-pronged approach. You need to master your trade while at the same time strive to achieve commercial success, primarily through marketing and networking. When you're a great mediator and everyone in your market knows it, you've reached the pinnacle of your profession.

Success as a Mediator For Dummies addresses both sides of success. If you're just beginning to set your sights on mediation as a career, this book helps you get there. If you're already in the field, this book makes you better at your profession. And if you have everything required to be a top-notch mediator but you have no idea how to manage and market a business, this book shows you how to shore up the business end of success.

Conventions Used in This Book

I use several conventions in this book to call your attention to certain items. For example:

- ✔ *Italics* highlight new, somewhat technical terms, such as *anchoring* and *logrolling,* which I follow up with straightforward, easy-to-understand definitions.

- ✔ **Boldface** text indicates key words and phrases in bulleted and numbered lists.

- ✔ `Monofont` highlights web and e-mail addresses.

- ✔ When this book was printed, some web addresses may have needed to break across two lines of text. If that happened, rest assured that I haven't put in any extra characters (such as hyphens) to indicate the break. So, when using one of these web addresses, just type in exactly what you see in this book, pretending as though the line break doesn't exist.

What You're Not to Read

You can safely skip anything you see in a gray shaded box. I stuck this material in a box (called a *sidebar*) for the same reason that most people stick stuff in boxes — to get it out of the way so you don't trip over it. However, you may find the brief asides in the sidebars engaging, entertaining, and informative.

If you're exclusively looking for how-to information, you can probably skip the many examples in the book, but I wouldn't recommend it. Seeing techniques and skills applied in real-world mediations is extremely valuable in learning when and how to use the techniques and skills to the greatest advantage.

Foolish Assumptions

In writing this book, I made a few foolish assumptions, mostly about your motivation and how much you already know about mediation:

- ✔ You want to be a peacemaker, and you think you have what's required to be an excellent mediator.

- ✔ You want to make mediation your day job. You don't merely want to be an excellent mediator; you also want to be a commercial success. The two really do go hand in hand. Without a lot of clients, you're not going to get the experience you need to become a master mediator.

- ✔ You're dedicated to becoming the best in your field and your market. You're reading this book, so you're obviously driven to excel.

How This Book Is Organized

This book is organized so you can read it from cover to cover or skip around to only those parts, chapters, or sections that capture your interests or serve your present needs.

As you'll soon discover, developing the skills required for understanding and practicing mediation — and doing it well — isn't always a linear path. In the process of discovering new strategies and techniques, you often must skip back to review what you thought you already knew and understood. This book is optimized for skipping around to find exactly what you need whenever you happen to need it.

To further assist you in finding specific information, I divide the chapters into the following five parts.

Part I: Acquiring the Keys to Mediation Success

The chapters in this part help you build a successful practice on a firm foundation. You discover what "success as a mediator" means, find out how to choose a market that matches your interests and holds the greatest potential for your commercial success, and explore resources for obtaining the training required to pursue your chosen market.

Part II: Becoming a Master Mediator

Part II equips you with the tools of the trade, so you have everything you need to conduct an effective mediation:

- ✔ Knowledge of the overall process.
- ✔ What to expect, whether you're mediating a litigated or nonlitigated dispute.
- ✔ Various mediation styles, including facilitative, transformative, and evaluative, along with guidance on when and how to conduct mediation in joint session and separate caucuses.
- ✔ Fundamental techniques, including anchoring, framing, trust-building, brainstorming, problem-solving, and logrolling.
- ✔ A deeper understanding of the conflict dynamics that often lead to disputes and make them more difficult to resolve.

Part III: Improving Your Success Rate

Skills and techniques are useful only if you know when and how to apply them in real-world disputes. In this part, I present various situations that you have to navigate during a mediation. In every mediation, you need to establish and maintain your own authority while also helping the parties find the authority and wisdom within themselves to solve their own dispute on their own terms; help the parties sort out the often confusing differences among rights, remedies, issues, and interests; use your people skills to deal with the human factor; and help the parties identify and solve problems.

Because the parties will inevitably reach *impasse* — the chasm that neither party believes can be crossed — you need to know how to help the parties break through what appears to be an impossible barrier to the achievement of a mutually satisfactory resolution. The chapters in this part explain how to do all this and more.

Part IV: Launching Your Own Mediation Practice

As a mediator, you're also a small-business owner, so you need to know how to set up shop, market yourself and your services, and grow your business through networking and referrals. The chapters in this part address the business end of mediation.

Part V: The Part of Tens

Every *For Dummies* title has a Part of Tens — a group of chapters, each of which provides a list of ten valuable tips, strategies, techniques, or related snippets of interest.

This particular Part of Tens presents ten practices of the super mediator, ten big mediation no-no's, and ten tips for breaking through impasse.

Icons Used in This Book

Throughout this book, you'll spot icons in the margins that call your attention to different types of information. Here are the icons you'll see and a brief description of each.

Everything in this book is important (except for the stuff in the shaded boxes), but some information is even *more* important. When you see this icon, read the text next to it not once but two or three times to tattoo it onto your gray matter.

Tips provide insider insight from behind the scenes. When you're looking for a better, faster way to do something, check out these tips.

This icon appears when you need to be extra vigilant or seek additional guidance before moving forward. Don't skip this important information — I'm warning you.

Throughout the book, I provide plenty of examples to show you as well as tell you how to conduct an effective mediation. Look for the examples to see how it's done.

Where to Go from Here

Success as a Mediator For Dummies is designed to take you from ground zero to master mediator. If you're just getting started, check out the chapters in Part I. For techniques and skill-building, set your sights on Part II. For guidance on how to deal effectively with situations you're likely to encounter, turn to the chapters in Part III. And when you're ready to start building or expanding your mediation business, head to Part IV.

Otherwise, read the book from cover to cover, skip around using the table of contents as your guide, or consult the index if you need direction on a more specific topic.

Part I

Acquiring the Keys to Mediation Success

The 5th Wave   By Rich Tennant

"My husband thinks I'd make a good mediator, my mother doesn't. So I sat them at a table and got them both to agree. Now, neither one of them thinks I'd make a good mediator."

In this part . . .

To become a master mediator, you need to start by being a mediator, and that's what this part is all about. Here I paint a picture of what success as a mediator looks like and describe some of the paths you can take to achieve that goal. I also assist you in selecting a mediation market that's right for you and in obtaining the required training to pursue that market.

In short, the chapters in this part ensure that you build a successful practice on a firm foundation.

Chapter 1

Achieving Success as a Mediator

In This Chapter

▶ Deciding whether you have the skills and personality to be a mediator

▶ Finding career opportunities in mediation

▶ Acquiring essential mediation skills, training, and education

▶ Launching and marketing your mediation business

Ask a dozen people what *success* means, and you're likely to get a dozen different definitions. For some, success means lots of money. Others define it in terms of happiness or freedom from worry. For others, success means spending quality time with loved ones. When focusing on success as a mediator, however, the word means two things:

✔ You're good at facilitating dispute resolution.

✔ You earn enough money to make mediation your career or, at a minimum, a significant source of new income.

To be a great mediator, you need to master the skills, techniques, and strategies required to assist parties in resolving their disputes. To earn enough money to make mediation a worthwhile career, you need to market yourself and network in ways that attract clients who can pay what your services are worth.

This book is dedicated to empowering you to achieve success as a mediator in both areas. This chapter serves as the *CliffsNotes* version, getting you up to speed in a hurry.

Do You Have What It Takes?

Not everyone has the makeup to be a mediator. Some people lack patience, are uncomfortable with conflict, or are unable to remain impartial. Others lack essential abilities, including critical thinking, problem-solving, and communication skills. Sure, you can develop some of what you may lack through education, training, and experience, but much of what's required to be a mediator is born and bred — it has to do with personality and attitude. In the following sections, you take a personality and skills inventory to see whether you have what it takes to be a master mediator.

Assessing your personality

Some people prefer to work in relative isolation, never having to deal with the messiness of human interaction and relationships. They focus on the task at hand and accomplish a great deal. The world needs people like that, but mediation doesn't. To be a great mediator, you need to be good with people, and that means having the following personality traits:

- ❑ Ability to inspire
- ❑ Curiosity
- ❑ Dogged determination
- ❑ Emotional stability/maturity
- ❑ Empathy/sympathy
- ❑ Impartiality
- ❑ Integrity
- ❑ Open-mindedness
- ❑ Optimism
- ❑ Patience
- ❑ Persistence
- ❑ Sensitivity

In short, you need to genuinely like people and enjoy helping them solve their problems and get along with one another.

Taking inventory of your skills

In an emergency, people with relevant skills tend to be more helpful than the average Joe. Doctors, nurses, emergency medical technicians (EMTs), police, and firefighters have the skills, equipment, and experience necessary to respond to disaster and help the victims. Those without the skills required for the task tend to just get in the way. Similarly, you need a few fundamental skills to help parties in dispute, which is a crisis in human interaction, including the following:

- ✔ **Interviewing:** You should possess the ability to ask open-ended, curiosity-driven questions and to follow up those questions with more inquiries to elicit detailed narratives along with the emotions and subjective perceptions driving the conflict story. If you're naturally curious about people and what motivates their behavior, you're probably good at interviewing people.

✔ **Critical thinking:** You must have the ability to figure out what's really bothering each party by breaking down problems into discrete issues and helping the parties problem-solve those issues in light of their conflicting or overlapping interests.

✔ **Creative problem-solving:** Mediation is often more than just figuring out how much of the pie each party is entitled to. It's about identifying each party's interests or needs and matching them up with the available resources.

✔ **Communication skills:** You need to be able to communicate orally, in writing, and in nonverbal ways. *Nonverbal* means without words, through body language. You must be able to pick up on what certain postures and facial expressions mean and to communicate confidence and optimism through your own body language.

Choosing Your Path

The paths that lead someone to a career in mediation are too varied and numerous to describe. Attorneys weary of litigation often pursue mediation as a more attractive alternative. Educators may go into mediation to help parents and school systems resolve their disputes. Healthcare providers may enter the field to help patients and doctors resolve malpractice claims outside the courtroom.

Generally speaking, however, two paths lead to a career in mediation, and the path you take requires that you learn or unlearn what you already know:

✔ **From attorney to mediator:** As an attorney, you need to unlearn what you already know about dispute resolution and embrace a collaborative rather than adversarial approach. In mediation, disputes are no longer about rights and remedies or who's wrong and who's right. Disputes are opportunities to locate and allocate available resources to provide the parties with as much of what they want as possible and, in some cases, to mend the relationships damaged by the dispute.

✔ **From non-attorney to mediator:** If you're not an attorney, you need to get up to speed on the basics of the law and legal process whether or not the dispute is being litigated, because the parties' right to sue each other is often the better (or worse) alternative to a negotiated resolution. You also need to learn what you may and may not legally do or say as a mediator working with parties whose dispute is, or may be, the subject of a lawsuit.

In either situation, Chapter 5 eases the transition.

Checking Out Mediation Opportunities

As a mediator, you can choose to ply your trade in a variety of ways. You may want to specialize in litigated or nonlitigated cases, pursue an opportunity in a court-annexed panel, seek out prospects in the public sector, or even go global with international diplomacy. Here's a short list of the many possibilities:

- ✔ **Litigated cases:** These are the meat and potatoes for many mediation practitioners because this is where most of the money is. Depending on the nature of the dispute and the parties involved, you can often save the parties a considerable amount of money in legal fees while earning a handsome income.

- ✔ **Nonlitigated cases:** Not all mediation originates inside the courtroom or even within the legal system. Plenty of opportunities exist in mediating agreements, contracts, and disputes in a wide variety of venues. Mediators are often needed for employer-employee disputes, in congregation-clergy contract negotiations, in prenuptial negotiations for couples planning to get married, to assist in no-fault divorce proceedings and public policy and environmental mediations, and much more.

Some mediators practice a form of mediation known as *deal mediation,* in which they help people build better deals upfront instead of resolving disputes that result from bad deals. It's the legal industry's version of preventive medicine.

- ✔ **Court-annexed practices:** Courts often order the parties involved in lawsuits to mediate their dispute at some point in the litigation. Some businesses require their customers or clients to mediate before they're permitted to pursue litigation. Some market sectors, such as the California real estate industry, have written mediation clauses into their recommended forms, including real estate sales and leasing contracts.

    When you join a court-annexed panel, your name and qualifications are listed on its roster, which is provided to the attorneys. In most instances, you're required to provide free services for a limited number of hours but can then charge the parties if the dispute continues beyond that time.

- ✔ **Public sector opportunities:** Government-sponsored programs — such as family courts, the Equal Employment Opportunity Commission (EEOC), and even the United Nations — require mediators. Some of these opportunities are provided as contract work, while others are employment opportunities.

- ✔ **Ombuds work:** An *ombuds* works for an organization, such as a hospital or university, to investigate and resolve complaints lodged against the organization. The ombuds may be an internal position or an external consultant hired by the organization.

✔ **Restorative justice and victim-offender programs:** Unlike the criminal justice system, which punishes or tries to rehabilitate offenders, restorative justice and victim-offender programs attempt to help the offender right the wrong of the crime he has committed, mend the broken relationship between the offender and the community, and restore to the offender and the community the sense of safety that everyone needs to thrive in collaborative ventures.

✔ **International diplomacy:** If you've always dreamed of playing an active role in achieving world peace, international diplomacy may be the field for you. Track 1 diplomats represent states or nations, and Track II diplomats work at the grassroots level to improve relationships among states and countries. They're often referred to as *citizen diplomats*.

✔ **Consulting, speaking, training, and publishing:** After gaining some experience in mediation, you can share your expertise with other mediators, members of the public, and people in the market niche you serve through consulting, speaking, training, and publishing opportunities — like writing this book!

For additional details about these and other opportunities in the mediation field, check out Chapter 2.

Consider looking for opportunities in your *natural market* — the field you're in right now. For example, if you're a real estate agent and you want to become a mediator, look for opportunities in resolving real estate disputes. If you're a human resources manager, you may want to look into resolving disputes between employers and employees.

Mastering Essential Skills and Strategies

To conduct effective mediation sessions efficiently, certain skills, techniques, and strategies come in very handy. Mediation has been around a long time, and mediators have discovered through trial and error what works and what doesn't. You need to become familiar with the tools of the trade to save yourself a lot of trial and error. The following sections give you a glimpse of what you need to do in the thick of many mediation scenarios and what's covered in the bulk of this book.

Recognizing different approaches to mediation

You can take several different approaches to mediation based on your philosophy, what you believe to be most effective, and what your market prefers:

- ✔ **Facilitative:** Through the use of trust-building techniques, diagnostic questions, concessions, reciprocity, and other negotiation strategies and tactics, you help facilitate the negotiated resolution of a dispute.

- ✔ **Transformative:** You preside over a process in which the parties use the dispute to reach a deeper understanding and appreciation of each other's issues, positions, and interests and develop communication and problem-solving skills to resolve the dispute, strengthen the relationship, and be better prepared to resolve other disputes with other people in the future.

- ✔ **Evaluative:** You analyze, or help the parties analyze, the strengths and weaknesses of each side's case to help them calculate the risks and benefits of proceeding on the course they're already on or bringing the dispute to a close by resolving it. This method requires the parties to conduct a risk/benefit analysis.

Although many mediators hold strong opinions about which approach is best or constitutes *real* mediation, each approach has its place. For example, transformative mediation may be best in family or community mediation, where the parties probably want or need to maintain a relationship long after they've resolved their current dispute. In other situations, parties may want the mediator to help them objectively evaluate the pros and cons of mediation versus litigation. For more on different mediation styles, flip to Chapter 6.

Knowing the essential skills and techniques

The goals of mediation are to resolve the dispute and to help the parties use the resolution process as a way of deepening their understanding of themselves in relation to others with competing interests. You have many tools at your disposal to accomplish these goals. The following list describes the most essential skills, techniques, and strategies you may employ during a mediation:

- ✔ **Asking diagnostic questions:** Disputes, especially those in litigation, tend to shut down communication and restrict the flow of information. To resolve the dispute, you need to find out what's driving it. To uncover the underlying reasons the parties have fallen into conflict, you need to ask open-ended questions, which always begin with *Who? What? When? Where? Why? How?* or *Tell me more about that.* The narrative responses you elicit lead to further questions seeking clarity and completeness. Answers to these questions expose issues, interests, and potential solutions that you, the mediator, couldn't possibly have guessed at.

- ✔ **Anchoring:** An *anchor* is any relevant number (or idea) that enters the negotiation environment and ultimately influences the outcome. You don't drop the anchors — the parties do — but you can encourage the parties to get the ball rolling by explaining that the party who puts the first number on the table or suggests the first solution sets the bargaining range that will influence the course of the negotiation until the parties reach agreement.

- ✔ **Framing:** This is a technique to help the parties take a look at the problem from a different perspective. The mediator often accentuates the positive and encourages the parties to engage in a collaborative effort to resolve their differences. Mediators often reframe the parties' dispute from an adversarial contest to a problem-solving exercise and from trying to find out who's right to searching for solutions that serve everyone's best interests.

- ✔ **Logrolling:** This concessions-and-reciprocity problem-solving technique enables the parties to gain a lot while giving up little. Each party trades something that's low-cost to him but of high value to the other party in exchange for something that's of high value to him but low-cost for the other party.

- ✔ **Bracketing:** This strategy enables a party to make an offer or demand conditional upon the other party's offer or demand in order to narrow the gap that separates them. For example, if Party A's offer of $175,000 in response to Party B's demand for $350,000 leads to impasse, you can ask Party A whether he'd be willing to increase his offer to $225,000 if Party B would drop her demand to $275,000. This can get the parties talking hypothetically without committing to a certain offer or demand.

- ✔ **Interest-based negotiation:** Through interest-based negotiation, you attempt to help the parties expand the thing being valued (the "fixed pie" being negotiated) beyond the money value that's so often the focus of disputes. The parties identify each other's interests — needs, desires, preferences, priorities, fears, and appetite for risk — and look for mutually beneficial exchanges that serve as many of those interests as possible. For example, if a disgruntled former employee is demanding a certain amount of money that her former employer is unwilling to pay, you can ask questions about what nonmonetary relief may satisfy the employee's needs, such as job training or a referral to another employer.

- ✔ **Distributive bargaining:** Through distributive bargaining, you help the parties figure out an equitable division of the fixed pie of benefits. Even in an interest-based negotiation where the parties expand the pie of available benefits, they ultimately create a fixed pie that needs to be distributed.

- ✔ **Forming contingent agreements:** Contingent agreements make the deal conditional upon certain events occurring. Such agreements often help alleviate a party's concern over a possible future event that could harm the party's interests. These agreements can also call a party's bluff. For example, if a party refuses to accept $500,000 as a buyout for his share of a mutual business venture because he claims that the business will earn a profit of $1 million in the next three years alone, the parties can agree to protect against future uncertainty by deferring part of the seller's payment until a date certain in the future while at the same time making the sum of the payment contingent upon the business reaching a certain level of profitability.

✔ **Appealing to higher values:** You can use shared beliefs or principles to reach agreement, such as both parents' desire to do what's best for the children.

Getting the required education and experience

You can start mediating with little more than a desire, people skills, and perhaps a certification from a 28-hour, court-required, alternative dispute resolution (ADR) course. To be a master mediator, however, you should constantly be learning more about your trade and mediation-related topics. Here are some opportunities you may want to consider:

✔ **Bachelor's degree in conflict resolution or a related field:** Colleges and universities are beginning to offer degrees in conflict resolution, conflict analysis, negotiation, and peace building.

✔ **Bachelor's degree or informal study in humanities:** Any formal or informal education that increases your understanding of human nature is beneficial, including courses in psychology, philosophy, literature, criminal justice, law, sociology, social work, and anthropology.

✔ **Bachelor's degree in any field of study:** A bachelor's degree in any field of study, especially in a field in which you want to mediate, such as business or agriculture, is useful.

✔ **MDR degrees:** Many universities now offer a master's degree in dispute resolution (an MDR degree). Anyone with a bachelor's degree, for example, can apply to the Straus MDR program — a 32-unit course of study with several required and many elective courses.

✔ **LL.M and doctoral degrees:** The Master of Laws (LL.M) in dispute resolution is a recent addition to curricula at many law schools. In addition, some law schools offer doctoral programs in various areas of dispute resolution study.

✔ **Basic course in law:** Courts that permit non-lawyers to mediate litigated disputes usually require them to take a short course that covers the legal process and general substantive law. Such a course covers contracts, *torts* (wrongful acts that result in injury to others), real property, and civil procedure.

✔ **Dispute resolution certification:** Some courts may require certification for acceptance on court-annexed panels. Certification may require a minimum number of hours in mediation training that covers confidentiality, ethics, convening, negotiating, caucus strategies, effective communication techniques, cross-cultural challenges, and methods for breaking impasse and closing the session.

Private sector certification is also available through any number of mediation training firms. Some certifications are meaningless, while others carry a lot of weight.

✔ **Law school courses for specific types of cases:** If you plan on mediating certain types of disputes — malpractice lawsuits, for instance — take a course or seek out continuing education programs related to the law that governs that type of dispute.

✔ **Trade-specific courses, experience, or training:** If you've been working in a field and plan on conducting mediations in that same field, you probably already have plenty of trade-specific experience and training. If you're in an industry that changes rapidly, however, you need continuing education. Read trade journals, attend conferences, and talk shop with people in the field.

For more on mediation education, turn to Chapter 3.

Obtaining additional training

Additional, less formal training is always available, and you should actively pursue that training to stay on top of your game. Following are some suggestions on where to look for continuing education opportunities:

✔ **Mentor or sponsor:** Learn from the best by asking a seasoned mediator whom you respect and admire to serve as your mentor. This person may eventually become your sponsor and introduce you to her contacts, expose you to potentially profitable networking opportunities, recommend you for speaking engagements or writing assignments, and vouch for the quality of your work.

✔ **Local mediation associations:** A mediation association is a great way to get to know your market, talk shop with other mediators, and establish yourself in the field, especially if you choose to serve in the organization. For a long list of mediation associations, visit www.mediate.com/ organizations.

✔ **Observations:** Ask other mediators in your area of specialization if you can sit in on a mediation. You can often pick up new techniques and strategies from your colleagues.

✔ **Mediation conferences and seminars:** All good mediators attend (and often speak at) mediation conferences and seminars held by mediation and bar association organizations. By attending these seminars and speaking at them you expand your network of mediators, improve your practice, and make yourself known in the industry. The more geographically distant the mediators you meet, the more likely you are to receive referrals from them because people rarely agree to fly mediators from their home state to the state in which the disputing parties live or work.

For more on mediation training, check out Chapter 3.

Building a Successful Mediation Business

Most mediators are also small-business owners — freelancers who set their own rates and fees, buy their own office equipment and supplies, do their own marketing and advertising, and often manage their own finances and taxes. To be successful on the business end of mediation, you need to be part business manager and part marketing maven. The following sections give you a taste of what's involved.

Launching your business

Launching a successful business requires the right timing and having the necessary resources in place to operate the business through the initial lean months that every start-up encounters. The following steps guide you through the process (for additional details, check out Chapter 15):

1. **Know when you're ready.**

   You're ready to make the move from part- to full-time mediation when you have clients lined up and you're earning at least half as much as you've been earning from your day job and at least ten times the amount you need to run the business.

2. **Draft a business plan.**

   Your *business plan* is a summary of how you intend to launch your practice and stay in business. It should include a vision/mission statement, market and competition analyses, short- and long-term goals, a list of income sources and projected expenditures, your location, and some ideas on how to market your services.

3. **Draw up a budget.**

   Your budget should include your projected income along with an itemized list of expenses, including living expenses, office space, professional services (such as a bookkeeper), Internet and communications (phone), office equipment and supplies, marketing costs, membership dues and fees, liability insurance, and taxes.

4. **Choose a name and location.**

   In most cases, your name is your business name and you run your business out of a home office. If you're planning to join a mediation panel, however, or rent office space, you should have a business address in mind.

5. **Prepare the necessary paperwork.**

   You need a few forms to get started, including a scheduling letter, a contract that each client signs, a settlement agreement that the parties flesh out with details of what they agreed to, and a follow-up letter.

6. **Purchase liability and property insurance.**

   Though mediators are rarely the target of lawsuits, you should have liability insurance in place just in case. Don't worry — it's very affordable. In addition, consider purchasing property insurance to cover damage to or theft of equipment or furniture and any personal injury claims by clients who slip and fall during office visits.

7. **Set your rates and fees.**

   Mediation rates and fees may vary from free for pro-bono work to upward of $20,000 a day for commercial litigation. Call around to mediators in your market to find out what they charge.

8. **Market and network to attract clients.**

   Being a master mediator isn't enough. People in your market need to know about you, so you need to market yourself online and off, as I explain in the following section, to increase demand for your services.

Mediation is a low-overhead business venture. If you run your practice out of a home office, your biggest expenses are income tax, payroll tax (FICA), and liability insurance.

Marketing yourself and your services

Mediators tend to be fairly humble people who are uncomfortable singing their own praises. Fortunately, marketing isn't about selling yourself. It's more about establishing yourself as a trusted expert and giving your clients something of value — typically information that saves them money or makes their lives easier or better. With that goal in mind, here are some of the marketing and networking activities you need to engage in to achieve that goal:

- ✔ **Identify your market.** Where are you likely to find new clients? Through law firms, corporate lawyers, or individual attorneys? From other mediators who have an overabundance of clients? From businesses in a specific industry? In school systems?

- ✔ **Immerse yourself in your market.** Before you can give your market something of value to remember you by, you must know its needs and the most significant issues and problems its members face. Engage in an ongoing conversation with your market and perform relevant research — read what your market reads.

- ✔ **Build a marketing database.** Collect names and contact information and enter into some sort of contact management program. Also, record details about each person you meet, including when and where you met, what you discussed, the kind of work the person does, details about the person's family, and more.

✔ **Launch a website, blog, or combination website/blog.** A website or blog gives you a permanent presence on the web, enables potential clients to find you via search engines like Google and Bing, and simplifies the process of branching out to social networking communities, including those on Facebook and Twitter.

✔ **Establish a presence on Facebook, Twitter, and LinkedIn.** These are the three major social networking venues. Though people don't want to be sold to on these venues, they do expect to find businesses there. In addition, being present in these venues makes it easier for people in the community to talk about you and generate buzz.

✔ **Claim your online business listings.** People often search Google Places, Yelp, and other online directories when they need a product or service. If you don't have a listing, add it. If you're already listed, claim the listing, so you can populate it with additional information, including your website or blog address.

✔ **Post press releases.** Whenever something important occurs, such as when you open your business or are planning to speak at a mediation conference, post a press release and be sure to link back to your website or blog.

✔ **Distribute newsletters.** Compose a monthly newsletter with articles relevant to your market and distribute it via e-mail or postal mail according to each recipient's preference. Be sure to have a system in place that allows recipients to opt out of future mailings.

✔ **Build a brand presence.** Design business cards, brochures, letterhead, and your website or blog so they all have a consistent look and feel. As people view your marketing materials, they begin to recognize your brand.

✔ **Network.** Join organizations where you're likely to mingle with people who need your services, and then take a leadership role in those organizations. Engage everyone you meet in conversation to really get to know people and what they do. In the process, distribute and collect business cards to add to your marketing database.

✔ **Contribute to online discussions.** Join mediation discussion forums online and contribute your insight. LinkedIn has several discussion forums dedicated to a wide range of mediation topics. Be sure to research the discussion group and get a feel for the community before posting anything.

For more on marketing yourself and your business, see Chapter 16.

Chapter 2

Choosing the Right Niche

· ·

In This Chapter

▶ Discovering a mediation market in your area of expertise

▶ Checking out opportunities in court-annexed mediation programs

▶ Finding out what you can do in the public sector

▶ Exploring ombuds, restorative justice, victim offender, and diplomatic opportunities

▶ Branching out into consulting, speaking, training, and writing

· ·

*I*n the mediation field, general practitioners are few and far between. Almost everyone specializes. Some mediators are lawyers, most of whom mediate litigated disputes. Others are social workers, human resource professionals, therapists, insurance claims adjusters, engineers, teachers, university professors, physicians, nurses, or artists. Some work exclusively on court-annexed panels or in restorative justice and victim-offender programs. Many focus their efforts and expertise on divorce and other family disputes or in the field of community mediation. Some even specialize in international diplomacy.

This chapter presents your options so you can choose a niche that's right for you and begin to prepare for and pursue that niche.

Identifying Your Natural Market

Your *natural market* is the field you're in right now. Corporate law, bankruptcy law, personal injury, commercial real estate, human resources, education, you name it — whatever field you're in, your area of expertise is your natural market. This is the best place to start carving out a niche because you already have the experience and connections to get started.

The following sections reveal some of the opportunities you're likely to find in both the litigated and nonlitigated arena, along with opportunities in specific industries.

Exploring opportunities in litigated cases

The market for mediating litigated cases is the most coveted in the business because litigated cases are generally where the money is. But the profit potential varies depending on which end of the litigated market you're considering:

✔ **Low end:** At the low end of the litigated market are lemon law claims, low-value personal injury cases, landlord-tenant disputes, small collection matters, and an infinite variety of cases with less than $50,000 in dispute. These are the majority of cases handled by *pro bono* and reduced-fee, court-annexed panels, which is where many mediators get their start. For more info, see the section "Considering a Court-Annexed Mediation Practice" later in the chapter.

✔ **Mid-market:** In the mid-market are

- Family law proceedings

- More serious personal injury actions

- Lawsuits for professional malpractice

- Breaches of commercial leases

- Partnership and minority shareholder lawsuits

- Actions to recover benefits from insurance policies

- Suits for breaches of fiduciary duty by people in a position of trust, such as financial advisors and real estate agents

- Every other dispute for which a legal claim is available

✔ **High end:** This is where you find the superstars making as much as $25,000 a day mediating bet-the-company litigation — cases seeking upward of $1 billion in damages. Here you may be called upon to mediate in class action lawsuits against pharmaceutical companies, intellectual property disputes between software companies, labor discrimination lawsuits against large corporations, and so on.

Transitioning from judge to mediator

Not so long ago, retired judges had a corner on the alternative dispute resolution (ADR) market, and for good reason — they have significantly more trial experience than most lawyers. No one understands the way jurors think better than a trial judge. She has heard thousands of lawyers question thousands of witnesses and has seen hundreds of juries return hundreds of verdicts. A retired judge also has an aura of authority that no attorney can match. Clients who've been waiting for months or years to be heard often want the person doing the listening to be a judge — the authority figure that clients anticipate would be the final arbiter of their dispute.

However, judges aren't always the best fit as mediators. To successfully transition from judge to mediator, you must be able to do the following:

- **Converse, not command:** As judge, you can order parties what to do. As mediator, you must take an interest in areas of the parties' dispute you'd consider irrelevant to its resolution under the law. You also have to persuade and cajole. More important, you must listen to a disputant express feelings and help that party move from fear or anger to a more rational and pragmatic state of mind. You can't hold a disrespectful party in contempt. You must bear the insults of people no longer able to hold their tongues or control their tempers. If you can't let down your hair, shed your robe, climb down from the dais, and mix it up with the rabble, you're not well suited to be a mediator and will soon leave the profession for a calmer retirement.

- **Negotiate, not merely evaluate:** A purely evaluative mediator merely tells the parties which side is likely to prevail and for how much if the case goes to trial. That's not enough. Mediators must engage the parties in the process of mediation so both parties feel satisfied at the end. The great mistake of too many mediators is to assume the parties don't know the weaknesses and strengths of their own case as well or better than any mediator does. Mediators aren't in the business of overwhelming the parties' will but rather finding out what motivates that will and then addressing ways to satisfy it. You must be able to get under the parties' positions — their opinions about the rectitude of their claim — to address the interests they're trying to serve, which may appear to be but aren't always monetary.

Don't expect to announce your retirement as judge and immediately land a spot on a private ADR panel. Most private ADR rosters are beginning to list as many attorney-mediators as retired judges. Furthermore, these panels expect their judge-mediators to market themselves by joining bar associations and speaking at their events, sending out e-mail newsletters, and networking at industry and legal conferences as well as in electronic social networks such as LinkedIn, Twitter, and Facebook.

Becoming an attorney-mediator

Though attorney-mediators may not carry the same authority that judges do, they tend to have more experience working with clients in the trenches. If you've been representing clients in litigation for 10, 20, or 30 years, you know what keeps counsel awake at night, how a case can go from great to unwinnable overnight, what clients really want, and how damaging litigation can be, both financially and emotionally, to the parties.

Attorneys are used to explaining to lay people how the law and the facts must come together to entitle their clients to victory at trial. They're used to performing cost-benefit analyses for their clients — for instance, predicting a good chance of winning but a bad chance of obtaining a high award of damages; explaining the many obstacles between the filing of a lawsuit and a jury trial; and understanding client-reporting relationships that require someone else to be responsible for a bad result.

That said, making a living as a mediator after a successful career as an attorney is rarely easy. The rule of thumb in the Los Angeles market is that the transition from attorney to mediator requires three to five years to replace the income from the legal practice. Attorneys who were making more than $150,000 per year before becoming mediators may well never replace their income. Now and perhaps until the end of time, far more money is devoted to war than peace.

Checking out opportunities that don't require a law degree

You don't need a law degree to be a top-notch mediator, even when it comes to mediating litigated disputes. Consider building on what you already know. If you're a therapist or counselor, for example, you may want to consider mediating litigated family disputes, such as divorce and child custody. Business professionals may be well suited to mediate litigated commercial disputes. Human resource specialists are often the perfect choice for mediating labor disputes and discrimination lawsuits. An insurance claims examiner may want to consider serving as a neutral in personal injury litigation.

You may not need a law degree to mediate litigated disputes, but you do need to brush up on the fundamentals, as explained in Chapter 3. You also have to know what you should and shouldn't say and do if you're not a lawyer but are helping lawyers and their clients settle a lawsuit. If you're not a lawyer, giving advice about a litigated dispute can get you into legal trouble.

Entering the world of litigated disputes is relatively easy, but the competition is stiff. Even attorney-mediators often have trouble drumming up enough work in the litigated-mediation market to stay busy full time. But don't let that discourage you. You may be better than those attorneys at resolving disputes outside the courtroom.

Identifying opportunities in nonlitigated disputes

Mediation opportunities are readily available outside the legal system. Many mediators earn a living mediating agreements, contracts, and disputes in a wide range of venues, including the following:

✔ Workplace issues within corporations or within and between small and family businesses. (A number of successful mediators around the United States have busy practices in business and workplace disputes in which lawyers never become involved.)

✔ Congregation/clergy contract negotiations.

✔ Prenuptial negotiations and mediations.

✔ Large-scale public policy and environmental mediations, including Superfund cleanups.

✔ Environmental and land use cases.

I urge anyone who has a true talent for entrepreneurism to bring quality mediation out of the legal market and directly to the people, where it can do them the most good.

Investigating industry-specific opportunities

Plenty of mediation opportunities exist in specific industries, particularly healthcare, human resources, special and higher education, assisted living and long-term care, and small business in general. Google the name of your industry followed by "mediation" and you're likely to find resources for industry-specific mediation opportunities. Networking with mediators is also a good way to find out which local mediators specialize in a particular industry and then contact them for guidance.

You should already have credentials, experience, or, at a minimum, a passionate interest in the industry you choose. To be successful, you need to bring all your own resources to market yourself and the practice of mediation-without-lawyers to your prospective clients.

Considering a Court-Annexed Mediation Practice

If you're not a retired judge, serving on a free or low-cost court-annexed mediation panel is likely the best place to familiarize yourself with the mediation of litigated cases. The court "convenes" these mediations for you, listing your name and your qualifications on its roster and providing that roster to attorneys, many of whom have been ordered to mediate their case and report their progress back to the court. Court-annexed mediations are a great training ground for new mediators and an excellent way to make yourself known in the legal community.

Mediation to the rescue!

Nearly three decades ago, many courts were so overburdened with lawsuits that they took as long as five years to schedule a case for trial. To ease the load, the courts turned to mediation, often providing training for mediators and creating the panels and rosters that live on in courthouses all over the country today.

Though many state legislatures originally provided funding to pay these court-annexed mediators a small fee, the money soon ran out. But the courts continued to need mediators, and people continued to want to become mediators. Many courts decided to ask mediators to volunteer their services, hoping that the opportunity to introduce themselves to their market would be enough to induce novice mediators to work for free. Others permitted their panel members to charge a minimal fee, and some created rosters of mediators available to provide their services at market rates.

Some of the largest mediation panels in the country — like the Los Angeles Superior Court Pro Bono roster — don't require their mediators to be attorneys. Hundreds if not thousands of nonattorney mediators were thereby given the opportunity to practice their new profession with lawyers and their clients — free for the first few hours and charging market rates thereafter.

These court panels required minimal training — between 28 and 42 hours — and the pay, if the mediation went overtime, was enticing — $150 to $450 per hour, depending on the case's size and subject matter. Unfortunately, in some markets, like Los Angeles, the lawyers and their clients came to feel as though free mediation was their right, an entitlement like the courts themselves. No one pays the judge, after all, and the courts appeared to be providing mediation services in the same way they offered judicial officers to the general public — for free.

The following sections explain how to find court-annexed mediation programs in your area and what qualifications may be required.

Don't spend more than a year on one of these pro-bono panels. Otherwise, you may begin to feel used and abused. The attorneys in these mediations are all paid for their services, as is the staff of the court-annexed mediation program. The judges who order the cases are also paid, as are the court clerks and bailiffs who make their jury rooms available for you to mediate with the litigants. You should get paid, too.

Finding court-annexed mediation opportunities

Almost all state and federal courts have court-annexed mediation programs. To find out about programs in your area, visit www.courtadr.org, click the Court ADR Across the U.S. link, and then scroll down and choose your state from the Browse State Resources list. This lands you on your state's ADR Resource Center page, where you can access general information, resources, and contacts. In addition, all state and federal courts have their own websites where you can find out more about their ADR programs or at least get the contact information of someone who can point you in the right direction.

If you don't yet know any mediators, call or send an e-mail to someone who practices in the area you'd like to practice in yourself. Most mediators are happy to share the good, the bad, and the ugly of their court-annexed programs. Ask several people about their experiences and their knowledge of the system. Join a mediation association and become involved in its activities. These are all extremely low- to no-cost means of making sure that mediation is a worthy pursuit and something you'll enjoy.

Qualifying for membership on court-annexed mediation panels

Qualifications for membership on a court-annexed mediation panel vary from one court to another. Some accept only attorneys, and others may recruit only attorneys who've practiced in that court for a significant period of time (like ten years!). Some courts conduct their own training, and others require a certificate from a mediation-training program. Minimum training ranges from about 20 to 42 hours, and you may need to take continuing-education courses. Some courts require panel members to work for free for a certain number of hours before they're permitted to charge for their services, and others permit their mediators to charge for every hour spent in mediation. (Unfortunately, most courts don't allow mediators to charge for the time spent in preparation.) Some require expertise in certain practice areas like employment, probate, or family law.

Before you take your first mediation course, find out whether you meet all the other requirements. Training alone may not guarantee acceptance into the program, and you don't want to waste time getting the training if something else is likely to disqualify you.

Checking Out the Public Sector

As an aspiring mediator, you may want to consider working in the public sector, either as a freelancer or employee. As a freelancer, you can join government specialty-dispute resolution panels such as the Equal Employment Opportunity Commission (EEOC). If you're looking for employment, here's a sample of conflict resolution openings found on the Straus Institute for Dispute Resolution website (www.law.pepperdine.edu/straus) at the time of writing:

✔ **Family Court Mediator** to provide evaluation and mediation in unresolved custody and visitation matters, conduct investigations, testify in court, prepare reports, and conduct meetings for parents and children in custody proceedings.

✔ **Director of Student Mediation & Dispute Resolution** at a for-profit university to receive and track informal student complaints, safeguard the integrity of the university's informal resolution process, and ensure that the process helps the parties facilitate a mutually acceptable agreement.

✔ **Ombuds** for a medical school to provide an informal, impartial, confidential, and independent resource for faculty, staff, and physicians to voice concerns within the institution and explore options to make informed decisions.

✔ **Food Safety Ombuds** for the Office of the Secretary of Agriculture in Washington, D.C., to respond to employee concerns related to the humane handling and slaughter of animals and other duties pertaining to the food safety mission.

✔ **Policy Analyst** for the National Center on Dispute Resolution in Special Education (CADRE) to promote appropriate and effective dispute resolution among families and schools.

✔ **Alternative Dispute Resolution Supervisor** for the Mohave County Superior Court Conciliation Court Services division to oversee, supervise, and participate in the day-to-day functions and operations of alternative dispute resolution programs.

Check out the job listings on the following websites to see more of what's available in the public sector (head to the site and look for the Jobs and Careers link or its equivalent):

✔ JAMS: www.jamsadr.com

✔ Center for Peacemaking and Conflict Studies at Fresno Pacific University: http://peace.fresno.edu

✔ The Conflict Resolution Information Source: www.crinfo.org

✔ Ombuds Blog: http://ombuds-blog.blogspot.com (blog has no jobs or career section, but businesses and government agencies often post job openings here)

✔ Mediate.com: www.mediate.com (must be a member to access job postings)

✔ National Association for Community Mediation: www.nafcm.org

Don't forget to search larger, more generic job listing sites such as Monster.com, CareerBuilder.com, and Indeed.com.

Pursuing Ombuds Work

An *ombuds* (originally called an ombuds*man* but since modified to reflect the fact that the profession includes as many or more women as men) is a conflict resolver similar but not identical to a mediator. An ombuds responds to complaints against organizations such as hospitals, universities, and news organizations. Mediators are typically hired by parties with an active dispute who share the cost of a mediation, whereas ombuds are employed by institutions on whose behalf they investigate and attempt to resolve complaints lodged by the public or the people the institutions serve, such as students or patients.

The International Ombudsman Association classifies ombuds in six categories:

- ✔ **Classical ombuds** are elected or appointed by governments to receive complaints, conduct investigations, and propose remedies for disputes between governments and their citizens.

- ✔ **Advocate ombuds** work in both for-profit and nonprofit organizational settings. Though hired by the organizations for which they work, the job of advocate ombuds is to represent the interests of individuals who lodge complaints against the organization. Hospital and university ombuds generally fall into this category.

- ✔ **Hybrid ombuds** also work in for-profit and nonprofit organizations to use informal dispute-resolution processes to resolve grievances. These ombuds are empowered to conduct investigations and publish annual and special reports about the results of their inquiries and dispute-resolution activities, often resulting in policy changes.

- ✔ **Executive ombuds** serve both public and private-sector organizations with a focus on complaints concerning the activities of the organization's officials, employees, and representatives. These ombuds assist the organization by holding it accountable and improving its performance.

- ✔ **Legislative ombuds** are generally civil servants who respond to issues raised by the general public to ensure that congressional bodies remain accountable to the people who elect them.

- ✔ **Media ombuds** promote transparency within and resolve complaints raised against news organizations. Media ombuds also explain to the public the responsibilities that the press owes to the people in a democracy and the standards that journalists must respect.

Qualifying for ombuds work

Qualifications for becoming an ombuds vary a great deal depending on the field and the specific position. Many ombuds have mediation training and experience, and some have obtained formal degrees or certificates in conflict resolution. Positions may require a bachelor's degree or better, investigative and legal experience, conflict-management training, or even experience in a particular field, such as education, healthcare, or criminal justice.

At the bare minimum, an ombuds, like a mediator, must be capable of neutrality and have active listening, communication, and negotiation skills. The ombuds should be nonjudgmental, a creative problem-solver, proficient in cross-cultural communications, respectful of people from all walks of life, and a skilled critical thinker. Ombuds come from many fields, including academics, law, human resources, the media, management, engineering, accounting, and healthcare services.

Finding ombuds work

Ombuds work is a *job*. It's not the entrepreneurial venture that most working mediators actively pursue. That's good news for people who are looking for stability and security and who break out into a cold sweat when they hear the terms *business plan, cash flow,* and *marketing.* If you're interested in pursuing a career as an ombuds, join an ombuds organization in the field in which you want to work, make yourself known there, be sure you have the necessary qualifications to land the job, and then commence your job search in the usual manner — networking, searching job sites on the web, and so on.

Scoping Out Restorative Justice and Victim-Offender Programs

Though the existing criminal justice system has punishment (and sometimes rehabilitation) in mind, its sole purpose is first to determine guilt and then to prescribe an appropriate punishment. The justice sought is primarily punitive or retributive; the criminal must pay for the crime, which is considered an offense against the community rather than the individual.

Restorative justice is relational rather than punitive. Its practitioners view crime as a profound rupture in the offender's relation to the victim and the community in which the crime occurred. Rather than punish the perpetrator, restorative justice seeks to instill accountability in the offender, help the offender and the victim agree on the type and extent of restitution that fits the victim's loss, assist the victim in forgiving the offender, and help the offender return to the community as a law-abiding citizen.

Most of the pretrial restorative justice programs in the United States serve the juvenile population because young people are considered the most likely to mend their ways and reenter society as law-abiding citizens. To accomplish this goal, restorative justice gives perpetrators the opportunity to meet with their victims, listen to their victims describe the profound damage they experienced as a result of the crime, explain their own motivations for the crime, set aside bitterness and blame, agree upon restitution, and be restored to the community which their criminal behavior shows they long ago excluded or felt excluded from.

Restorative justice programs also work inside prisons with people serving time for crimes whose victims are unable to put rage, bitterness, resentment, hatred, and grief behind them for the purpose of moving forward with their lives. These programs work separately with victims and prisoners to prepare them for a process in which the perpetrator acknowledges his accountability for the damage caused and the victim describes the horror, loss, trauma, and lifelong damage arising from the crime. Ideally, the victim expresses forgiveness, the perpetrator expresses an effort to make amends, and the two reconcile, either within themselves or, in some dramatic cases, with each other.

On the international level, the field of restorative justice also includes peace and reconciliation programs. Criminal prosecutions are generally insufficient to restore order to societies in which people have committed crimes against humanity — often by half the population against the other half. A society that jails half its people, if that's even possible, can't function. Therefore, in post-apartheid countries like South Africa and post-genocide countries like Rwanda, the governments have created truth and reconciliation programs with the goal of reconciling entire victimized populations with the entire perpetrating classes.

To qualify as a mediator in the restorative justice field, you should probably have a background in social science, international diplomacy, criminal justice, or law, and have conflict-resolution education and experience. Though an international community of volunteers work in restorative justice programs, paid positions are available, but you're likely to be job-hunting rather than building your own practice.

 To find out what's available, visit www.restorativejustice.org/job-openings-in-restorative-justice and http://peace.fresno.edu/rjjobs.php, where you'll find actual job listings complete with job duties and qualifications.

Giving Peace a Chance

Most mediators consider themselves peacemakers. They see their mission as greater than merely settling a lawsuit. They're making their little corner of the world a more peaceful place. Even mediators who see themselves primarily as agents of settlement tend to possess a passionate interest in the non-violent resolution of disputes, from the fight over a neighbor's boundary line to the achievement of peaceful relations among nations.

Local may lead to international

Many citizen diplomacy councils work with the U.S. State Department's International Visitor Leadership Program and the National Council for International Visitors. I personally learned of these programs from a fellow mediator in San Diego who was an active participant in her city's citizen diplomacy council. In response to a request by the State Department through the auspices of the diplomacy council, we dined with lawyers and leaders of restorative justice programs in Mali, Rwanda, Republic of the Congo, Benin, and South Africa. Our discussions played a part in leading the Republic of the Congo to take the first steps toward instituting ADR processes there.

If you're interested in playing a more active role in diplomacy, you can do so at two different levels:

- ✔ **Track I:** Track I diplomats are those who the word "diplomacy" call to mind — people who act with the authority of their state or nation or on behalf of multinational organizations such as the United Nations to resolve conflicts and foster peaceful relations among governing bodies.

- ✔ **Track II:** Citizen or Track II diplomacy is conducted by organizations and individuals who don't represent any state or nation. They work at the grassroots level to support the institutions of a civil society, which in turn support Track I diplomats in their efforts to achieve peace in civil conflicts or cross-border disputes.

The pursuit of Track I diplomatic employment is outside the scope of this book. If you have the inclination, however, hundreds of thousands of opportunities are available to participate in Track II diplomacy through both governmental and nongovernmental organizations. Nearly every city boasts a *citizen diplomacy council.* These nonprofit, nonpartisan organizations promote peaceful relations through cultural and professional exchanges and dialogue among U.S. residents and world leaders.

If you're more interested in working on an international level, consider getting involved with Mediators Beyond Borders International (www.mediators beyondborders.org). This organization is all-volunteer, but volunteer work enables you to hone your mediation skills and develop valuable contacts that may lead to paid positions.

Consulting, Speaking, Training, and Publishing . . . for Experienced Mediators

Knowledge isn't only power; it's also a valuable commodity. After you gain experience as a mediator, you may yearn to share your knowledge and earn some money doing it. Consulting, speaking, training, and publishing offer three major benefits that you as a mediator have to offer. These opportunities allow you to grow your practice in the following ways:

- **Money:** You may talk to some organizations for free when you're starting out on the talk circuit, but eventually, you can transition from those freebies to paying gigs, earning upward of a thousand dollars or more, plus expenses, for a single appearance. Having another income stream can carry you through the slow periods.

- **An opportunity to market yourself:** You can employ two effective methods to sell yourself as a mediator. The first is to mediate for someone and show the person how good you really are or probably will be in a year or so. The second is to speak to people in your market about what you do and why it's good for them. Speaking establishes you as a credible authority — just what people in mediation need and want.

- **A learning opportunity:** When you speak, you meet a lot of lawyers and business people with conflict problems. They pose questions that reveal the interests you need to address as a mediator and ways to market your mediation services. In the process, you get to know what the people in your market most want to know, what their greatest concerns are, and what they like and dislike about the voluntary resolution of their disputes. You get to know your market and your competition that much better.

In the following sections, you explore opportunities in consulting, speaking, training, and publishing and find out how to pursue these opportunities.

Checking out opportunities

Experienced mediators have plenty of opportunities to consult, speak, train, and write. At least a dozen mediators in my own local market have written books on mediation and negotiation. Some of them also teach at local universities, law schools, and dispute-resolution institutes. One of them has formed his own mediation institute, where he has gathered some of the best mediation trainers in the country. He also rents out office space to other mediators.

The gig economy

Tina Brown, former editor of *The New Yorker*, famously said that we're now living in a gig economy. A *gig* is something that calls to mind rock bands who play a wedding here and a bar mitzvah there. Occasionally, they open for a more famous band locally or get hooked up with a national or international tour. They sell T-shirts, mugs, and CDs. They give free concerts on summer evenings at the local art museum or shopping mall, where they sell their merchandise.

In the increasingly competitive global economy, many people can't rely on a single job with a steady income to sustain them. Their work has been offshored to Bangalore, and their 401(k) has evaporated in the financial meltdown of 2008. They don't have jobs; they have gigs. As a mediator, you're part of this gig economy, and one of the secrets to survive and thrive in this environment is to develop multiple income streams. That way, if one stream dries up, you don't go thirsty.

Another mediator acquaintance of mine is also a magician who performs locally and who uses magic tricks to break deadlock — "If you think settling this case is impossible, what do you have to say about my disappearing card trick?" Another friend has brought mediation into a local women's prison, training women lifers the conflict-resolution skills necessary to resolve prison fights that can have fatal outcomes.

The ADR opportunities available to you are limited only by your own imagination and your market's needs. Move in the direction of what you love and you'll find the work most suited to you and the audience most in need of your services.

Landing some gigs

Consulting, speaking, training, and publishing gigs are a natural extension of what you're already doing or should be doing as a successful mediator. A large part of landing these gigs consists of personal marketing — becoming a well-known and respected member of the community. Accomplish that feat and you don't have to solicit business. People will find and approach you about speaking engagements, workshops, articles, books, and more.

Start by assessing your education, experience, interests, and skills. Define your market — the people who could use what you know and are willing to pay for it. Direct your attention and your marketing efforts to that market and say "yes" whenever an opportunity to make money there arises. For more about marketing, check out Chapter 16.

Chapter 3

Training for Your Chosen Market and Niche

- -

In This Chapter

▶ Grasping the fundamentals of the legal process

▶ Transforming yourself from a lawyer to a mediator

▶ Getting mediation experience and education

▶ Becoming certified in mediation

▶ Gaining experience and knowledge on the job

▶ Adhering to mediation ethical standards

- -

*A*ny discipline worth pursuing, including mediation, requires preparation. If your background is in something other than litigation, you need to brush up on the law and the legal process. If you are an attorney, you need to balance your adversarial view of dispute resolution with collaborative dispute resolution techniques. Although you don't need a degree in mediation to practice, formal training and classes certainly help. And if you're specializing in a particular industry or market, you need to find out as much as possible about it so you can serve your clientele more effectively.

This chapter explains how to prepare yourself for what lies ahead. You find out what training is required, how to shift your thinking from an adversarial to a collaborative approach, how to pursue certification, and more. You may already have much of the knowledge and many of the skills you need to get started. This chapter helps you take inventory and plug any gaps in your education and training.

Acquiring Essential Legal Skills

You don't have to be a lawyer to practice mediation, but you do need to understand the basics of substantive and procedural law in the jurisdiction in which you practice:

✔ **Substantive law** consists of written rules that govern the rights and obligations of those who are subject to it. To mediate contractual disputes, for example, you need to know the basics of contract law. To mediate marriage disputes, for instance, you must know something about the laws that govern divorce, custody, and distribution of property. (For more on contract law, check out *Contract Law For Dummies* by Scott Burnham, published by Wiley.) The same is true of all other areas of the law applicable to your mediation niche.

✔ **Procedural law** consists of the rules a court follows in hearing and determining what happens in criminal or civil proceedings. Chapter 5 takes you through the legal process that applies to most civil lawsuits.

In addition to getting some formal training, you also need to understand how lawyers think and what they have to deal with so you can form constructive relationships that benefit the parties in a dispute. I discuss these points in the following sections.

Acquiring formal training

Courts that permit people other than lawyers to mediate litigated cases on court-annexed panels usually require that they take a full- or multi-day course that covers the legal process and the general substantive law that all attorneys learn in their first year of law school, including contracts, torts (wrongful acts that result in injury to others), real property, and civil procedure.

If you intend to specialize in mediating certain types of disputes — construction defect cases, for instance — take any reasonably priced course a local law school offers or a continuing education program related to the law that controls that type of dispute.

Knowing the law gives you a deeper understanding of the interests and motives of, and pressures on, the parties and their attorneys. Many of those pressures arise from procedural forks in the road and the substantive law that controls the outcome if the case goes to trial.

Gaining insight into the litigator's mind-set

To successfully mediate litigated cases, you need to understand the litigator's mind-set, which can be summed up as this: *Control* the field and *win* by any legally permissible means. A party in a dispute doesn't generally hire an attorney to collaborate, cooperate, compromise, accommodate, ingratiate, reconcile, conciliate, yield, give up, give way, ease, or concede. The attorney doesn't want to settle. She wants to win. Unfortunately, by the time lawyers bring their clients to you, they've usually decided that they can't win or that the cost of winning is too great to justify the expense of trial. So they shift their attention from winning the litigation to "winning" the mediation. They hope you'll overpower the will or break the spirit of the other side.

A lawyer who fights for her client is doing her job. She's not an obstacle. Helping her settle litigation is *your* job. I've heard more than one mediator say, "I could easily have settled the case if it weren't for the lawyers." But the lawyers, my friend, have *convened the parties to the mediation for you.* In the absence of a complaint and summons, most people wouldn't willingly sit down with their adversaries to resolve their dispute.

Try to see the situation from the lawyer's perspective. The client is upset, he's convinced he's right, and he tells the lawyer his side of the story, conveniently omitting any details that cast himself in an unflattering light or make his adversary appear reasonable. The lawyer doesn't get to hear the other side's version of events for months, or sometimes years, after the litigation has commenced.

By the time the attorneys bring their clients to see you, most of them are pretty tired of battering and being battered by the other side. Sometimes they have trouble delivering bad news to their clients, so they haven't fully clued their clients into just how messy their case has become. They need *you* to do that. They're hoping you'll help.

When presented with a case, ask each lawyer what you can do to help her resolve the dispute. I guarantee she'll tell you.

Brushing up on some basic concepts and terminology

When you're mediating litigated disputes, you need to transition the parties from an adversarial litigation mind-set to a collaborative mediation mind-set. To navigate the transition effectively, you need to be aware of and sensitive to the litigation mind-set they've been engaged in and the concepts and terminology they've become accustomed to dealing with, including rights, obligations, and remedies.

Rights

Rights are entitlements granted by law, custom, and agreement. Rights come in various forms depending on their source:

- **Constitutional rights:** Federal and state constitutions often grant rights to citizens. For example, the U.S. Constitution grants citizens the right to free speech and the right to bear arms.

- **Legislative rights:** State legislatures may enact any law that is reasonably related to a legitimate public interest, that conforms to federal law, and that doesn't violate the provisions of the United States or that state's constitutions. The U.S. Congress may enact any law that is both reasonably related to a legitimate public interest and that is within the federal powers granted to it by the U.S. Constitution. If Congress enacts a law that violates federal constitutional provisions, the Supreme Court may grant a petition to overturn it. Legislatures enact laws, and the courts enforce, interpret, and apply them to disputes that parties bring to the courts for resolution.

✔ **Ordinances:** Municipalities may grant rights and impose obligations upon their residents by enacting ordinances that apply only to the municipality.

✔ **Case law:** As appellate courts interpret and apply the rules of law to disputes between or among people, they often set precedents that result in granting additional rights or imposing additional obligations on the people and institutions regulated by both statutory and case law.

✔ **Contracts:** Individuals and institutions generally have the freedom to enter into a contract imposing private obligations and granting private rights that control the conduct only of the parties to the contract. The courts are required to enforce the parties' contract so long as it doesn't violate state or federal law or public policy. In other words, you can hire someone to mow your lawn but you can't hire someone to beat up your competitors.

Obligations

The law not only grants rights but also imposes *obligations*. For example, you have the right to contract with someone to work for you, but you have an obligation to pay the person at least the federally mandated minimum wage. Individuals of legal age have a right to marry, but they also have a legal obligation to support each other financially while they're married. A tenant is obligated, by contract, to pay rent, while his landlord is obligated, often by law, to provide his tenant with habitable premises — a living space in which the plumbing, electricity, and heating are all in working condition.

Just because an individual possesses a legal right to a material benefit or has a legal obligation to provide one doesn't mean that the parties will voluntarily enforce their legal rights or abide by their legal obligations. The parties are free, in almost all circumstances, to contract around their legal rights and obligations as long as they don't violate a law or public policy in doing so. The freedom to contract is very powerful.

Remedies

Remedies are the legal solutions available in adversarial proceedings. Remedies for breach of contract, for instance, are most often in the form of money damages for the harm suffered as a result of the broken promise. Less commonly, courts will force a party in breach of contract to perform. In some types of cases remedies are limited by statutes seeking to serve other purposes.

In California, for instance, no individual injured by a healthcare provider has been permitted to recover more than $250,000 in "pain and suffering" damages for the past 40 years. California lawmakers placed that cap on intangible damages because they believed that limiting awards of that type would relieve what was then perceived to be a physician-malpractice and medical-liability insurance crisis.

In litigation, parties tend to focus on legal rights, obligations, and remedies and overlook their interests — what they want and need to make the problem go away. As a mediator, part of your job is to help the parties shift their focus from rights, obligations, and remedies to issues, positions, and interests, as explained in Chapter 12.

Beware of the unauthorized practice of law

Two of the greatest hazards of mediating disputes, especially litigated cases, are the unauthorized practice of law and professional malpractice. You encounter the greatest risk of crossing the line between mediation and legal practice when you act as an evaluative mediator, and the parties and their attorneys, if attorneys are involved, expect you to tell them what you believe are the merits and demerits of their legal claims. As mediator, you can avoid these potential pitfalls in the following ways:

- ✔ If the parties have lawyers representing them during the mediation, tell them that you're certain their attorneys have provided them with all the legal advice necessary to analyze their chances of winning and the potential for an award of damages in a certain range.

- ✔ Raise doubts in the parties' minds about the merits of their claims and defenses by asking probing questions about their factual or legal positions. If you have an opinion about the merits of a claim or defense, keep that opinion to yourself. Ask the parties questions that would help them reach your same conclusion instead.

   Contracts for the sale or lease of real estate, for instance, must be in writing. If the parties have a dispute about the sale of property but they don't have a written contract, you're better off asking something like, "Do you worry about the lack of a written contract that evidences your agreement?" than saying something like, "You're going to have a hard time enforcing that agreement in the absence of a written contract." This is better mediation technique in any event, because the more confrontational approach puts the party on the defensive. Posing a question gives the party a chance to evaluate his chances of success or failure for himself, and he's going to be more receptive to the conclusions he draws for himself.

✔ When the parties don't have counsel to represent their interests, warn them that you're either not an attorney or, if you are a lawyer, that you don't represent their interests and won't be providing them with legal advice. Tell them that they may have rights, obligations, or defenses of which they're unaware unless they seek legal advice from an attorney who has agreed to represent their interests.

✔ If the parties know what they want and don't care what the law says they're entitled to, reaffirm that during the mediation and proceed without discussing the legal merits or demerits of their claims or defenses. If they tell you they do care about their legal rights, obligations, and defenses, encourage them to seek legal advice before mediating further or, if they reach an agreement, that they may want to condition the enforceability of that agreement on the advice of an attorney they consult within a set period of time.

Because part of your job when performing evaluative mediation is to raise doubts in the parties' minds about their chances of success at trial, you may be tempted to give your opinion concerning the merits of the parties' claims and defenses. This is a risky strategy because it could be viewed as legal advice down the road if either party catches a case of mediation remorse. If you're not a lawyer, you could be accused of practicing law without a license, and whether or not you're a lawyer, you could be charged with legal malpractice.

Transitioning from Lawyer to Mediator

As a lawyer, you may have a leg up on those who have little or no experience in the legal system, but in a way, you're at a slight disadvantage. You've been indoctrinated in the philosophy and practice of resolving conflict through legal means — an adversarial process. Now, you have to unlearn some of what's been ingrained since law school and start to think like a mediator. The following sections provide guidance to make a successful transition from litigation to mediation.

Ditching the rights and remedies approach

The litigation story starts when a relationship is disrupted (contract breached, partnership dissolved, marriage terminated, and so on) or someone is injured (property stolen, pedestrians injured, consumers ripped off, and so on). Everything was good until one person's bad behavior set in motion a series of events that resulted in another's loss.

In an effort to deliver justice and establish rational and universally applicable rules of civil behavior, the law focuses on facts, rights, obligations, and remedies, as explained in the preceding section. It strips the parties' dispute of nearly everything that makes it unique, complex, ambiguous, multidimensional, and intricately textured. The law ignores context. It also ignores *feelings,* presuming that people are capable of making entirely rational decisions.

To transition from lawyer to mediator, you need to stop telling the adversarial litigation story, which names, claims, and blames, and start telling a story in which disputes arise more commonly from miscommunications, inadvertence, and outside influences rather than from an opponent's bad faith or evil motives.

Shifting focus to interests

Your job as a mediator is to help the parties place their dispute in context again and restore their right to express their emotions — the feelings of injustice that made them file suit in the first place. You do this by steering the conversation away from black-and-white formulations and into the gray zone where people actually live. You then encourage and assist the parties in a collaborative effort to resolve their conflict mutually rather than to stage a morality play in which one party emerges victorious while the other is crushed in defeat.

As a mediator, you help the parties locate and address their interests rather than focus on the factual and legal positions they must take to prevail in litigation.

Recognize the difference between rights and interests. *Rights* are entitlements granted by law, custom, or agreement, and courts typically enforce rights by granting monetary rewards. *Interests* are what motivate people to action and inaction — fears, desires, needs, preferences, priorities, and attitudes about the future. If you don't pay your rent, I have a *right* to evict you, but I also may have an *interest* in keeping you as a tenant:

- ✔ My right is to file an action for unlawful detainer, obtain a judgment against you, and send a sheriff to evict you. Then I can plant a "For Rent" sign on the scorched lawn and watch the weeds grow until the economy improves. Those are my *rights.*

- ✔ I may also have an *interest* in keeping you. I'm in a down market and tenants are difficult to find. I have to pay the mortgage, and to do that, I need tenants from whom I collect rent. Maybe I'm tired of dealing with rental properties, so I really want to sell the house I'm leasing. To obtain the best price, I have to fix up the property and keep it on the market long enough to find a buyer willing to pay top price for it. I might be better served to keep you on the property and ask that you maintain it than to evict you and have to maintain it myself.

We may also have *mutual interests* that we can work together to serve. Maybe you don't have money, but you have time, tools, and skills to help me manage and fix up the property. If you fix up the premises, you can have a place to live, and I can move closer to my goal of selling the property some day. If we sit down to have coffee or a meal together, we may well find other interests we have in common, other ways we can be of service to each other. Perhaps you have a real estate license but haven't been able to sell a piece of property for the past six months. That's why you don't have the money for rent. After fixing up the property, you're willing to waive your commission on a sale if I defer the rent for six months. The possibilities of an interest-based solution to our undeniably mutual problem are endless. The probabilities of a rights and remedies solution are narrow, unpredictable, and sometimes worse than the problem they're meant to resolve. Someone *always* loses.

If you remember that the law is for people who can't solve their own problems, you're halfway through your transition from lawyer to mediator.

Getting Schooled

You finally decided what you want to be when you grow up — a mediator. Now you want to know how to get from where you are now to the mediator you want to be. That requires experience from the college of hard knocks, along with some formal education. The good news is that you may already have some of what you need.

The following sections describe the premediation experience/education you need (and may already have) and the type of mediation-specific educational programs available.

Warming up with premediation experience and education

Premediation experience and education typically consists of what you've already experienced and what you know:

- ✔ **Experience:** Experience counts, whether it's as a social worker, therapist, human resources manager, physician, nurse, small-business owner, or even a gangbanger who wants to work in victim-offender mediation.

- ✔ **Education:** Formal or informal education in psychology, philosophy, criminal justice, law, sociology, social work, or anthropology is especially valuable when transitioning to a career in mediation. You may want to supplement what you already know by reading about the social psychology of conflict, negotiation, peace work, international relations, and the like whenever you have a chance.

Anyone at any age can become a mediator. I've coached children as young as 10 who could leave many of my mature mediator colleagues in the dust. A friend of mine was serving as a New York City police detective when he became interested in mediation. He wanted to add conflict resolution to his tool kit and ended up as a full-time mediator with the department. The only essential qualifications you need are an interest in peaceful conflict resolution and an attraction to the field.

Obtaining an ADR program certificate of completion

Numerous programs offer *certificates of completion* to satisfy the requirements of community mediation and court-annexed alternative dispute resolution (ADR) programs. Certificates from these programs attest to the completion of a 28-, 36-, or 42-hour course that covers the theory and practice of mediation; negotiation; different mediation styles; ethics; legal processes; communication and counseling skills; cross-cultural conflict resolution; and the psychology of conflict. Courses typically involve some role-playing activities in which students can test out a theory and practice on hypothetical disputes with their classmates.

Pursuing a formal dispute resolution education

No one *needs* an advanced degree to practice mediation, but many people love the work so much that they want to know everything about the field. If you take a mediation course, you too may find yourself hungry for further and deeper education about your new profession. This section describes some ways you can pursue formal education in mediation.

University certificate programs

Several universities offer certificate programs in conflict resolution, requiring students to spend between 480 and 810 hours of classroom study and externships combined. These programs may be affiliated with law schools, such as the Straus Institute's certificate program at Pepperdine University School of Law; with state colleges, such as the post-master's degree certificate from California State University at Dominguez Hills; or with state universities, such as the University of California's certificate program at its Santa Barbara campus.

MDR degrees

Many universities now offer Master Dispute Resolution (MDR) degrees. Anyone with a bachelor's degree can apply to the Straus MDR program, a 32-unit course of study with several required courses and many elective courses. The required courses are arbitration, communication and conflict, cross-cultural conflict and dispute resolution, interviewing, counseling and planning, introduction to legal processes , mediation or investor advocacy clinic, mediation theory and practice, negotiation theory and practice, and the psychology of conflict. (For details, visit www.law.pepperdine.edu/straus.)

The Straus MDR degree is also offered as a joint JD-MDR degree for law students. Lawyers interested in earning a degree in conflict resolution are welcome to seek the MDR degree, but most go on to obtain a Master of Laws degree (LL.M) in dispute resolution, which is a lengthier program available only to those who've earned their Juris Doctor (J.D.).

Bachelor's degrees and minors

Some universities offer bachelor's degrees in conflict resolution. California State University at Dominguez Hills, for example, offers a Bachelor of Arts in negotiation, conflict resolution, and peacebuilding. It also offers a 36-semester unit Master of Arts degree. Antioch University Midwest in Ohio offers a Master of Arts degree in conflict analysis and engagement, as well as a bachelor's degree in dispute resolution.

Many colleges and universities feature minors in conflict resolution, even if they don't offer a bachelor's degree in it. Consider majoring in just about any of the humanities, especially psychology or anthropology, and minoring in conflict resolution.

LL.M and doctoral degrees

The Master of Laws (LL.M) in dispute resolution is a recent addition to law school curricula. The Straus Institute for Dispute Resolution offers LL.M degrees for attorneys. Other law schools that award LL.M degrees in dispute resolution include the University of Missouri-Columbia School of Law, the Vermont Law School, the Benjamin N. Cardozo School of Law in New York City, the U.C. Hastings College of the Law in San Francisco, and the Moritz College of Law at Ohio State University.

Doctoral programs are available at Southeastern University in Florida, the University of Kent in England, State University of New York at Buffalo, Fresno Pacific University in California, and the Werner Institute for Negotiation and Dispute Resolution at Creighton University School of Law in Nebraska.

A little background on law degrees

The three-year law school degree is a Juris Doctor (J.D.), but the subsequent advanced law degree is just a master's (the LL.M). The reason for this is part history and part status envy. In Britain, where the common law system of the United States originated, law school is an undergraduate degree. U.S. legal education followed that historic practice, awarding LL.B (Bachelor of Law) degrees well after law schools in the U.S. began to require students to first obtain Bachelor of Arts degrees before commencing their legal studies.

In the 1960s, lawyers got tired of having two bachelor's degrees rather than a graduate degree denoting the post-university education the law required. Hence the creation of the J.D. The older forms persisted, however, so that the post-J.D. degree is an LL.M, followed by the S.J.D for doctoral-level legal studies.

Becoming a Subject Matter Expert

Whether you're a former gang member, civil litigator, social worker, therapist, physician, HR administrator, or sous chef, you know more about how and why the people in your profession and community start, escalate, and fail to resolve conflict than any former judge or PhD in conflict resolution. In fact, the first step in becoming an industry and subject matter expert is to realize that, to some degree, you're already an expert. Mentally walk yourself through an ordinary day, remaining sensitive to the conflicts that surround you. Where do you see conflict over scarce resources ripening into a fresh dispute? Do you work in an office in which the staff gossips about and then shuns a critical member of the sales team? Are you the only member of your family capable of getting Grandma and Dad on speaking terms over the Thanksgiving turkey? Are you a registered nurse who successfully manages patient care, family conflict, staff and physician relations, and fights among the custodial workers better than anyone else on the floor? Can you calm a gymnasium full of teenagers or break the legislative budget impasse? If so, you already have industry expertise.

If you're not well-versed in your chosen niche, however, you'd better get up to speed. You probably already have some specialized knowledge, but you can never have too much. To gain knowledge and insight and keep abreast of changes in the industry, develop a continuing education program of your own that includes the following:

✔ Read industry journals and other industry or niche-focused publications.

✔ Attend trade shows and conferences where you have the opportunity to talk shop with leaders in the field.

✔ Network locally with people in the same industry or niche.

✔ Get involved in online communities and discussion forums related to the industry or niche.

Getting Certified or Qualified

Certification in the mediation profession is controversial and confusing. Some state courts certify mediators who meet specified requirements — among these are courts in the state of Florida and the probate court in New Hampshire, which certifies marital mediators. Other courts, however, including the Massachusetts courts, have no certification system. Instead, mediators are "approved" or "qualified" by their education and experience.

Certification or qualification may or may not improve your mediation knowledge and skills, but it signals to courts and prospective clients that you've met at least the minimum requirements to skillfully conduct a mediation. The word *certified* or *qualified* implies that an individual has met certain professional standards. It's not the same as licensing. Doctors, lawyers, social workers, and hairdressers all need licenses to practice their professions. Mediators don't need to be licensed to practice mediation. Some court programs, however, require a certificate or a certain number of hours of training by approved mediation education programs to be included in their court-annexed programs. These mediators are said to be "qualified" or "certified," but those designations aren't standardized and don't give mediators the imprimatur of any state or federal agency other than the court on whose panel they might serve.

Agencies that license or certify professionals to practice in their field generally audit educational programs, requiring accredited schools to offer certain curricula and resources. They usually test applicants or require assessors to provide documentation showing that the applicants have been observed at work and are qualified to provide the services the profession renders. None of the certification programs mentioned in this book are within that category of program.

Whether qualification or certification is required before you're permitted to mediate for a particular court or agency and how you go about getting certified vary among the courts and the organizations that require it or provide it. The following sections explain what to expect, how to find information about certification requirements, and how to pursue certifications through court programs and the private sector.

Becoming certified or qualified for court-annexed and government programs

Every court-annexed mediation panel requires minimum qualifications and training for acceptance to the panel. You can usually find information about the court's mediation training and experience requirements on the court's website. If the court doesn't have this information on its site, find a phone number to call or an e-mail address to contact someone who can steer you in the right direction.

Some courts, such as the Los Angeles Superior Court, permit lawyers and others to serve as civil mediation panel neutrals as long as they meet the following requirements:

- ✔ They must have a minimum of 40 hours of mediation training, 20 of which are from a single trainer who teaches mediation theories and styles, confidentiality, ethics, convening, negotiating, caucus strategies, effective communications techniques, cross-cultural challenges, and methods for breaking impasse and closing the session emotionally and legally. Ten of the mandated 40 training hours must include role play, observation, and lecture. All mediators are also required to complete five mediations that are at least two hours in length.

- ✔ Applicants without law degrees must also possess a bachelor's degree and take three hours of "litigation nuts and bolts training" on legal terminology, processes, rules, and procedures.

- ✔ Attorney applicants must be members in good standing with any state bar.

New York's state courts also require mediators on their roster to complete 40 hours of approved training. The system has no formal educational requirement beyond this; anyone with the requisite training can serve.

Eighty of the 94 federal district courts have some sort of ADR program. Each of these trial-level federal courts has its own training and experience requirements. Some of them, like the federal District Court for the Central District of California, provide the necessary training for their "settlement officers" free of charge, but these neutrals must have at least ten years of experience as attorneys admitted to practice before that federal court.

To find information about the federal district courts for your state, start at www.uscourts.gov. You may not be able to find information about requirements and training on the court's website, but you'll find contact information for offices that can help you find the information. Some nonprofit agencies also offer basic to advanced levels of mediation training. Check out www.vorp.com for an example.

Getting certified or qualified in the private sector

Unless you want to work on a court-annexed mediation panel, you don't need to be certified or qualified through any particular certifying authority. Anyone can hang out a shingle as a mediator with no education or training. However, hundreds of mediation training firms offer certifications. Some are all but meaningless, but others signify that you're an A-lister, a master mediator. The following sections describe some of the better certification programs.

ACR Family and Divorce Mediator Advanced Practitioner

Although the well-known Association for Conflict Resolution (ACR; www.acrnet.org) doesn't certify its members, it does allow a qualified practitioner to designate herself as an ACR Family and Divorce Mediator Advanced Practitioner. The qualifications for that designation include a minimum of 60 hours of family mediation training and 250 hours of face-to-face family mediation experience.

International Academy of Mediators Certification

One of the most prestigious mediation certifications is granted by the International Academy of Mediators (www.iamed.org), which describes itself as a "fellowship of preeminent commercial mediators." The standards for certification aren't public. To be certified by this organization, a current member must nominate you for membership and members must approve the nomination.

The International Mediation Institute

The International Mediation Institute (www.imimediation.org) is another nonprofit organization that provides its members with certification that they've satisfied its professional standards. IMI was founded in 2007 by American, Dutch, Chinese, and Bahrain mediation providers, including the prestigious American Arbitration Association (AAA). Qualifications for membership in this exclusive, world-class mediation association are strict because the IMI strives to serve its mission of driving transparency and high competency standards into mediation practice across all fields, worldwide.

Mediators who want to be certified by IMI under the qualifying program instituted by the AAA must

- Mediate a minimum of 25 disputes (15 of them for pay) for no fewer than 200 hours
- Complete at least 40 hours of training in mediation theory and skills in programs approved by AAA/ICDR

✔ Complete at least 100 additional hours of study or training in dispute resolution generally

✔ Submit to live-action mediation skill, performance, and competence assessments by AAA-appointed assessors

The Massachusetts Council on Family Mediation

The Massachusetts Council on Family Mediation (MCFM; www.mcfm.org), a private not-for-profit organization, was the first organization to certify family mediators. It has some of the most stringent requirements for earning an MCFM certification, including a formal educational requirement of a J.D. or a master's degree or doctorate in dispute resolution, mental health, or a related behavioral science. This certification, like all others in the U.S., isn't a license to practice mediation and isn't required to practice family mediation in Massachusetts or anywhere else. It simply indicates that the certified individual has met the requirements of the MCFM. You can be a member of the MCFM without being a certified member.

Other well-known organizations that have certification standards include the Washington Mediation Association (www.washingtonmediation.org) and the Idaho Mediation Association (www.idahomediation.org).

Arranging for On-the-Job Training

Every great mediator has at least one world-class mediation mentor, several subject-matter and marketing mentors, and as many sponsors as she can find. The difference between mentor and sponsor is important:

✔ A *mentor* helps you learn your trade by permitting you to observe his mediations, giving you tips for improving your mediation techniques, and making suggestions about resources available in the local community to continue your practical training.

✔ A *sponsor* puts her own skin in the game on your behalf. She introduces you to her contacts, brings you into the organizations that have helped her build her business, recommends you for speaking engagements or writing assignments, and vouches for the quality of your work.

Mentors are, of course, easier to find than sponsors because a sponsor puts her own reputation on the line by recommending you. Here are some of the most effective ways to find both mentors and sponsors:

✔ Join your local mediation association and volunteer your time. Doing so gives other association members an opportunity to evaluate your performance and see how reliable, energetic, creative, intelligent, and hardworking you are.

- ✔ Join industry groups in your area of specialty and volunteer your time.

- ✔ Contact a mediator who has a good reputation in town and ask whether he'd permit you to observe one or more of his mediations, noting your respect for the work he does and the high esteem in which he's held in the community.

- ✔ Take well-known mediators out to lunch to ask them about how they built their own practices and how they improved their mediation skills.

Some mediators refuse to allow others to observe their mediations because confidentiality is a mediator's stock in trade. Some mediators believe that allowing a stranger to observe a mediator at work leaves the mediator vulnerable to liability in the event that the observer breaches the confidentiality of the session.

Even those mediators, however, often agree to permit observation so long as they know the observer well or someone else who they know well vouches for the observer's good character. In all cases in which an observer attends a mediation, the mediator must first ask the disputants whether they'll agree to the presence of an observer, and the observer should agree to the same degree of confidentiality as the mediator does.

Brushing Up on Ethical Standards for Mediators

As a mediator, you belong to an elite group of dedicated professionals, and your colleagues expect you to behave accordingly. Although this group has no single set of rules to follow and the rules that do exist are open to debate, many ADR associations have crafted and adopted their own standards of conduct for mediators. The most widely accepted is the *Model Standards of Conduct for Mediators* (www.abanet.org/dispute/documents/model_ standards_conduct_april2007.pdf), which has been approved by the American Bar Association and adopted by the American Arbitration Association and the Association for Conflict Resolution.

The *Model Standards of Conduct for Mediators* addresses several areas, including party self-determination; mediator competence, confidentiality, and impartiality; responsibility for ensuring the quality of the process; truthfulness in advertising; accuracy of information regarding fees and other charges; and more. In the following sections, I explain the basics.

If you serve or plan on serving on a court-annexed panel, find out whether the courts have any ethical standards in place for practicing mediation. Though the *Model Standards of Conduct for Mediators* contains guidelines you probably *should* follow, rules set by the court are rules you *must* follow. Programs can lose their approval to provide services to the courts, and neutrals can be removed from program panels for failure to honor these ethical duties.

Ensuring party self-determination

One of your roles as mediator is to ensure party self-determination, which is a fancy way of saying that the parties determine the process and the outcome — that they're not coerced in any way to enter into a settlement agreement or a process for resolving their dispute with which they're not satisfied.

You're not a used car salesman, and you don't represent the "deal." Whether the parties have been ordered to mediation or have reluctantly decided to "give it a shot," remind them that the entire mediation is a voluntary process. Tell them that

   ✔ You're not the boss of them; they are. Nobody else is the boss of them either — not their representatives, and not anyone else who may be pressuring them to do something they don't feel comfortable doing.

   ✔ Your role is to ensure that they're not coerced into doing anything they don't want to do, particularly by you.

   ✔ Your job is to make sure they understand the consequences of resolution and the consequences of impasse.

   ✔ They're free to reject an offer or demand and terminate the mediation at any time, even if it may not be in their best interest to do so.

Self-determination extends to the process the parties follow to resolve their conflict, but you're ultimately responsible for ensuring the quality of the process. See the section "Ensuring procedural and substantive fairness" later in the chapter.

Don't sideline the clients in a litigated dispute. Mediators are often lawyers who are more comfortable dealing with other lawyers than with the parties. And lawyer representatives often prefer to deal directly with the mediator, reach agreement with the lawyer on the other side, and then ask the mediator to play the heavy, selling a resolution to their clients. Don't play that game. Your job is to help counsel and their clients find the sweet spot — where a proposed resolution is equally satisfactory to them both.

Remaining impartial

As a mediator, you must remain *impartial* — don't play favorites or allow any bias or prejudice to govern the way you conduct the mediation. You can and probably will form opinions about each party's motives, veracity, the pros and cons of their positions, or even the interests that are driving them. That's okay. But don't give any party preferential treatment.

As a mediator, you don't represent either client. You must remain impartial and avoid any behavior that may be perceived as a breach of impartiality. Following are some formal rules regarding impartiality that you should keep in mind:

> A mediator must maintain impartiality toward all participants in the mediation process at all times. [California Rule of Court 1620.5(a)]

> Mediators should not have any substantial personal or business relationships with any of the parties and have a continuing duty to disclose potential areas of conflict that might affect their impartiality. [California Rule of Court 1620.5(b)]

> A mediator must not accept any gift that might raise a question concerning his or her impartiality. [California Rule of Court 1620.9(d)]

Standard II of the *Model Standards of Conduct for Mediators* requires a mediator to conduct a mediation in an "impartial manner" and describes impartiality as "freedom from favoritism, bias, or prejudice."

Remaining impartial often is most difficult in separate caucus, because that's when the parties and their representatives tend to make the most inflammatory remarks, when they try to get you to be an advocate for their side, and when you're called upon to answer to your better angels.

In a collection case, the attorney for the claimant and I engaged in a cost-benefit analysis during separate caucus. We both agreed that his clients would lose even if they won in litigation because the defendant would probably declare bankruptcy if the case went to trial. The attorney heaved a deep sigh and said that I didn't understand his clients' motivations. He said, "They would rather destroy this guy and talk about it over cigars and 20-year-old scotch than take less than \$X."

I have strong judgments about attitudes like that, and it's not easy for me to stay centered and impartial, but that's what I had to do if I was going to continue to assist the parties in resolving their dispute. I counted to 10 and proceeded to ask open-ended diagnostic questions to ascertain whether the attorney's harsh characterization of his clients was accurate or whether he was bluffing, playing the tough guy, and hoping that statements like this would influence me to lean more heavily on the defendants to make the concessions he wanted.

Recognizing how easily clients can be misled into believing that you represent their interests

Parents often teach you valuable lessons, sometimes unwittingly, as my own mother did several years ago when she entered into a foolish investment with her employer without consulting an attorney (me!) first. The first time she told me about her investment was the day on which she lost all her money. As I was bemoaning her failure to consult with an attorney, she told me she had:

"Who did you hire, mom?"

"I didn't hire anyone," she said. "My boss invited me to an attorney's office in downtown San Diego, and that attorney explained the deal to us."

"But that was *his* attorney," I moaned, "not *yours*."

"He told me that," she said, as I quietly writhed on the other end of the telephone line. "But he wouldn't lie to me, and one attorney's advice is as good as another; it seemed wasteful to hire my own."

That's how easily a litigant can form the belief that you're representing his interests as well as the interests of his opponent. And though you may believe that their interests overlap, it's critical for you to explain, as often as necessary, that your role is not to get a better deal for one disputant or the other. Your role is to help them find a deal that's satisfactory to both of them.

I helped the parties close most of the gap between their purported bottom lines. Finally, after a grueling day, Mr. Tough Guy walked out of the mediation. When I delivered this news to the defendant, she burst into tears, and we spend the next 20 minutes talking about the wisdom of making a counteroffer that I was pretty certain the plaintiff would accept. She agreed and I called the plaintiff's attorney's cellphone. He came back and we inked the deal that night.

If you lose your cool and your impartiality, don't beat yourself up over it. You'll fail from time to time. Learn from it and move on. Your most painful recollections of your *partial, judgmental* responses will be your best teacher. Reflect on them, use them as guides to the future, and work on your own issues so that they don't intrude into the mediation space.

Impartiality also means refraining from any behavior that would help one party more than another. Unsophisticated parties may assume that you represent their interests. You need to disabuse them of this notion as often as necessary during the mediation process.

The "black letter" rules in my jurisdiction on this topic are as broad as they are unhelpful, but they do accurately state the ethical obligation to remain neutral:

A mediator must inform all participants, at or before the outset of the first mediation session, that during the mediation he or she will not represent any participant as a lawyer or perform professional services in any capacity other than as an impartial mediator. [Rule of Court 1620.7(d)]

A mediator may also assist the parties in preparing a written settlement agreement, provided that in doing so the mediator confines the assistance to stating the settlement as determined by the parties. [Rule of Court 1620.7(h)]

The Virginia Standards of Ethics and Professional Responsibility for Certified Mediators is more descriptive of what a "neutral" does. Those Standards provide that mediation "is a process in which a neutral facilitates communication between the parties and, without deciding the issues or imposing a solution on the parties, enables them to understand and to reach a mutually agreeable resolution to their dispute."

Being upfront about your compensation

Success as a mediator means getting paid commensurate with your services, but you need to be upfront about how much you charge and who's footing the bill. The following guidelines apply to most locations:

- ✔ Disclose to the parties in writing any fees, costs, or charges to be paid to you by the parties.
- ✔ Inform the parties about the source of your compensation, especially if only one party is paying for your services.
- ✔ Abide by any agreement you reach with the parties concerning compensation. In other words, charge the parties only what you promised to charge them in your written fees, costs, and charges disclosure.

- ✔ Don't base your fees on the outcome of the mediation. Though an attorney may charge a contingency fee of 25 to 40 percent of the settlement, receiving a percentage of the settlement is not an option for you as a mediator. Contingency fees tend to undermine impartiality, compromise neutrality, and may even interfere with party self-determination.

Practicing in your area of competence

One of the fuzzier areas of mediation ethics involves competency. Theoretically, a well-trained mediator should be able to help disputants resolve any conflict. After all, as one of my mentors told me, "People don't have *legal* problems. Only lawyers have legal problems. People have *people* problems."

However, I refrain from certain types of disputes that I think I lack the competence to mediate, including the following:

- ✔ Any mediation in which one party isn't legally competent and doesn't have a representative to protect his interests; that is, teenagers, the mentally ill, or people in abusive relationships where a mediated resolution could cause harm to the abused party. This includes any mediation that involves the welfare of children in a divorce or custody proceeding where the children don't have representatives and their interests are therefore not being represented.

- ✔ Any mediation in which one party is likely to understand the legal consequences of any resolution and the other isn't, unless both are represented by legal counsel.

Many attorneys believe that non-attorney mediators aren't competent to mediate the resolution of litigated disputes because they don't understand the law or how the facts relate to the probable outcome of any legal claim. I know several highly successful and well-respected mediators who handle litigated cases without being lawyers. Sometimes, they do a better job than the lawyer mediator because they don't get caught up in the legal analysis. Mediation, after all, seeks interest-based solutions that satisfy both parties' needs, desires, preferences, priorities, and the like. In a litigated case, both sides generally are represented by attorneys who know the law. The mediator doesn't necessarily need to know the particular laws governing the legal resolution of the matter, although understanding civil procedure and how the substantive law affects the parties' attitudes about the potential resolution of the lawsuit is critical.

Some mediators believe that a mediator should be able to demonstrate cross-cultural competence if she's going to mediate a dispute with people from different cultures; for example, between an Asian immigrant and an African American from Beverly Hills.

All mediators should understand cross-cultural dynamics, but to require every mediator to have specific knowledge of diverse cultures and customs would make it tremendously difficult for people to find competent mediators and for competent mediators to find work in major metropolitan areas. That said, general training in cross-cultural understanding is a must for all mediators.

Ensuring procedural and substantive fairness

To varying degrees, mediators are responsible for ensuring procedural and substantive fairness:

✔ **Procedural fairness:** Often referred to as *procedural justice,* this is simply a sense of fair play, or as the California Rules of Court put it, "a balanced process in which each party is given an opportunity to participate and make uncoerced decisions." If you're impartial, competent, and disclose any potential conflicts of interest, you're well on your way to ensuring procedural fairness. (For more about ensuring a sense of procedural justice, see Chapter 11.)

✔ **Substantive fairness:** Substantive fairness means that the deal is equitable to both parties. Unfortunately, determining what's fair and what's not is often impossible, and sometimes what may be considered lopsided is best for both parties. As a result, mediation standards vary widely concerning the mediator's responsibility to ensure substantive fairness. Mediators often ensure substantive fairness in as unobtrusive a manner as possible by, for instance,

- Asking the parties whether they're aware of their legal rights and obligations and, if not, whether they would change their agreement if they knew they were entitled to more or obliged to part with less.

- Recommending to the parties that they seek legal advice so they can make a truly informed decision; that is, knowing their legal rights, they choose to follow informal or formal agreements that the law would likely not enforce.

Consult the mediation rules and standards in your jurisdiction and community to determine guidelines for ensuring substantive fairness. California has resolved this question by providing that a mediator "is not obligated to ensure the substantive fairness of an agreement reached by the parties" [Rule of Court 1620.7(b)]. Other states may require that the mediator ensure the substantive fairness of the final agreement.

In my opinion, requiring mediators to ensure the substantive fairness of an agreement runs counter to many of the other standards mediators must follow. For example, the principle of substantive fairness runs counter to the principle of self-determination — if a third party has to tell the two disputants what's fair, they're not free to determine for themselves what's fair. In addition, for a mediator to protect one party's interests against the other would require the mediator to set aside her duties of impartiality and neutrality.

Keeping mediation and arbitration separate

When you've engaged parties in a mediation, don't shift gears to a different alternative dispute resolution (ADR) procedure, such as arbitration, without the consent of both parties. And where the parties aren't represented by counsel, it's wise never to act as an arbitrator after you've acted as a mediator, because you're in possession of confidential information from both sides that would never be disclosed to a neutral who's going to resolve the dispute for the parties rather than help them resolve it themselves.

Know the difference between mediation and arbitration:

- ✔ **Mediation:** A process in which you help the parties resolve their misunderstandings and resolve their conflict to their mutual satisfaction.

- ✔ **Arbitration:** A process in which you review the evidence presented to you and present what you believe would be a fair resolution.

Don't do arbitration and simply call it mediation.

Maintaining confidentiality

Confidentiality is essential in achieving success as a mediator, so protect the information the parties share with you in mediation very carefully. Specifically, adhere to these rules of confidentiality:

- ✔ Don't disclose information that one party has shared with you in confidence to another party unless the revealing party has authorized you to do so.

- ✔ Don't discuss details of the mediation process or outcome with anyone not involved in the mediation.

- ✔ Don't use information you acquired in confidence in the course of a mediation outside of the mediation for personal gain. In other words, if you know that a major corporation is going to benefit by reaching a settlement with the claimants, don't use that information to purchase stock in the company.

You should also discuss with the parties the confidentiality of the information they share or the agreement they reach in mediation if their dispute eventually ends up in litigation. For details, see Chapter 4.

State law may have a say in your obligations as a mediator regarding confidentiality. For example, if during a mediation you encounter evidence that makes you suspect that someone is abusing a child, you may be obligated by law to report what you know to law enforcement authorities. In addition, if you're subpoenaed to testify in court regarding knowledge you obtained during a mediation, you may be legally obligated to testify. In California, state law makes a mediator "incompetent" to testify — a provision about which most mediators *and* judges are unaware. When mediators are subpoenaed, they should seek help from their local mediation association. In Los Angeles, they've received *pro bono* legal help to resist the subpoena from an association of mediation professionals. If you're subpoenaed as a result of your participation in a court-annexed program, ask the program to provide you with legal counsel. Most mediators carry mediation insurance. You should check your insurance policy to see whether it provides coverage for retention of counsel when you're asked to testify to anything other than the fact that you served as a mediator and the mediation took place.

Improving the profession

Part of your role as mediator is to improve the profession, which benefits not only mediation clients and the community, but you, too! The *Model Standards of Conduct for Mediators* sums up what improving the profession really means:

> A mediator should demonstrate respect for differing points of view within the field, seek to learn from other mediators, and *work together with other mediators to improve the profession* and better serve people in conflict. (Emphasis mine.)

Improving the profession means continually improving your own practice by attending advanced training, soliciting feedback, reading, and writing. I've personally found that I've improved my practice more by writing about my mediations (even if only in journal form) than through any other practice. When you reflect and write about your interventions, you see much more clearly how you may have done better.

Following are some further suggestions on how to improve the mediation profession:

- ✔ Foster diversity.
- ✔ Make mediation accessible to those who are least able to afford it.
- ✔ Be active in mediation associations and outreach and education programs.
- ✔ Help novice mediators through training, mentoring, and networking.
- ✔ Engage in discussions in the mediation community to share your knowledge, experience, and insights.

Maintaining integrity in advertising

Most of the rules that govern solicitation and advertising apply to truthfulness in advertising and not using client names or information without their express permission:

- Don't be misleading when presenting your qualifications, experience, services, or fees.

- Don't include promises concerning the outcome, such as a 90 percent settlement rate.

- Don't claim that you're certified by a government entity or private organization unless the organization has procedures in place to certify members.

- Don't advertise in a way that shows favoritism to a certain type of client (for example, personal injury claimants) or in any other way that may undermine the integrity of the mediation process.

- Don't mention client names in your advertising unless they've given their express permission to do so.

Exploring additional standards

I've highlighted some of the most important ethical standards in the mediation field, but you can find additional information by exploring other resources, including the following:

- *Model Standards of Practice for Family and Divorce Mediation,* developed by the Symposium on Standards of Practice and approved by the ABA House of Delegates in February 2001, at `www.americanbar.org/content/dam/aba/migrated/family/reports/mediation.authcheckdam.pdf`

- The ABA's *National Clearinghouse for Mediator Ethics Opinions* at `www.americanbar.org/directories/mediator_ethics_opinion.html`

- *Model Rules of Professional Conduct Amendments* (2002) at `www.abanet.org/cpr/mrpc/mrpc_toc.html`

- *Principles for ADR Provider Organizations,* drafted by the CPR-Georgetown Commission on Ethics and Standards of Practice in ADR (May 2002), at `http://cpradr.org/Resources/ALLCPRArticles/tabid/265/ID/623/Principles-for-ADR-Provider-Organizations.aspx`

- ✔ *Mediation Ethics Guidelines,* published by JAMS, at `www.jamsadr.com/mediators-ethics`

- ✔ The *Uniform Mediation Act,* adopted by the National Conference of Commissioners on Uniform State Laws and recommended for enactment by states in August 2001, at `www.nccusl.org/Act.aspx?title=Mediation%20Act`

- ✔ The *Uniform Rules on Dispute Resolution* at `www.mass.gov/courts/admin/legal/newadrbook.pdf`

Take your ethical duties very seriously. If you fail to honor the ethical standards established for mediators in your jurisdiction, you could potentially be sued for malpractice or be removed from a prestigious panel. It also harms the reputation of the field at large and undermines public confidence when mediators fail to honor ethical codes of conduct, whether the standards are recommended or required. Consider taking a mediation course in your area that covers ethics.

Part II
Becoming a Master Mediator

The 5th Wave   By Rich Tennant

H. FELDER
MEDIATION
SERVICES

"Before we begin mediation, I'd ask that you leave your animus, stress, and blowguns in the hallway."

In this part . . .

Successful mediation requires mastery of a highly specialized skill set. You must understand the overall process, know what to expect whether you're mediating litigated or nonlitigated disputes, and be able to choose the best approach to a mediation based on the nature of the dispute. You must also grasp fundamental techniques, including anchoring, framing, and logrolling; know how and when to apply them; and use your knowledge of conflict dynamics to recognize and disrupt any counterproductive tactics a party may employ.

In this part, I present tried-and-true mediation strategies and help you acquire and hone the essential skills of a master mediator. You'll probably want to revisit the chapters in this part again and again as you practice these strategies and techniques in real-world mediations until they become part of you.

Chapter 4

Navigating the Mediation Process

*B*efore you can become a master mediator, you have to be a mediator, which entails navigating the mediation process from point A to point B. This chapter leads you through the mediation process from start to finish — from the time someone contacts you to request your services to when the parties sign off on their agreement.

Convening a Mediation

Convening a mediation means getting the parties to agree to mediation instead of litigation (or violence!) as the means to resolve their dispute. More often than not, someone else convenes the mediation before you step in:

▬ Community mediation centers hire skilled conveners who spend a large part of their day convincing one of the disputants to mediate a claim that an aggrieved party has brought to the center. If you're doing community or private litigated-case mediation, the convener calls you after she's convened the mediation and asks you to serve as a *neutral* (mediator).

▬ If you're on a private mediation panel — such as JAMS, Judicate West, or ADR Services, Inc. — attorneys who want to retain mediators to help them settle a litigated case contact the panel's case manager and request the services of a specific mediator or ask who the case manager believes is most qualified to conduct their mediation. Your case manager calls you to ask for your availability and whether you have any conflicts.

✔ Third parties also convene court-annexed mediations. Often, the court itself orders a case to mediation or strongly suggests that the parties hire a third-party neutral to help them settle the matter. Usually, the attorneys acting under court compulsion or suasion repair to the court's alternative dispute resolution (ADR) office to choose a panel mediator they agree on. The attorneys generally communicate their choice to ADR office personnel, who provide the necessary paperwork to the chosen neutral.

Even when someone else convenes a mediation for you, you're always in the process of convening the parties. That is, you're always helping the parties understand the wisdom of staying in the process long enough to find a solution to their mutual problem. Even though the parties arrive on the scheduled date prepared to engage in the process, many still don't see the value of mediation and have no intention of settling their lawsuit or resolving their dispute.

If you run a solo practice and people contact you directly to request your services, you have to convene the mediation yourself and screen their dispute for appropriateness (not every case is suitable for mediation) and possibly for issues such as domestic violence or caretaker neglect, as I explain in the following sections.

Convening a mediation yourself

When a party to a dispute contacts you directly and requests your help in convening a mediation, you need to do the following:

✔ Gather information about the dispute and the disputants from the person who contacted you. Find out as much as possible about each of the following:

- The nature of the dispute.

- The quality of the parties' relationships with each other.

- Any history of their attempt to resolve the dispute.

- Reasons why the requesting party believes the dispute can't be resolved without third-party support.

- Reasons why this party believes it's in her dispute partner's best interest to resolve the matter. How will resolution improve the quality of the other party's life, and what other benefits would flow from a mediated resolution?

- The reluctant party's conflict resolution style. If the parties have had disputes in the past, how did the disputes unfold, and by what means were they resolved, if they've been resolved? (For more about conflict resolution styles, see Chapter 8.)

✔ Build credibility for yourself as a mediator and for mediation as an effective process for resolving disputes.

✔ Establish rapport with the disputants.

✔ Ascertain whether mediation is likely to serve the needs, desires, fears, preferences, or priorities of all parties involved. (More about this in the following section, "Assessing the situation and screening for potential issues.")

After your in-depth conversation with the person requesting the mediation, contact each of the other parties as you'd approach a frightened animal — hand extended in a manner that shows you mean no harm, using a soft and inviting tone of voice, and making it clear that you have no agenda other than to help.

Hear them out. Empathize and clarify. Assume everything they say is true. Assuming all those circumstances are accurate, would the party resisting mediation nevertheless find some benefit from the process? If so, ask questions to help the party recognize that potential benefit.

Some mediators suggest writing a letter first, but I'd use the telephone. Written correspondence is easy to ignore and equally easy to misconstrue, with no potential for the correction of misimpressions. Ask the same questions of the recalcitrant party as you've posed to the party seeking the mediation. If you encounter harsh words or negative characterizations of the individual's "adversary," remain nonjudgmental.

Don't argue or state persuasive reasons for mediation *in general*. Probe for the specific reasons this person may have to engage in or avoid the initiator of the process. The recalcitrant party may well have very good reason not to mediate or never to lay eyes on the person who called you in the first place.

Assessing the situation and screening for potential issues

Not every dispute can or should be mediated, so you need to carefully screen the parties and the dispute to ensure that the dispute is one you're qualified to mediate safely and that the parties are likely to benefit from mediation and from the services you offer. Following are some recommendations to help you screen out situations you may be best to avoid:

✔ **Assess the parties' relative bargaining power.** Many mediators believe that mediation is desirable only if the parties have relatively equal bargaining power. Unfortunately, "relatively equal bargaining power" covers an extremely large gray zone that's tough to ascertain. Here are some benchmarks that may help:

- If both parties are represented by counsel, you can safely assume that they have relatively equal bargaining power.

- Plaintiffs often have more bargaining power than defendants if the plaintiff's attorney has taken the case on contingency because the plaintiff isn't paying legal fees, while the defendant usually is. However, this imbalance of power doesn't automatically rule out the mediation option.

- Any repeat player in the litigation market has more bargaining power than the day-in-court novice for a host of reasons, including a deep and lengthy experience with the way the system works, a greater ability to withstand loss, and often better legal representation. However, determining whether a better-heeled party genuinely has the power edge over the less economically powerful party is almost impossible to tell. For example, corporate counsel may be no match for a superstar lawyer who's built a career around representing injured plaintiffs.

✔ **Screen for the potential of emotional or physical coercion or harm.** If you're convening without the benefit of attorneys, chances of encountering a dispute in which a power balance may lead to physical or emotional harm is greater, so be more careful in such situations. When screening for the potential of physical or emotional coercion or harm, keep the following in mind:

- In family mediation, always ask whether the family has a history of violence. If it does, identify the nature and severity of all acts of violence, the frequency and timing of those acts, whether lethal force was used, what the frequency and nature of contact between the parties is now, and whether the abused or threatened party has access to alternative living arrangements if the mediation results in violence or threats of violence.

- If you're not a trained and licensed psychotherapist, social worker, psychologist, or other professional with experience in mental and emotional health, you may want to exempt disputes in which either or both parties have been victims of domestic violence, physical or emotional abuse, sexual abuse, family violence, drug or alcohol abuse, or where the act of bringing the parties together risks the emotional or physical health of the participants.

- If you have the requisite training and are dealing with emotionally volatile parties with a history of violence, draw up a safety plan to ensure that the parties can escape from or resist acts of violence. (Court bailiffs, for instance, are armed and trained to deal with violent parties.)

- If you suspect that one or more of the parties has so little bargaining power vis-à-vis one or more of the other disputants, you must make sure that she clearly understands she can opt out of mediation without experiencing any negative repercussions.

> ✔ **Screen out cases that might expose you to physical harm.** Take your own safety needs into account. I was once assigned to mediate a case on my court's *pro bono* mediation panel involving prominent gang members who had accused each other of committing murder. Recalling courthouse shootings that had recently occurred, I politely declined the invitation to serve.

Starting Off on the Right Foot

So you receive a call from your local community mediation center or private ADR panel telling you that you've been chosen to mediate a dispute. You open your mail to find that you've been assigned the task of helping warring parties settle their differences. Or you've managed to convene a case yourself after talking to all the parties through the proposed mediation.

What do you do now?

First you do the happy dance. After all your training, planning, researching, and marketing, you finally have the opportunity to prove to your market just how good a dispute resolver you are. Now you need to get down to work.

Contacting all stakeholders

The first thing you do is contact all the lawyers or, in non-litigated cases, the parties to let them know what you need from them prior to the mediation's commencement. If the dispute is a litigated dispute with attorneys representing the parties, ask the attorneys to file mediation briefs at least a week before the mediation. If attorneys aren't involved, ask each party to provide a written description of the dispute's history.

At a minimum, ask that the briefs address the dispute's general nature, the status of the parties' previous efforts to resolve it, the names of the individuals who will be present at the mediation, and the parties' opening offer or demand for settlement. Also ask that the briefs identify all *stakeholders* — whoever will be affected in some way by the dispute's resolution.

Identify *all* potential stakeholders, especially those who may exert substantial influence over the decision makers. If a wife is in a dispute with someone, the husband may need to be present. If an agent is representing a business, the business owners or managers probably should have a seat at the table. Only by exploring the basis of the dispute and the available avenues of settlement do you discover who should be present during the mediation.

If attorneys are involved, after you receive the parties' briefs, call the attorneys to ask any questions that the briefs don't answer. Gather information to gain insight into the following:

✔ **Personality issues:** Briefs rarely contain information about personality issues that may lead you to believe that addressing the matter first in a separate caucus is the best approach. Those personality issues include individuals who, though not violent, are nevertheless prone to engage in bullying behavior or name-calling, as well as those who tend to escalate conflict or are otherwise temperamental. You can coach many of these people in separate caucus to hold their tongue until their dispute partner has finished talking, to avoid ad hominem attacks, and to use their "inside voice" during the course of any disagreement.

✔ **Unidentified stakeholders:** The attorneys may identify stakeholders that the parties failed to mention. If the parties identify stakeholders whose presence can help settle the matter but who aren't planning to attend, the attorneys may help you bring these stakeholders to the table.

✔ **Case history:** Ask the attorneys to give you their candid, informal opinions about their working relationships with opposing counsel, any problems with their own clients, and any other matters that may be helpful to you.

When you contact the attorneys and stakeholders, you get both sides of the story. As you speak with the parties, take copious notes. If certain details are fuzzy, confusing, or contradictory, ask follow-up questions until you're clear about the dispute's history, the major players, and the efforts to resolve it.

Creating a comfortable atmosphere

Prior to conducting a mediation, attend to the participants' needs. In addition to establishing an atmosphere that's conducive to negotiation, demonstrating sensitivity to the participants' needs signals your concern for their welfare, which helps build trust. Following are suggestions for making everyone comfortable:

✔ **Accommodate any special needs.** Find out whether either party has special needs, such as the need for an interpreter or a meeting place that's wheelchair-accessible, and attend to those needs. You might also ask if either party has special dietary needs; for example, the need to avoid certain ingredients because of a food allergy. In communities with many different cultures, be alert to religious and other customs with which you should comply if violating them would cause offense. In my local, ultra-orthodox religious community in Los Angeles, for instance, I've learned not to offer my hand to a religious Jewish man unless I first ask whether a handshake is permitted, as it often is not between the genders.

✔ **Choose a location that has private space to conduct separate caucuses.** The ideal arrangement has two conference rooms with enough chairs to accommodate everyone and tables they can work at while you're out of the room. If two conference rooms aren't available, any sitting area that guarantees privacy is sufficient.

✔ **Set a comfortable temperature.** Start in your comfort zone and then ask the participants to let you know if they're too hot or cold.

✔ **Provide food and beverages.** When people eat, their bodies release a hormone called oxytocin (not to be confused with the pain reliever OxyContin!) that brain scientists believe boosts positive social behavior, making people more willing to enter into a relationship of trust.

✔ **Provide newspapers and magazines.** The parties may have some down-time during the mediation. Reading material fends off boredom and may serve as a pleasant distraction.

✔ **Check the restroom locations.** Know where the restrooms are located so you can direct the participants to them.

Introducing the participants

When you and the other mediation participants gather for your first session, introduce the parties to each other in a manner that begins to build trust between them and between the parties and you.

Ask the parties to introduce themselves to each other as if they were strangers meeting for the first time at a block party. Say something like, "Tell everyone your name, explain what you do, and then talk briefly about something good that's happened to you recently." Then, model the introduction by introducing yourself.

When people fight with each other, they often cut off communication for long periods of time or have hostile communications. They depersonalize and demonize the other person (as I explain in Chapter 8) because doing so makes the person easier to despise and fight with. By having the parties introduce themselves and engage in small talk before the session begins, you rehumanize the parties and begin to separate the people from the problem.

One of the best ways to begin breaking down the wall is to engage the parties in small talk. By its very nature, small talk is inconsequential, but it's a great way to establish a sense of shared interests. Choose topics strategically to:

✔ **Identify shared interests:** Talk about the weather, the performance of a popular home team, or a movie or TV show everyone's talking about. Shared interests make people feel a connected.

✔ **Establish a sense of community:** Discuss local road construction or traffic congestion, community events, local sales or businesses, or whatever happens to have the community buzzing.

✔ **Remind everyone of their shared humanity:** Steer the conversation to children or parents, school events, family issues, pets, and so on. People generally have a tough time demonizing someone who volunteers at the local food pantry or serves as president of the PTA.

Selling the joint session approach

You can mediate in a *joint session* (all parties in the same room) or in separate caucuses, in which each party is in a separate room and you scurry back and forth between them. The custom and practice in community mediation is to conduct most of the mediation in a joint session, and that's what I recommend. If you start off in separate caucuses (not recommended), the parties may be reluctant to transition to a joint session. Here are a few ways to convince the parties that a joint session is best for them:

✔ **Emphasize the cost of time.** Say something like, "If we do separate caucuses, I'll be spending a lot of time repeating to your negotiating partner what each of you has said. It would be much more efficient and less costly if everyone came into the same room so that you can explain yourself to each other. You're paying me for my time as well as your attorneys for their time. I hate to see you spend money unnecessarily while you're trying to save it by settling the litigation."

✔ **Assure the parties that they won't be bullied, insulted, or purposefully intimidated by the other.** You may say something like, "I've asked your negotiating partner whether he believes he's capable of talking with you without blaming or ridiculing you or anything you assert. If you're also able to talk about the dispute without making accusations, by simply telling your own side of the story, I believe a joint session would be very valuable to you both."

✔ **If you're mediating the case with attorneys present, brainstorm ways that they can preserve some degree of control over their client's statements.** Ask the attorneys to help their clients explain their version of events by asking them the type of questions they'd ask on direct examination. Sometimes, the parties want to ask each other questions. Attorneys usually feel much more comfortable with a question-and-answer session if everyone understands that the attorney can say she doesn't want her client to answer some of the questions.

> ✔ **Emphasize the parties' ability to solve problems better together.** Tell them that because they know the dispute better than anyone else possibly can, they're more likely to think of creative ways to solve it if they're in direct communication with each other.

Avoid starting the mediation process in separate caucuses. In the litigated mediation market in the United States, parties are often escorted to separate rooms when they arrive and talk to their bargaining partners only in special circumstances. Often, the mediator believes that a joint session would make the process move more efficiently and effectively, but by that time the parties have decided they're far more comfortable apart, and moving them together is difficult.

By the time the mediation commences, you should already have had private telephone conferences with each of the parties to talk about their unique situations and to explain your own general guiding principles. If the parties are expecting to commence the mediation in separate caucus, for instance, but you begin all your mediations in joint session, you risk harming the chance you have to establish an atmosphere of hope and safety in the parties.

Clearing the air about confidentiality and neutrality

Prior to negotiating with each other and disclosing information to you, parties are typically concerned about confidentiality and neutrality. The purpose of *confidentiality* in mediation proceedings is to provide the parties with a safe venue to resolve their disputes without fear that anything they divulge will be used against them in a court of law. The purpose of *neutrality* is to ensure that you don't favor one party over another. The following sections provide guidance on what to tell the parties and what not to tell them about confidentiality and neutrality.

Confidentiality

You have an obligation to inform parties about the confidentiality of mediation proceedings. Be cautious, however, about telling them that what they say in mediation can't be used against them in the court of law. In some jurisdictions, parties *can* be required to disclose something that's been said in mediation if the matter proceeds to trial. If you advise the parties that what they say can't be introduced as evidence in court or disclosed to the judge and you're wrong, you can be sued. Therefore,

✔ Consult an attorney to ascertain the laws that govern mediation confidentiality, and

✔ Remind the parties that you're not their lawyer, that you don't give legal advice, and that they should consult their own attorneys to learn the full extent of the applicable protections for communications between the parties to a mediation.

State laws don't govern the federal courts. In a federal case brought against Facebook creator Mark Zuckerberg, the federal Ninth Circuit Court of Appeals opined that no federal law protects communications made during the course of a mediation. Therefore, any mediator who assures the parties that what they say can't be used against them in a court of law will be misleading them if their dispute is being heard or may be heard in a federal court under the jurisdiction of the Ninth Circuit.

I practice mediation in California, where the state law strongly protects the principle of confidentiality as it's expressed in California's Evidence Code (see the nearby sidebar, "Mediation confidentiality in California"). During the writing of this book, my confidentiality statement went something like this:

> Even though I know your attorneys have advised you about the confidentiality of this mediation, I'd like us to all be on the same page. If anything I say is contrary to what your attorneys have told you, please trust that they have properly instructed you in the law — that is not my role.
>
> That being said, nothing you say during the mediation today can be used against you in any proceeding pending in a California state court, an arbitration pending in California, or an administrative proceeding. That doesn't mean you can't talk about what was said here or what happened here with your friends, your family, or even the press. It simply protects anything you say here today from being offered in evidence or discovered in pretrial proceedings.
>
> If you reach an agreement today, you'll likely write up that agreement to make it binding and enforceable on all the parties. Your attorneys are aware of the provisions contained in the California Evidence Code that permit that agreement to be offered in evidence if one party has buyer's remorse and challenges its enforceability.
>
> That is the first layer of confidentiality in these proceedings. The second layer is my promise that I won't communicate anything that you say to me in a separate caucus to your negotiating partner unless I have permission to do so.
>
> In the unlikely event that you or your negotiating partner takes your dispute to a federal court located in California, your communications may not be protected in the absence of a written contract requiring the parties to keep all mediation communications confidential.

Mediation confidentiality in California

In California, the state's Evidence Code protects confidences exchanged in mediation. It prohibits the introduction into evidence of any written or oral communications made "for the purpose of, in the course of, or pursuant to, a mediation or a mediation consultation." This same law protects parties in mediation from being required to respond to pretrial discovery that would reveal the substance of those communications.

However, the state's statutory mediation confidentiality provisions protect confidentiality only in civil proceedings, arbitrations, administrative adjudications, and other *noncriminal* proceedings in which testimony can be compelled to be given. In other words, California law doesn't prohibit the parties from talking to the press about information disclosed during mediation or from testifying about that information in criminal proceedings.

If you're a practicing mediator in California, you'd have to give the parties so many warnings about the exceptions to mediation confidentiality that they'd probably think they had no protection at all, when in fact California law provides a great deal of protection. Here's what those warnings may look like:

If you don't have a written confidentiality agreement, you can't count on confidentiality under the following circumstances:

- Someone seeks to discover what was said or exchanged in this mediation in an action pending in a federal court;

- You or any one of the other parties seek to learn in discovery or prove in court that a writing allegedly summarizing an agreement reached during mediation is binding and enforceable against you;

- Someone contends that this proceeding is not a mediation but is, instead, a settlement conference;

- Even though your dispute is being litigated in a California court, the law that applies to your dispute is the law of another state;

- The writing that one party insists constitutes a binding agreement is sufficient to satisfy California statutory law that permits the disclosure of such an agreement.

As you can see, wading into the confidentiality morass usually isn't worth it. Let the parties' attorneys advise their clients on matters of confidentiality.

Neutrality

After wrapping up your statement on mediation confidentiality or passing the buck to the parties' attorneys, instruct the parties about your neutrality, an issue that's not nearly as strewn with land mines as confidentiality. Feel free to compose your own neutrality statement using mine as a starter:

> As a mediator, I am neutral. That doesn't mean that I don't form opinions during the course of the mediation. It simply means that I don't take sides in your dispute and that I don't let any of my own personal experiences or opinions influence anything I do or say in my attempt to help you resolve your dispute.

Setting the ground rules

People in conflict are angry, afraid, and discouraged, so as early as possible during the mediation, establish an atmosphere of respect, safety, and hope. One way to establish a suitable atmosphere is to set ground rules, but not all mediators believe in setting ground rules. You're likely to encounter three different schools of thought on the topic of ground rules:

- ✔ **Set ground rules:** Some mediators establish and present their ground rules prior to any joint sessions.

- ✔ **Don't set ground rules:** Some mediators dispense with ground rules entirely, for any or all of the following reasons:

  - • Ground rules sound patronizing and may imply that the parties would have behaved badly without such rules.

  - • If the mediator imposes rules, then the mediator is placed in the often uncomfortable situation of enforcing them.

  - • Ground rules may inhibit the parties from addressing the very issues that have them mired in their dispute.

- ✔ **Have the parties establish the ground rules:** Encourage the parties to set the rules that govern their behavior. This gives the parties a chance to warm up their collaborative skills while helping them develop rules that they both agree to ahead of time.

Whether you choose to have ground rules in place is up to you. It often depends on your philosophy and on the situation and the parties involved. If you decide to use ground rules, here are some suggestions:

- ✔ **Treat each other with respect.** This means no name-calling, no personal attacks, and no physical displays of disrespect such as rolling of the eyes, vigorous head shakes, sighs, snickers, or any other verbal or non-verbal expressions of shock, outrage, disbelief, and the like.

- ✔ **Listen without comment.** If you're afraid that you'll forget what you want to say at the moment, jot it down and come back to it when it's your turn to speak.

- ✔ **Wait to ask questions.** When the other party has had his say, you can ask follow-up questions in a respectful manner.

- ✔ **Tell your own story from your own viewpoint.** Avoid the temptation to accuse the other party or speculate on your adversary's motives.

- ✔ **Talk *to* each other, not *about* each other.** Don't play the blame game or "he said, she said."

> ✔ **Remain open and flexible to resolutions you haven't considered.** Avoid taking hard-line positions.
>
> ✔ **Make a genuine effort to understand and credit what the other party is saying.** Think about *what* the other party is saying, not *who's* saying it.
>
> ✔ **Speak up if something's not working or feels uncomfortable.** Nobody can read minds, and when the mediation has ended, you'll regret what you didn't say. When it's your turn to speak, let people know what's bothering you.
>
> ✔ **If you need a break, say so.** Physical discomfort makes people grumpy.

Let the parties know that you'll do your best to protect them from any emotional bullying and physical harm by separating them whenever any of them begins to feel threatened.

Fostering a sense of collaboration

In a joint session, encourage the parties to consider each other partners in the joint effort to find a solution. Let them know that you won't make binding decisions based on the strength of any arguments or appeals they make to you. The parties can't form a resolution team when one is trying to impress a third party with the rectitude of his positions and opinions or making the other party look like a liar, a cheat, and a thief.

The resolution team grows stronger over the course of the mediation as the parties take greater responsibility for resolving their own problem on their own terms according to their sense of personal responsibility and basic principles of fairness.

Defining and Prioritizing the Issues

Whether you open a mediation in a joint session or a separate caucus, take the following steps to help the parties define and prioritize the issues:

1. **Give both parties the opportunity to fully state their views of the problem and their desired solution.**

   As a party expresses her side of the story, avoid any temptation to cut off narratives of events that seem irrelevant. Not everything a person says is critical, important, or relevant, but what sounds unimportant at first often holds the key to resolving the dispute.

2. **Ask the parties open-ended questions to ascertain the minor issues that they must address in order to resolve the major issues, and jot down their answers.**

   Open-ended questions are those that can't be answered merely by "Yes" or "No." For example, instead of asking whether a party performed as promised in the contract, ask Party A something like, "What did you expect Party B to do in return? And what is it that Party B actually did?" Open-ended questions elicit more detailed responses than yes/no questions. The solution is often in the details.

3. **Prioritize which issues to resolve first and develop an agenda for addressing them.**

   Prioritizing is called *sequencing*. One of the most effective ways to sequence problems is to tackle easier issues first and then work up to more complex issues, where the degree of difference is greater.

   By starting with issues that are relatively easy to resolve, the parties

   - Grow more confident as they solve issues they didn't believe they'd ever reach consensus on

   - Develop respect for each other's competence

   - Become more deeply invested in the process as they reach more agreements

   - Grow more hopeful as they experience the effectiveness of the mediation process

The agenda — whether suggested by the mediator or the parties — for a dispute about the dissolution of a business partnership may look like this:

1. **Ascertain the business's value or agree upon the means by which the parties can agree upon its value (appraisal by a neutral third party, for instance).**

2. **Brainstorm ways to compensate both partners for their interest in the partnership.**

   Does the business have assets other than cash that the partners are willing to trade?

3. **Brainstorm ways of generating the money necessary for Partner A to buy out Partner B.**

4. **Ascertain the means by which Partner A can determine whether Partner B has taken more than his rightful share out of the business and, if he has, how much?**

5. **Determine what the available grounds are for dissolving the partnership (usually found in the partnership agreement).**

6. **Determine any limitations that Partner A may have on competing with Partner B, assuming Partner A buys out Partner B's interest.**

7. **Determine whether both partners would be willing to continue in business with each other if certain changes were made.**

8. **Evaluate the changes necessary and provide for a means of resolving any disputes between the partners regarding those changes.**

   Decide what's likely to happen to the partnership business in the event that the changes aren't satisfactory to either party.

Tackling One Issue at a Time

With your dispute resolution agenda in place, you're ready to begin the problem-solving process. Mediation has no step-by-step process for solving problems and resolving disputes between the parties, but you can employ a number of techniques, choosing the one you think is most effective for each problem. The following sections explain the most common and effective techniques for resolving differences.

Don't give up if one approach doesn't yield results. Instead, go with plan B or C or D — try one of the other techniques. When you can't think of any other suggested means for resolving the problem, ask the parties for help; they may be withholding information that can aid them in resolving the dispute but may think you need to raise it first. Give them permission to be proactive problem solvers, not mere bystanders.

Summarizing the conflict narratives

Before you engage in any serious problem-solving, summarize the parties' conflict narratives so that everyone's on the same page and is working with the same facts. A *conflict narrative* is one party's side of the story, which invariably begins at the moment of loss and describes the reasons why the other party is responsible for that loss. Here's an example of conflicting dispute narratives from Dad and Mom:

> Dad says, "I was picking the kids up for their weekly visitation and she (Mom) pushed me down the stairs. I broke my arm and haven't been able to work at my job delivering the mail since then, so I'm suing for personal injuries."

> Mom begins her conflict narrative at a slightly earlier point in time. According to her, "Megan had a cold and Johnny had an out-of-town soccer match that I knew his dad wouldn't be able to take him to. I called Dad and asked him to switch weekends but he refused. Half an hour after our phone call, he stormed into the house and grabbed both kids from me. Megan was screaming so I tried to pull her back. In the struggle, he fell down the stairs. I never would have intentionally pushed him."

Mom's insurance company has been defending her in the litigation but refuses to contribute to the settlement because the policy excludes coverage for intentional acts; it only covers negligent ones.

After listening carefully to the parties' conflict narratives, you have two limited perspectives of what happened. To elicit additional details and form the bigger picture, ask the parties

✔ Open-ended questions — Who? What? When? Where? Why? and How? — to obtain additional details that may have been omitted.

✔ To rewind to an earlier point in the story, prior to when the alleged wrongdoing occurred, so you have a better understanding of what happened in context.

✔ What they've done to resolve their differences and the outcome of those efforts.

✔ If they could live the injury-causing event all over again, what they'd change in their own behavior.

For example, in the specific dispute between Mom and Dad, you can ask a number of questions, including

✔ How long have you been divorced?

✔ Have you had problems with visitation in the past? What have you done to resolve those problems?

✔ Was there a time when you were cooperating with each other about the visitation schedule? When was that? What happened to change that?

✔ How were the children before you began fighting over visitation issues? How have they been since that time? How are they now?

✔ What effect has the litigation had on the quality of your lives? What effect has it had on the children?

✔ In the best of all possible worlds, what would you each like the visitation schedule to look like?

Become an active listener by engaging in dialogue with the parties. Listen without judgment. Ask open-ended questions to gather information. Summarize in your own words what the speaker has said to demonstrate that you were listening and to give the speaker an opportunity to correct details you may have misunderstood. Recharacterize your own understanding based on the speaker's corrections, ask for clarification, and resummarize the heart of the speaker's communication.

If you're in a joint session, the respect you show to both parties by actively and uncritically listening to their (often opposing) narratives of the same event initiates a self-reflective process during which the parties begin to see that the people they're asking to resolve their dispute (the judge, jury, or mediator) may see things the way their adversary is describing them. And people who come to their *own* opinion that their case isn't watertight are usually ready to settle their differences and move on.

Moving from narratives to issues

As you clarify the narrative through your retelling of it, the parties naturally start to take a more objective view of the situation and begin to see how they may have contributed to it. At this point, they should be open to questions that lead them in the direction of accountability, forgiveness, amends, and reconciliation. You may now pose more focused questions that function as a sort of cross-examination: Do you, Mom, believe that you played some role in Dad falling down the stairs and breaking his arm? Do you, Dad, still believe yourself to be entirely without blame for the accident? And do you, insurance carrier, see how likely it is that a jury will find Mom to have been negligent and that your company will be obliged to pay the damages awarded against her?

When the parties stop fighting over their differing interpretation of past events, they can let go of the anger and fear that too often causes impasse. Rather than concentrating on who said what to whom and who did what to whom, the parties can begin to profitably brainstorm potential solutions. Dad has been receiving unemployment insurance, and his insurance carrier has been paying 80 percent of his medical bills. Mom has been receiving $2,000 per month in child support, and Dad has filed papers with the court seeking to reduce that sum during the time he's unemployed. The homeowners insurance policy has limits of $50,000, and Dad's total losses could exceed those limits. If a jury found that Mom had intentionally pushed Dad down the stairs, the insurance carrier's failure to settle the case within the policy limits could expose it to an action for bad faith.

With all those issues on the table, the parties have innumerable opportunities to maximize the upside and minimize the downside for everyone.

Identifying miscommunications and incorrect assumptions

Classic comedies always start with everyone getting along. Then, usually because of miscommunications and false assumptions, the characters turn against one another. Eventually, the cause of their conflicts is revealed, and everyone's back together at the end. This is pretty much the formula for every comedy from Shakespeare's *Much Ado About Nothing* to modern movies like *The Hangover*.

Active listening can clear up many of the miscommunications, incorrect assumptions, and conflicting details that led to the misunderstanding. In

Chapter 7, I provide guidance in how to ask open-ended and follow-up questions to identify areas of miscommunication and misunderstanding, so the parties clearly understand the issues and can address them more effectively. It's actually pretty easy to make sure you and the other parties to the mediation clearly understand what's being said. For instance, you can say, "I heard you say x, y, and z, Barbara. Is that what you meant?" If Barbara says "Yes," ask Zack whether that's what he understands Barbara said. If the parties say "No," ask the speaker to say it again. Paraphrase it again. Ask whether it's accurate again. Rinse. Repeat.

Understanding the cognitive biases that often drive people to misunderstand one another is also a big help. For example, *confirmation bias* is a universal human tendency to recall and highlight everything that supports your existing views and discard as unworkable, irrelevant, or simply wrong those facts that do not. Chapter 8 describes the most common cognitive biases and provides guidance in helping the parties overcome these biases.

Uncovering the personal issues underlying the legal issues

Behind every legal issue is a personal issue. As one of my own mentors used to say, "People don't have legal problems. People have people problems. Only lawyers have legal problems." Often, the sole reason the parties can't agree on a solution to their mutual problem is that they're emotionally involved and can't admit that personal issues caused the event that triggered the legal problem.

Many people don't want to deal with their personal problems and hope that they can resolve the legal issues without having to address the personal ones. If the people are unwilling to address these problems or even to meet their adversary in a joint session, you may need to resort to strategies for breaking impasse, as explained in Chapter 13.

For now, simply note that one of the early challenges in a mediation is to dig down beneath the legal problems to the root causes of the disagreement — personal differences and emotions. Ask the parties diagnostic questions tailored to elicit information about these underlying issues. "What happened?" is one of my own favorite ways to enter this difficult terrain:

Mediator: "What happened?"

Party: "What do you mean 'what happened?'"

Mediator: "Well, everything was going pretty smoothly, right? Dad was picking the kids up without trouble. When someone's schedule needed to be changed, you accommodated each other. Did something happen to change that?"

After you get the parties talking about the personal issues, just follow them in the same way you would if you were asking questions at a deposition or as a reporter seeking to cover the news but without any agenda other than to learn, acknowledge, support, understand, and care.

Brainstorming possible solutions

Engage in brainstorming sessions with the parties to develop possible solutions. Consider using a whiteboard to jot down everyone's suggestions or have everyone jot down possible solutions on strips of paper, fold them up, and drop them in a box; you can then draw from the box and write each solution on your whiteboard.

During the brainstorming session, let the ideas fly. Encourage creativity. After the brainstorming session, you can eliminate solutions that don't make the cut.

If you're lucky, the parties suggest or agree on one of the suggested solutions. If you're not so lucky, use the suggestions as a conversation starter with the goal of coming up with something that works for everyone. For more about problem-solving techniques, see Chapter 12.

Closing the Deal

After the parties resolve their dispute and negotiate terms that satisfy everyone, you want to close the deal and get everything in writing. How you and the parties close and memorialize the agreement in writing depends on the situation:

- ✔ **Lawyer-drafted agreement:** If either party has legal representation, one or both of their lawyers may draft an agreement that both parties can read and sign.
- ✔ **Party-drafted agreement:** You may supply the parties with a boilerplate agreement that they complete, which includes the following:
    - **Settlement agreement:** The settlement agreement states what each party agrees to give and give up, when the exchange will take place, and what happens in the event that a party doesn't meet his obligation.
    - **Mutual general releases:** The parties agree to release each other from any claims related to the dispute they just agreed to resolve.

- **Terms:** The terms are the details of what the parties agree to in the event of a breach of contract — which jurisdiction's laws will govern the breach, who must pay any attorney fees, and so on.

- **Stipulation for the entry of judgment:** A stipulation for the entry of judgment, which often includes a hammer clause, provides the party that's responsible for paying a strong inducement to honor his end of the agreement. For example, a hammer clause may state that the party agrees to pay a certain amount on such and such a date or will pay a stiff penalty for not doing so.

For more about closing and memorializing the parties' agreement in writing, see Chapter 14.

Even if you're an attorney, you're better off leaving the legal details of agreements between the parties up to the parties and their respective attorneys. As the mediator, you're a neutral third party, so even if you are a lawyer, you can't represent either party's interests.

Chapter 5

Mediating with and without Lawyers

*M*ediators deal with two types of cases — litigated and nonlitigated, each of which requires a different approach. With litigated cases, the parties consider at least two possible outcomes — what happens if they win the case and what happens if they lose. Most parties are optimists, so they usually focus more on what they stand to gain than what they stand to lose, which is one of the reasons they hired you.

With nonlitigated cases, the parties are often unaware of possible outcomes, including the possibility of hiring a lawyer and suing someone. Though they're focused on what they believe to be fair and unfair, they often don't know their available legal rights and remedies. They generally have an easier time focusing on their interests (their needs, desires, priorities, preferences, fears, and the like) than on the narrow set of facts that may lead to victory or defeat in a legal proceeding. Nonlitigated cases require a different kind of preparation on your part and the drawing of firm boundaries to ensure that you don't compromise your neutrality or engage in the practice of law (regardless of whether you're a lawyer).

This chapter explores the differences between mediating litigated and nonlitigated disputes and shows you how to effectively approach each type.

Mediating Litigated Cases

The most important understanding you can have when mediating a litigated case is the adversarial context in which the participants try to resolve the dispute. In a perfect world, the lawyers' interests would align exactly with those of their clients, but that's not usually the case.

In the imperfect, real world, your goal is to assist the lawyers to assist their clients in settling the case out of court. Your role in achieving this goal varies according to the lawyers' needs and, to the extent the lawyers are compliant with your direction, with the parties' interests. Here are just a few of the ways you can help improve the outcome for all participants in a litigated dispute:

- ✔ Team up with the lawyers to help their clients discover solutions that are mutually beneficial and satisfactory.

- ✔ Play bad cop, delivering bad news to the lawyers' clients that the lawyers don't feel comfortable communicating, such as the fact that the client has a slim chance of prevailing in litigation.

- ✔ Bring the lawyers' own expectations of their likely success into the realm of reality. Lawyers are sometimes more married to their legal positions than their clients are. They may be more convinced of their chances of victory because they've spent so much time massaging the facts and interpreting the law as favorable to their client and fatal to their opponent. Lawyers working on a contingency may also be driven to maximize their client's monetary benefit so that their own share of the settlement is correspondingly higher. And they may be dedicated to prolonging the litigation out of self-interest (attorney's fees) or afraid to settle prematurely and leave too much money on the table.

The following sections explain how to develop the skills and techniques you need to effectively team up with or negotiate separately with attorneys and their clients.

Tracing the path of a litigated dispute

Although the legal process may vary depending on the jurisdiction and subject matter of the dispute, every civil lawsuit follows a similar path through the justice system. To help lawyers release themselves and their clients from this expensive and uncertain venture, you must understand the process, which usually goes like this:

1. **The aggrieved party, universally referred to as the *plaintiff,* files a *complaint* with a state or federal trial court, stating only the facts that give rise to legal claims.**

A judge or jury decides who wins the lawsuit based only on the facts that are relevant to the legal claims raised in the complaint and the affirmative defenses asserted in the *answer* (the defendant's response to the plaintiff's complaint). Although the court (or the jury the court instructs in its duties) is limited to considering the relevant facts, the mediator can use the entire story of the dispute to resolve it, even if parts of that story are completely irrelevant to the legal claim.

2. **The court issues a summons.**

A *summons* is a court order that requires the defendant to file an answer or other defensive pleading within a certain number of days or have his default entered. If the court enters an order of default, the plaintiff can proceed directly to obtain a money judgment and the case is over, unless the defendant has a good reason for failing to respond and petitions the court to set aside the default.

3. **If the defendant responds to the complaint in time, he files an answer to it with the court and, if warranted, files cross-actions against the plaintiff or any other party who may also be legally liable for the injuries or damages claimed.**

Alternatively, the defendant may file a *demurrer* or motion to dismiss the complaint, contending that the alleged facts don't give rise to a legal *(actionable)* claim (called a *cause of action*). The demurrer or motion to dismiss challenges the plaintiff's right to legal relief even if the facts alleged in the complaint are true.

4. **Shortly after the plaintiff files a complaint and serves it on the defendant, the parties may begin *discovery* proceedings — seeking the production documents, answers to written questions, and admissions to certain undisputed facts.**

The parties may also demand that certain individuals submit to an examination *(deposition)* before trial, appear for a physical examination in the case of injury, or submit to an inspection of property in the event that the property has suffered damage. At a deposition, parties and other witnesses testify under oath. Their testimony may be used at trial to tie a party down to a particular version of the facts in dispute or to impeach a witness's credibility.

5. **After most discovery, one or both parties may file a motion for summary judgment.**

A *summary judgment motion* is based on undisputed facts. The party filing the motion (the *moving party*) lays out for the court all the facts that the party claims to be undisputed and asks the court to enter judgment in her favor without a jury trial. Because a jury's sole function is to resolve disputed issues of fact, the court can constitutionally decide the matter without a jury if the uncontested facts entitle the moving party to judgment as a matter of law.

6. **In cases where the judge or jury can't be expected to understand scientific or technical issues important to the dispute's resolution, expert witnesses are retained to explain the science or technology in lay terms.**

   Each side hires its own expert witnesses, all of whom testify to their opinions in pretrial depositions and, if necessary, again at trial. Lawyers often ask a mediator to help them settle a case before experts are retained because experts are expensive, and their retainers are rarely fully recovered by the prevailing party.

7. **During the last 90 days before trial, all discovery must be completed and all pretrial motions heard.**

   Within the last few months before trial, the parties are generally required to exchange witness lists and to describe the documents they intend to introduce in evidence at trial. If a jury will decide the case, the parties submit dueling jury instructions, and the court decides which side's submission accurately states the law or sends the parties back to the drawing board to make the instructions less partisan and more neutral.

8. **Assuming a judge or jury decides the case, the court enters a judgment based on the verdict or enters a *judgment notwithstanding the verdict* (JNOV).**

   If the judge thinks the jury acted irrationally or based its decision on passion or prejudice, the court may enter a judgment different from the one the jury's verdict would support — a JNOV.

9. **One or both parties may appeal the judgment, asking for reversal and sometimes for a new trial.**

   When a new trial is granted, the parties are permitted to engage again in pretrial discovery, to make motions to the court, and to present their case to a judge or jury for final judgment a second time.

Even the most straightforward cases take at least two years of discovery and pretrial proceedings to get to trial. If a party appeals, the appellate process takes another two years. Because of the state and federal budget crises at the time of this writing, many courts are cutting back on staff and reducing the number of available courtrooms. These cutbacks may result in additional delays.

Obviously, litigation is a long, drawn-out, expensive process, and the outcome is never predictable. In addition, overburdened courts are interested in clearing their dockets, so they tend to set for trial only cases that aren't amenable to settlement and to order (or strongly recommend) that the parties resolve their dispute in mediation. Even if the court doesn't order or recommend it, most attorneys now hire mediators whenever they're serious about attempting to settle litigation.

More than 90 percent of all litigation settles before trial, with or without a mediator. The only difference between the settlement of nonmediated cases and mediated cases is that the parties are generally better satisfied with a mediated outcome than they are with a settlement conducted only between the lawyers.

Ensuring procedural justice for satisfactory results

Procedural justice is the way people perceive the fairness of the rules that regulate how resources are distributed, rights are granted, remedies are provided, and disputes are resolved. Research demonstrates that people care as much about the fairness of the process as they do about the outcome *(distributive justice)*.

To ensure that the parties are satisfied with the mediation's procedural dimensions, do the following:

- ✔ Explicitly assure the parties of your impartiality and then be impartial throughout the mediation.

- ✔ Map out for the parties, or assist them in mapping out, the process by which the dispute will be resolved, including plans and predictions for joint session and separate caucus proceedings. (See Chapter 6 for more about mediating in joint session and separate caucuses.)

- ✔ Clearly explain the rules of confidentiality that apply to the parties' conversations and exchange of documents during the mediation.

- ✔ Give the parties the opportunity to object to any process, including separate caucus communications.

- ✔ Encourage the parties and attorneys alike to fully express themselves and their view of the conflict, even if they become emotional when doing so or the details seem irrelevant to the case.

- ✔ Treat all parties with respect and dignity, affirming their right to assert their claims and defenses.

- ✔ Tell the parties that you trust and respect their ability to handle their own affairs and resolve their dispute in the manner they see fit.

- ✔ Assist the parties and their counsel in brainstorming credible reasons for demands, defenses, and offers, particularly when offers are rejected and counteroffers are presented.

- ✔ Encourage the parties and their counsel to brainstorm freely without risk of ridicule by the mediator, counsel, or the other parties in word, facial expression, or body language.

✔ Model respectful behavior for all parties. If a party shows disrespect for his adversary or engages in discourteous conduct, ask the party to give reasons for such behavior.

✔ When a separate caucus becomes lengthy, check back with the parties waiting for a response to let them know as much about what's going on in the other room as your obligation to maintain confidentiality permits. Give them an estimate of when you believe you'll get back to them.

✔ Make sure you understand what the parties and their counsel have told you by repeating your understanding of what they've said (active listening).

✔ Tell the parties that they may terminate the mediation at any time without coercion by their attorneys or the mediator.

As long as the participants perceive the dispute-resolution processes as fair, they generally accept the outcome and express satisfaction with the proceedings even if they don't get precisely what they want.

Improving attorney-client communication

The attorney-client relationship often involves too much advice by and too few questions from the attorneys. Lawyers often shut down potentially productive dispute-resolution discussions because they believe that the information the clients want to communicate is irrelevant to the legal proceeding. As a result of the narrow legal channel of communication, the client usually knows far more than his lawyer possibly could about both parties' interests — knowledge that can often help resolve the dispute.

Don't make any assumptions about an attorney before you have a chance to size up the attorney and the situation you're dealing with. Not all attorneys are pit bulls determined to wring the life out of their adversaries. Collaborative lawyers are becoming increasingly common, especially in situations involving family and business disputes. Heading into a mediation with a mistaken expectation that the lawyers are going to be adversarial could offend the lawyers and put you at a disadvantage.

To find out where the attorney's knowledge ends and the client's begins, listen for instances in which a client raises an issue, only to be silenced by the phrase "that's not relevant." The attorney has probably been telling her client for months or years that some of her most pressing concerns aren't material to her chances for victory. These "irrelevant" facts often concern emotional issues, hidden interests, or unknown constraints that are most relevant to settlement and are keys to unlock the door of impasse.

Part of your job as a mediator is to help bring issues that have been suppressed in the adversarial process to the forefront. To accomplish this goal, become aware of what the plaintiff really wants from the defendant and what the defendant really wants to express to the plaintiff:

✔ **Validation:** Plaintiffs are often more interested in the intangible rewards of the dispute-resolution process — feeling that their grievance has been fully heard and validated, for instance, or that they've had a chance to explain the context in which the dispute arose and the injustice that they've suffered as a result.

✔ **Concessions:** The number of concessions the parties make are more important to party satisfaction than the deal's dollar value. Contrary to the prevailing belief, money doesn't have a single, objective value. To test that proposition, ask yourself whether you spend credit more freely than cash, treat gift money differently from money you've earned, or are more willing to give than loan $100 to a friend. To an injured party, nonmaterial concessions have considerable intangible value that can reduce the size of the settlement a plaintiff is willing to accept or induce a defendant to place more money on the table.

✔ **Something tangible:** Plaintiffs often have plans for spending the money they win in litigation — plans they never share with their attorney. Often, what the clients want to purchase with the money they expect to receive costs much less than they imagine and far less than their attorney once told them they could likely recover at trial.

Ask the plaintiff, "Have you thought about what you're going to do with the money?" Asking this question often leads to an effective brain-storming session about ways to achieve the same ends for less money than the defendant is willing to pay. Every time I've asked a party this question, her attorney has been surprised at the relatively modest goals the client has for the dispute's resolution. This question also provides clients with the opportunity to mention their intangible desire to be heard and validated.

Providing another perspective instead of a second opinion

Your clients, both the lawyers and the parties to the dispute, have come to you *in part* to receive a second opinion on the wisdom of choosing trial over settlement. Their BATNA, or *best alternative to a negotiated agreement* (settlement), is always more litigation (expense) and trial (uncertainty). But just because attorneys and clients *say* they want your opinion on the merits of their case doesn't mean they really do. What they want is to be told that they're right. Your job is to help them see the circumstances in which they may be found to be wrong.

When participants seek a second opinion, you can respond in two ways — the right way and the wrong way. The wrong way is to tell the parties what you believe their odds of success are at trial. The right way is to ask the parties probing questions about their own doubts and fears to help them evaluate their chances for success. The first way is a strategy for failure; the second, a strategy for success. Here are just a few of the questions you may want to ask the parties (and their attorneys) to help them see the situation in a different light:

✓ What do you see as the weaknesses in your own case?

✓ Do you believe your case is stronger on the facts or stronger on the law?

✓ Who are your most reliable/credible witnesses?

✓ Who are your least reliable/credible witnesses?

✓ How important to your case are your least reliable/credible witnesses?

✓ Do you believe the jury will be capable of understanding the scientific or technical aspects of your case?

✓ If opposing expert witnesses testify, which ones do you believe would have the easiest time of selling their opinion to the jury?

✓ What do you think your judge will do with summary judgment (or other dispositive) motions? Is he known for being decisive or do you believe he'll let the case go to the jury no matter what?

✓ Are the juries in the venue where your case is pending known for giving large judgments to plaintiffs or generally returning verdicts in favor of defendants in cases like this?

✓ Is your opponent's attorney (or law firm) known for taking cases to trial or settling everything before trial?

✓ How many cases of this type have you tried to a jury in the past? How were those cases resolved?

I can list hundreds of questions like these. The precise nature of the answers rarely matters. What's important is that each question sparks a discussion in which counsel and their clients are forced to take a hard look at their own chances for success and failure in the legal process.

Avoid the temptation to say something like, "I believe you'll have a serious problem prevailing on your statute of limitations defense." If you try that approach, nine times out of ten you'll trigger an argument with an attorney who knows the facts and the law of his own case 99.9 percent better than you do. A mediator who has studied the facts and law for an hour or so can't possibly win an argument with the attorneys who've been living with the case for months or years. Even worse, instead of helping the parties evaluate the strengths and weaknesses of their own case, you'll strengthen their belief that their version of the events and their counsel's reading of the case law are right and that they'll therefore prevail. Finally, if you tell the parties that they're likely to lose at trial or even stand a less than 60 percent chance of prevailing, they often turn against you, and all the work you've done to create an atmosphere of hope and safety will evaporate.

Letting the parties decide

Your job is to empower the parties, not make their decisions for them. When my husband was diagnosed with prostate cancer, the first thing we did (true story) was buy *Prostate Cancer For Dummies,* which presented three options — surgery, radiation, and radiation seeds. We found out as much as we could from the *For Dummies* book and from various medical websites, but we wanted another opinion.

To gain more insight, we did what most people do — we consulted physicians. We didn't want just one perspective; we wanted at least three — one each from a physician who recommended surgery, radiation, and radiation seeds. Each physician presented insights from a unique perspective, but at the end of the day, we — really my husband — had to make the tough decision.

When asked for a second opinion, ask questions that increase the participants' awareness of the possible solutions and their potential outcomes. Then let them make the tough decisions.

Bridging the gap between law and justice

Legal rights and remedies don't always provide the parties with a just resolution of their dispute. The daily news produces a steady stream of stories about cases in which judges and juries complied with the law, knowing that the verdict or judgment was unjust. In one of the oldest lawyer jokes around, an attorney sends a telegram to his client saying, "Justice was done!" and the client responds, "Appeal immediately!" Lawyers and their clients are constantly at odds over this dichotomy. Lawyers seek a legal resolution, while their clients demand justice. One of your jobs is to bridge the gap by explaining lawyers to their clients and clients to their lawyers.

Here are some typical complaints that clients have regarding their attorneys:

- He tells me to forget about the most important losses I've suffered.
- She keeps *editing* my story.
- I don't understand why I can't . . . recover my attorneys' fees, cross-complain, sue for mental distress, and so on.
- He wouldn't let me tell the mediator everything I wanted to say.
- She didn't let me talk to the other side.

Here are the typical lawyer complaints I hear about clients:

- His expectations of success or recovery are completely unrealistic.
- When I explain the weaknesses of her case, she says I've become the enemy or asks which side I'm on.
- I've explained the limitations of the case to him, but he just doesn't seem to understand.

One of the easiest and best ways to explain the gap between law and justice is to draw a picture, like the one shown in Figure 5-1, and present the following explanation:

> The dispute you're having exists in the world of injustice, represented by the planet earth.
>
> Now picture a grain of rice somewhere on earth.
>
> The grain of rice represents the injustices the law will remedy.
>
> The earth represents the injustices the law won't remedy.
>
> You feel like your attorney is editing, shaping, or spinning your story of injustice because she *is*. The light gray square in Figure 5-1 represents the facts necessary to obtain relief in court (damages, an injunction, and so on) and defeat your opponent's claim for relief.
>
> The entire dispute — everything that happened inside the dark gray circle — is generally what you want to resolve. It often includes facts that could jeopardize your success in litigation.
>
> That's why your attorney doesn't let you talk in the presence of the other side and asks you not to discuss the dispute with your opponent anymore — because you may reveal something in the dark gray area that's bad for proving your case in the light gray area.
>
> Mediators work in the green area. Clients *almost always* want to resolve *all* the issues raised by the dispute (in the dark gray area), not simply the legal (in the light gray area). Perhaps more important, the dark gray mediation zone has many opportunities for resolution that no one has yet seriously explored because the dark gray area isn't the focus of the legal action. Only the light gray legal area is.

Mediation restores the dispute to the people engaged in that dispute. They're the only ones who know and understand that dispute in all its detail, texture, dimension, and meaning. Party *interests* — their hopes, fears, desires, needs, and so on — exist in both zones. The good news of mediation is that the party interests outside the legal zone can often be traded for concessions that are in *or* out of the legal zone.

Negotiate with more than one currency. When you have only one currency (dollars) to negotiate with, you often reach impasse. Both parties believe that it's unfair to give in, compromise, or split the baby in half just because the cost and aggravation of getting to trial is so high. When you have more than one currency to negotiate with — like dollars *and* saving face, dollars *and* unexplored business opportunities, dollars *and* apology, or dollars *and* an explanation for the dispute's events that has the ring of truth — you can trump legal impasse with party interests.

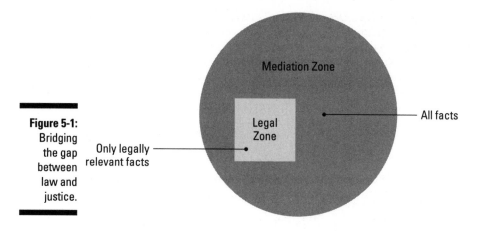

Figure 5-1:
Bridging
the gap
between
law and
justice.

Mediation Zone

Legal
Zone

All facts

Only legally
relevant facts

Mediating Nonlitigated Disputes

Parties who have legal representation know their rights and the available remedies; understand how the law may compensate them monetarily for non-monetary losses such as reputation, goodwill, or physical injury; and won't turn to you for legal advice. In nonlitigated cases, parties without legal representation rarely understand their rights and remedies, have little idea how to turn their losses into monetary damages, and are almost certain to request your legal advice. Some of these differences act in your favor, but you need to avoid giving legal advice.

The following sections explain the pitfalls of offering legal advice and describe a more productive approach to address each party's concerns, questions, and interests.

Avoiding the pitfalls of giving legal advice

Don't offer legal advice or conduct an evaluative mediation — that is, give your opinion about the merits of the case. Why? Three good reasons:

- ✔ **Giving legal advice compromises your neutrality.** Answering legal questions imparts knowledge to the party asking the question, thus improving that party's position in negotiations.

- ✔ **If you're not an attorney, practicing law without a license is against the law.** In California, practicing law without a license is a misdemeanor punishable by up to one year in county jail or a fine of up to $1,000, or both. If you practice law without a license because you've been suspended or disbarred from practice or you've resigned with charges pending against you, you may be charged with a felony.

> ✔ **Conducting an evaluative mediation is counterproductive.** Legal analysis often creates obstacles to satisfying both parties' interests. By answering legal questions, you may unintentionally convince a party that a legal solution is in his best interest, limit the possible solutions to legal remedies, and undermine your mediation efforts.

Questions that parties without legal representation commonly ask during a mediation may seem innocent enough, but they're likely to elicit an answer that could make you guilty of practicing law without a license. Such questions include the following:

✔ If I hire a lawyer and go to court, what are my likely remedies?

✔ I'm entitled to a restraining order if my boyfriend has threatened me with bodily harm, aren't I?

✔ What kind of damages am I entitled to recover if I sue my neighbor instead of settling with her now?

✔ Truth is a complete defense to defamation, isn't it? Doesn't everyone understand that that's the law here?

✔ If she takes me to court and wins, can she place a lien against my property or garnish my wages?

✔ What do you think my chances are of prevailing if I sue him for breach of contract?

✔ Here's the contract — it's absolutely clear that she's required to pay me. I'm entitled to enforce it in court, right?

✔ The contract says we have to mediate this case. What happens if I refuse to do so?

✔ They always award custody to the mother, right? I don't have a snowball's chance in hell of getting custody of my daughter as her father, even if my ex took her out of California without my permission and contrary to the court's order. Isn't that right?

✔ We weren't married, but we lived together for 16 years. Doesn't that make me her common-law husband?

✔ She rear-ended me, so that proves it was her fault, doesn't it? I'm sure to win that point if we go to court, aren't I?

Each of these questions calls for a legal conclusion. Answering "yes," "no," "maybe," or with a narrative almost certainly improves one of the parties' positions at the negotiating table, thus compromising your neutrality. More important, by answering these questions, you're holding yourself out as someone authorized to give legal advice. If you're not a lawyer or you've been disbarred or suspended, you're committing a crime. If you are a lawyer, you may be inadvertently establishing an attorney-client relationship with one or both parties, leaving you open to charges of malpractice or a breach of your ethical obligation not to represent parties with conflicting interests.

That's the bad news. Now for some good news.

Resolving conflict without legal analyses

Facilitative, interest-based mediation is almost always more effective than litigation in helping the parties craft a resolution. In fact, legal analyses often get in the way of the parties finding a way to satisfy as many of their interests as possible. Legal remedies are usually restricted to monetary compensation, which often falls short of compensating a party for what she believes is the worst behavior of her adversary.

For example, the law has no rules to govern the breaking off of a marriage engagement. In the past, a jilted fiancée was entitled to bring suit for the emotional and material damages inflicted when left at the altar, but that's not the case anymore. The law leaves it to the parties to work out an amicable split, except that some states have laws regarding the rightful disposition of the engagement ring. Should the recipient of the engagement ring return it? Unsurprisingly, some state courts say "yes" and others say "no," while etiquette guides say "usually."

In the absence of laws and attorneys, the mediator is limited to what most experts consider to be the most effective, efficient, and durable bargaining strategy — interest-based negotiation. (See Chapter 6 for more about interest-based negotiation.) Agreements that satisfy the parties' interests are far easier to reach and more durable than settling disputes at the point of the lawsuit "gun."

Consider the example of the engagement ring. Herman and Leticia are 25 and have been living together for two years. Last Christmas, Herman got down on his knee in the couple's living room, asked for her hand in marriage, and slipped a $5,000 engagement ring on her finger. Although the ring itself isn't a family heirloom, one of the small gems surrounding the center diamond was taken from his deceased mother's engagement ring. Needless to say, the ring has enormous sentimental value to Herman in addition to representing a substantial expense.

But Herman and Leticia decide to call off the wedding. Neither blames the other. It was a mutual decision. They don't believe they can still be friends, but neither wants to cause the other any additional harm.

Leticia's parents spent $10,000 on the wedding, including $3,000 on her wedding gown. They were unable to recover any of these expenses. Leticia believes she's entitled to keep the ring to offset her parents' financial losses. Herman knows that Leticia's parents will never ask her to repay them and believes she's keeping the ring to punish him for reasons he can't fathom.

Enter you, the mediator.

After establishing an atmosphere of trust and safety, as described in Chapters 4 and 11, you explore the interests that underlie Herman's and Leticia's positions, perhaps by asking the following questions:

- ✔ What sentimental value does the wedding ring have to each party?
- ✔ If Herman's attachment to the wedding ring is based primarily on his mother's gem, would he consider replacing it with a gem of similar size, clarity, and value? Would Leticia consider accepting this solution?
- ✔ Is either party interested in the ring's monetary value?
- ✔ What might the ring sell for if either Herman or Leticia decided to put it up for sale?
- ✔ What does Leticia intend to do with the ring if she gets to keep it?
- ✔ What does Herman intend to do with the ring if Leticia returns it to him?
- ✔ Why does each party want the ring?

These are the diagnostic questions (see Chapter 7) that negotiators ask to ascertain the needs, desires, preferences, priorities, and fears that drive the parties' positions. Knowing those party interests, you can engage the parties in a brainstorming session to figure out how most of both of their interests can be served.

Assume that Leticia wants to keep the ring as a memento of her love for Herman and that Herman has recently lost his job and needs the money he can sell the ring for on eBay. Leticia's interest is sentimental, and Herman's is monetary. You can ask whether the couple exchanged other items during their relationship that may satisfy Leticia's sentimental interest. Discovering at the mediation that Herman has just lost his job may put Leticia in a more generous mood, and she may offer to pay him all or a portion of the ring's market value. Determining whether Herman believes he'll find new employment during the next year may permit the parties to consider a contingency arrangement — perhaps a loan by Leticia to Herman secured by the ring. If Herman can't pay the loan in full within two years, Leticia gets to keep the ring in lieu of repayment.

The number of potential solutions to Herman and Leticia's dispute is unlimited after you find out what each of them is trying to accomplish by laying claim to the same piece of property. *That's* mediation.

Chapter 6

Exploring Different Mediation Styles

*P*rior to and during a mediation, you want to consider your mediation style options. They include whether to take a facilitative, transformative, or evaluative approach; whether to conduct the mediation in separate caucuses or joint sessions; and whether to rely on numbers to make your point. You don't have to pick one style and stick with it; you can mix and match to create your own style or change styles during the mediation to use whatever is likely to work best given the circumstances.

This chapter describes your options, helps you choose the most effective mediation style for whatever you're dealing with during a session, and offers guidance on how to prevent competitive bargaining tactics from derailing the process.

Practicing Facilitative Mediation: The Concessions and Reciprocity Route

Facilitative mediation consists of helping the parties reach a mutually acceptable resolution using both *distributive* and *integrative* or *interest-based* negotiation strategies and tactics, which involve concessions and reciprocity. (As I explain in Chapter 5, the goal of interest-based negotiation is to meet both parties' needs instead of attempting to reach an unhappy compromise. Distributive negotiation, which I discuss in Chapter 7, consists of dividing a fixed pie of benefits among the parties to the dispute.) To resolve a dispute using facilitative mediation, you

✔ Help the parties build trust with and empathy for one another

✔ Identify issues and interests by asking diagnostic questions

✔ Validate each party's point of view

✔ Soften hard offers and demands

✔ Help the parties brainstorm and analyze solutions

✔ Use concessions and reciprocity to achieve consensus

The following sections explain how to harness the power of the concessions and reciprocity approach.

Understanding and maximizing concessions

Your clients' satisfaction with the settlement you help negotiate depends more on the number and tenor of the concessions their adversaries make than on the final dollar value. Experiments in social psychology show that people tend to be more satisfied with the outcome of negotiations when the following occur:

✔ The other side makes numerous concessions, even if they're small or inconsequential.

✔ The outcome is as good or better than similar outcomes that colleagues or competitors have achieved.

✔ The person does better than he hoped to, regardless of how good or bad the outcome is based on objective factors.

✔ The person feels that the negotiation process was "fair and reasonable," as I explain in Chapter 5.

✔ The person doesn't feel that his will was overridden by a stronger negotiator on the other side.

Whatever a client's reservations about the outcome, by the end of the day he's made dozens of small decisions among dozens of attractive and unattractive choices. Because people tend to positively frame their most difficult decisions, in hindsight most people whose concessions have been reciprocated are more likely to be satisfied by the end result than those who cut to the chase.

The following sections explain how to maximize concessions, encourage reciprocity, and deal with cultural differences that may influence the way a party negotiates.

Maximizing concessions and encouraging reciprocity

Part of your job as mediator is to soften extreme demands or offers that can result in an immediate impasse. If one party opens with a ridiculous demand, consider telling the other party, "It's only their opening demand. They're willing to drop into the range of reason if you're willing to do the same." Following are some additional responses you may want to use to soften hard demands or offers. You can make some of these statements in joint session and others in separate caucus. Telling which is which should be easy; just ask yourself whether the statement would hinder progress or complicate your relationship with one of the parties if made in joint session. I've made it even easier for these examples by labeling each as best in separate caucus or joint session:

Separate Caucus	**Joint Session**
"It's a soft number."	"The negotiation doesn't really start until the parties reach impasse, and I don't believe anyone is close to that yet."
"It's their *opening,* not their final proposal — they're *negotiating.*"	"I don't want to let the parties leave the negotiation if I believe that their bottom lines may overlap."
"Someone has to eventually step up to the line of impasse. Frankly, I think you're the party with the bargaining power (or integrity or flexibility or courage) to do it."	"As long as the parties are moving in each other's direction, it makes sense to continue negotiating rather than cutting and running."

Some lawyers say that the mediator's sole function is to keep the parties in the room, and that notion has a great deal of truth. Help the parties plan the number and size of their concessions and normalize each other's responses, particularly if they continue to be outside the realm of reason. Nine times out of ten, doing so helps them settle their dispute.

Dealing with cultural differences regarding haggling

In planning concessions, remain sensitive to the cultural context in which the negotiation takes place. Americans are so used to buying retail that they become uncomfortable after just a few (three or four) bargaining moves; for example, an opening offer (one), a counteroffer (two), and a counter to the counter (three).

After three rounds of negotiation, many American negotiators get squirrely. They get angry, begin to accuse the other side of "bad faith," and suggest that if a deal isn't reached soon, they're leaving, and the other side can suffer the consequences of litigation or the burden of the unresolved conflict.

Other cultures expect the haggling to continue, sometimes even after the matter is settled or the parties have signed off on the agreement. This type of bargaining is also well-known to occur in the entertainment industry. Negotiating over every possible point, no matter how small, making extremely small bargaining moves, treating each concession as difficult to make and as important as any other concession no matter how important is called *haggling*. Bargaining after a deal is done is known as *nibbling*.

When negotiation cultures clash, you can ask the parties diagnostic questions about the likely source of their different negotiation styles in joint session or you can explain them to each party in separate caucus. Many people don't know that their style is culturally unique to them and if you raise the issue yourself in a joint session, you risk causing them embarrassment and to "lose face." I tend to deal with cultural differences first in separate caucus and follow the lead of the parties in regard to raising the issue in joint session.

To deal with cultural differences in separate caucus, consider the following approach:

1. **First ask both parties whether they sense that part of the impasse they're experiencing might be caused by culturally different negotiation styles.**

2. **If a party admits that cultural differences may be contributing to impasse, ask the parties what style of negotiation they're accustomed to:**

   • Small concessions, grudging delivery of pertinent information, demands for outsized displays of reciprocity from the other side, threats to leave if the most recent demand is not met, and the like.

   • Impatience with the negotiation process itself, wishing to "cut to the chase" immediately, interpreting the other party's slower, more aggressive style as evidence of bad faith, and the like.

3. **Ask each party whether he'd feel comfortable talking to the other about their differing styles and whether they might find the negotiation more effective if they spoke more frankly with one another about process.**

   The answer to this question is invariably "no" because the parties are used to their "style" and generally believe it to give them a tactical or strategic advantage that they rarely wish to give up.

4. **Soften the blow of conflicting styles by reminding the parties (usually in separate caucus) that they should not take those styles as evidence of bad faith but rather as a sign of cultural differences that needn't stop them from reaching agreement.**

If you practice a strict transformative mediation approach, this particular strategy may not be the best for you. Transformative mediators believe that any process by which the mediator intervenes to help the parties understand one another better is ineffective and limits the parties' "voice and choice" not only to resolve the matter on their own terms but to use any strategy they please without interference from the mediator.

Harnessing the power of reciprocity

Reciprocity makes the adage "It's better to give than to receive" literally true. When a party makes a concession, the beneficiary of that concession usually feels obligated not only to return the favor but also to outdo the other person. To maximize the power of reciprocity, when a party offers a concession, you can help move the parties to agreement by taking the following three steps:

1. **Counsel the offeree to express appreciation for (or, at a minimum, an understanding of) the offer or demand.**

2. **Suggest that the offeree explain the reasons why making a concession in response to the offer or demand is difficult if he is reluctant to make a counter-offer.**

3. **Help the offeree formulate a reciprocal concession if a concession seems warranted, including a request for a similar and equally difficult concession in return.**

If you're working in a more transformative mode and object to "coaching" the parties, you could respond in the following way in joint session:

> Say, "Thank you for making that concession," and ask the other party whether he believes the concession is sufficiently significant to justify a concession on her part or whether more problem-solving discussions are needed before a counter-offer is put on the table.

> Ask the offerer how easy or difficult it was to make his most recent concession.

> Either be silent and see where that intervention leads, or, if the parties have indicated that they need your continued assistance, ask the offeree whether he believes the concession calls for reciprocity on this part.

This type of bargaining is commonplace among family members. For example, you may respond to a request from your spouse in the following way:

> "I know how much you want to spend the winter holidays with your parents again this year." (This statement acknowledges the request and demonstrates your understanding of its importance to your bargaining partner.)

> "Last year our trip to see your parents in Timbuktu cost us twice as much as we budgeted for family entertainment for the entire year." (This statement explains why acceding to the request is difficult for you.)

> "I'm willing to spend the winter holidays with your parents again this year, but only if it fits in our budget after we spend a week at Disneyland with the children this summer." (This statement makes a concession conditional on its reciprocation.)

The "rejection-then-retreat technique" relies heavily on the pressure to reciprocate concessions. When one of the parties makes an extreme demand that's certain to be rejected, you can help the parties move in each other's direction by suggesting that the party making the extreme demand retreat to a smaller request even though the smaller request will likely be for more than she's willing to settle. As long as the opening offer isn't so outrageous that it completely derails negotiations, the second request is far more likely to be accepted because it's a tempting concession.

Using Transformative Mediation to Repair Damaged Relationships

When parties have a long-term relationship that's likely to continue beyond a dispute's resolution, consider taking a transformative approach to resolving the dispute. *Transformative mediation* focuses primarily on the personal interaction between the disputing parties. The goal is to improve the disputants' relationship or increase their insight, self-knowledge, and respect for each other. This type of mediation uses the crisis in communication that *is* a dispute as an opportunity to transform the parties' relationship with each other or transform their relationship to conflict itself. In the process, the parties' communication and problem-solving skills are also transformed, often leading to the dispute's resolution.

The dispute isn't the central concern of the transformative mediator; the focus is on the individuals and their relationship. Because conflict occurs at the intersection of problems people need to solve in order to grow and skills that they don't yet possess, the transformative conflict resolution *process* enables growth, and that growth often promotes or produces resolution.

The following sections make the case for transformative mediation, describe situations in which transformative mediation is probably the best approach, and explain how to use transformative mediation to achieve reconciliation.

Making a case for transformative mediation

Transformative mediation offers three important benefits over other mediation styles:

- ✔ **It increases satisfaction in the outcome:** When clients are allowed to put on the table whatever they want to — to talk about what matters most to them and make their own decisions — they're far more satisfied with the resolution because they rarely if ever feel pressured or manipulated to do something they really didn't want to do.

✔ **It allows for greater certainty about the settlement's value:** In the open forum of transformative mediation, the deal arises from richer, more textured information based upon the degree of detail and depth of experience the parties share with one another, increasing the value *to the parties* of what the parties have achieved.

✔ **It equips the parties with communication and problem-solving skills to resolve future disagreements.** Transformative mediation is more interpersonal than transactional; that is, the goal is to help the parties communicate more effectively. The parties' current dispute is an opportunity to transform the relationship between the parties, and resolution of the dispute is a welcome byproduct, but resolving the current dispute is not the primary goal.

You may or may not choose to use a purely transformative approach, but by understanding and practicing transformative mediation techniques, you add another tool to your toolbox of conflict-resolution strategies — a tool that can break impasse when all the parties' savvy negotiation strategies and tactics have failed.

Mediating in personal and professional relationships

Transformative mediation is particularly well-suited for disputes between partners in personal or business relationships — situations in which the parties need to repair and improve a damaged relationship. The transformative mediator serves as the parties' guide and mentor in the process of reconciliation. This process is more descriptive of healthy dispute resolution among people than it is prescriptive. It's human nature to apologize for wrongdoing, to make amends, and to seek reconciliation. The transformative mediator is merely the midwife to the rebirth of this process among parties for whom the conflict can serve as a transformative experience.

With transformative mediation, you often play the role of a relationship coach, which is a little too touchy-feely for some mediators. If you have a highly analytical mind but aren't much of a people person, you may want to stick with evaluative and facilitative mediation techniques.

Resolving community disputes

Community mediation is another arena in which transformative mediation shines. The people who seek out community mediation generally can't afford to hire attorneys to "make a federal case" out of disputes that don't justify the expense of litigation. As a community mediator, I've handled numerous cases of dogs barking loudly and incessantly, rowdy behavior in common areas, visitation issues between parents who've run out of funds to pay their attorneys, and complaints by tenants about landlord failures to keep their premises habitable.

Engaging in transformative mediation

When engaging in transformative mediation, start with the premise that all parties are experiencing confusion, fear, disorganization, vulnerability, uncertainty, indecisiveness, defensiveness, and suspicion. In litigated disputes, the parties *and* their attorneys wage wars of nerves and battles of wit and intelligence. This increases anxiety and makes the participants self-absorbed and self-serving, which impedes collaborative problem-solving.

To reduce the participants' anxiety and increase confidence in their ability to solve their own problems on their own terms, create an atmosphere of hope and safety. Ask questions, such as the following, to help the parties establish a structure and ground rules for their dispute-resolution process:

- ✔ What would be a comfortable way for you to talk about this dispute with your adversary?
- ✔ Can you think of ways to conduct your discussions that may help you have a productive conversation with each other?
- ✔ What ground rules would you like to establish before you begin your conversation?
- ✔ Would you like to ask your conflict-resolution partner to refrain from doing anything or to do something you'd like him to do in the course of your discussion?
- ✔ Can you think of any other ground rules that may help you have a productive conversation with each other?

By setting ground rules and structuring the way in which the conflict is resolved, the parties regain the control they relinquished when they turned their conflict over to the lawyers. As they take back the power to resolve their own dispute, they gain clarity, confidence, personal strength, and decisiveness. This movement from confusion and powerlessness to strength and clarity is the goal of transformative mediation.

The key to transformative mediation is giving the parties "voice and choice" — not only in the final solution but also in the process by which they reach the final solution.

As you observe and interact with the participants, listen for signs of their confusion, fear, feelings of powerlessness, and self-absorption. When you hear the parties expressing these feelings, seize the opportunity to help guide them from helplessness to strength, from confusion to clarity, and from self-absorption to recognition of the interests of their opponent. See Chapter 8 for specific techniques to empower the parties and assist them in recognizing each other's interests.

Remain alert to any shift in the parties' discussions from self-interest and self-absorption to empathy and respect for their adversary and appreciation of their adversary's situation. This shift can only happen in joint session mediation and only if you allow the parties to express all their concerns and the full range of their emotions without hindrance. When you notice these positive shifts, praise the parties for their progress.

The transformative mediator doesn't evaluate the merits of the parties' positions or facilitate a negotiation focused on getting both parties what they want. Transformative mediators don't carry messages back and forth between the parties, deliver the bad news an attorney can't bring herself to convey to her client, or "bang heads together" to induce the parties to settle on terms they dislike. They don't help one party improve his negotiation posture or depress the clients' expectations of victory. The transformative mediator encourages and empowers the parties to resolve the dispute on their own terms.

Reaching a peaceful end through reconciliation

The ideal goal of mediation is reconciliation, even if only to end commercial hostilities in or out of the courtroom. To reach reconciliation, the following principles of peacemaking come into play:

✔ **Accountability:** The person who committed the wrong needs to acknowledge his role in the wrongdoing. Acknowledgement may come in one of the following forms:

- Acknowledgment of moral culpability demonstrates moral character; for example, "I was wrong to have said or done. . . ." Sometimes all the damaged party wants to hear is the other party admit that what she did was wrong.

- Acknowledgment of the offense or wrongdoing demonstrates that the party recognizes the specific action that was wrong; for example, "This is what I did. . . ." The more specific the description of wrongdoing, the more receptive the injured party is likely to be.

- Acknowledgment of the behavior's impact demonstrates empathy or compassion; for example, "This is how I understand it affected you. . . ." The wrongdoer needs to show an awareness of how the deed inflicted pain on the injured party.

- **Apology:** The person who committed the wrong needs to apologize for the pain it caused. The apology may come in one of the following forms:

  - An expression of sorrow or regret at having caused offense demonstrates caring; for example, "I feel sadness that I did this to you. . . ."

  - Acknowledgment that nothing adequately or truly justifies the action demonstrates sincere sorrow; for example, "There's no excuse for my actions that caused you pain. . . ."

- **Amends:** The wrongdoer must describe what he plans to do to right the wrong. An intent to make amends may come in one of the following forms:

  - A promise to make restitution and/or alter behavior in the future.

  - An acceptance of the consequences, which conveys an admission of responsibility and the impression that the apology is sincere.

- **Forgiveness:** The wrongdoer must ask for forgiveness. This signals that the person responsible has done all he can and is now handing control over to the injured party and giving her the opportunity to be magnanimous.

Reconciliation in medical malpractice cases

I used to help attorneys, insurance adjusters, and patient/clients resolve medical malpractice cases — what most mediators mistakenly refer to as "pure money" cases.

The parties probably won't have a continuing relationship, but the principles of peacemaking — accountability, apology, amends, and forgiveness — are as relevant in these cases as they are in the resolution of disputes between business partners or husbands and wives.

Patients don't tend to sue their doctors primarily for the money. They sue to find out why they or their loved ones had an unexpectedly bad experience, to hear the physician express responsibility for the adverse result, and to ensure that the same thing doesn't happen to someone else. Studies also show that patients tend not to sue for malpractice if they respect their physician and feel that their physician has been honest with them.

In other words, the "pure money" case is a myth. Malpractice disputes are cases of conflict in which the plaintiff really wants respect, honesty, accountability, and reconciliation. Sometimes, money serves as a second-rate substitute.

Some lawyers and mediators, especially in commercial litigation, believe that transformative strategies are ill-suited for the justice system because an open acknowledgment of error or wrongdoing carries potentially serious legal consequences. Those consequences can be mitigated by confidentiality protections provided by the state or federal law in the jurisdiction in which the lawsuit is pending. Depending on the scope of the confidentiality provisions that control your mediation, the parties may be able to acknowledge wrongdoing and apologize without creating evidence that the other side can use in court. And if suit hasn't been filed, accountability, apology, amends, and forgiveness are not only good for the soul but also far more likely to avoid litigation than to spur it.

Bringing the Parties Down to Earth with Evaluative Mediation

Evaluative mediators help the parties analyze the strengths and weaknesses of each side's case to help them decide whether to continue litigating their dispute or settle it. If you're contacted by attorneys to mediate a dispute, they're often expecting evaluative mediation services.

Depending upon standard of practice in your legal locale, attorneys want an unbiased but skilled and experienced individual to help them assess the pros and cons of going to trial and to provide their clients with a second opinion on the choice between settlement and trial. What the parties often want and need most is an objective look at their chances of success in court.

Among the questions they want answered are the following:

- ✔ Will I find through the discovery process the "smoking gun" document or witness I believe will assure my victory at trial?

- ✔ Am I likely to win the pre-trial motions necessary to get my full story to the judge or jury or to stop the other side's case dead in its tracks?

- ✔ Will the jury tend to believe my expert witness testimony?

- ✔ Will my witnesses come across as credible? Will the other party's witnesses appear to be more credible?

- ✔ Will the jury believe my story and disbelieve that of my opponent? In other words, will I appear to the jury to be a credible witness? Will evasiveness in pre-trial testimony or apparent contradictions in my story harm my chances of winning?

✔ What type of jury will be deciding the case — an urban cosmopolitan jury or a suburban homogenous jury? How well will my case appeal to the type of jury that will ultimately decide the case?

Avoid engaging in arguments with either side and probe what truly needs to be evaluated — the cause of the conflict and the parties' inability to resolve it. When formulating questions to help a party evaluate his chances of success, make sure your questions cover the following sources of conflict between the parties:

✔ **Information:** Conflicts often arise over what happened and who said what when — the facts. Which of those facts are important to the resolution of the legal "case" and which are not is something the attorneys understand better than their clients. By asking open-ended and follow-up questions, you can help bring the parties' knowledge and understanding of the facts in the context of a legal proceeding closer together. You can also help the attorneys better understand their clients' views and vice versa. For more about asking open-ended questions, see Chapter 7.

✔ **Interests:** Parties invariably have actual or perceived conflicts of interest. Ask questions to reveal each party's interests in regard to the legal case itself — how much money and time have the parties devoted to prosecuting or defending the case; what toll has it taken on their business or personal lives; what would it be like for the parties to wake up tomorrow morning and have the case be over? Has the litigation itself caused more disputes and a greater degree of mistrust than existed when it started? Are there misunderstandings about how the case has developed over time between the parties or between the attorneys and their clients? For more about uncovering hidden interests, see Chapter 9.

✔ **Relationships:** Relationship conflicts may arise over bias, poor or miscommunication, or a history of bad behavior by one or both parties. You can help the parties settle *and* save face by getting to the root of relationship issues that have resulted in negotiation impasse and needlessly prolonged the legal proceedings by asking each party to describe what led them to distrust or demonize their opponent. For more about identifying and dealing with relationship issues, see Chapter 8.

✔ **Practical limitations:** Time constraints, geographical or physical barriers, environmental factors, and a lack of power or authority can all get in the way of enabling the parties to resolve their differences and serve each party's interests. To identify and overcome such limitations, engage in problem-solving with each or both parties, as explained in Chapter 12.

✔ **Values and beliefs:** Each party's belief system and values strongly influence what they feel is a fair outcome. As I explain in Chapter 7, you can often resolve a dispute by appealing to the parties' shared values. You also need to identify and address unshared or conflicting values and beliefs.

As an evaluative mediator, you may tend to focus more on conflicts regarding facts and other information, but you need to remain sensitive to the other sources of conflict. Failing to address any source of conflict is likely to result in impasse.

In the following sections, I explain what you need to do to prepare yourself for evaluative mediation and present various approaches for conducting evaluative mediation.

Being prepared

Evaluative mediators tend to be more concerned with the parties' legal rights and remedies than with their justice issues. If you're going to practice in a market that expects evaluative mediation, be very familiar with the substantive law that governs the dispute (personal injury, fraud, intellectual property rights, and so on), the industry in which the dispute takes place (manufacturing, insurance, entertainment, and so on) and the legal culture of the practice niche (employment cases in my legal market (Los Angeles), for example, are primarily settled in an evaluative manner by way of attorney- and judge-mediator proposals after the mediator performs a thorough legal and factual evaluation).

Conducting evaluative mediation

As an evaluative mediator, you assist the parties in reaching resolution either by pointing out the weaknesses of their cases or by asking tough questions of the parties and their attorneys about the strengths and weaknesses of their cases. The goals are to highlight weaknesses and create doubt, so the parties are more receptive to the idea of an out-of-court settlement. Your approach for achieving these goals may vary. Here are some common approaches to evaluative mediation:

- ✔ **Predict the outcome based on your experience.** Some evaluative mediators go so far as to predict what they believe a judge or jury would be likely to do given the facts they've been told and the law as the attorneys in the dispute have explained it. Sometimes evaluative mediators, particularly retired judges, rely on their own experiences to predict success or failure, comparing the legal "case" with other legal cases the judge has herself tried or that a jury has decided with the court's legal guidance.

- ✔ **Suggest your opinion of a possible resolution by way of a mediator's proposal.** You may make formal or informal recommendations to the parties or use a mediator's proposal to break impasse. (For more about mediator's proposals, see Chapter 13.)

- ✔ **Conduct shuttle diplomacy in separate caucuses.** Some evaluative mediators read the parties' written submissions ask each party to give oral presentations and show the mediator the evidence that supports their position in the case. The mediator gives her opinions about the relative risks to each party, and then simply carries offers and counter-offers back and forth between the parties. This approach is more likely to sideline the clients and have you dealing primarily with the attorneys.

✔ **Be directive as well as evaluative.** In some disputes, you may want or need to take charge to keep the parties moving forward. Some evaluative mediators, for example, tell the parties what counters they should make to offers on the table and may become very assertive to bend the parties to their will. The assertiveness can run from the fairly benign — *You'll never settle this case if you make that demand* or *You'll have to reduce it if you want me to carry it to the other side with a straight face* — to the malicious — *I'll keep all the parties here without food until they settle this ridiculous piece of litigation* or *I'm prepared to stay up all night if I have to.* In these ways, you directly influence the outcome of mediation.

Don't be afraid of challenging a lawyer's case. Often, the lawyers are counting on you to bring their clients' expectations back down to reality after the lawyers themselves have built up those expectations. Lawyers who seek out evaluative mediation expect you to denigrate each side's chances of success in court on the merits of their claim. Of course, each lawyer hopes that you'll do more to denigrate the other side's chance of success. The sophisticated attorney takes any praise of the other side's case and uses it to help manage his own client's expectations while redefining success in terms of the more realistic expectations.

As I explain in Chapter 5, there's a good way and a bad way to help attorneys help their clients make the choice between settlement and trial through an evaluative mediation process. (For more about helping attorneys settle their cases, see Chapter 5.)

Is the evaluative approach really mediation?

Some mediators claim that evaluative mediation isn't mediation at all. They say it's merely a cheap, fast substitute for the legal process, with the mediator doing what a judge would do — analyze the strengths and weaknesses of each side's case and then coerce a settlement rather than enter judgment.

Other mediators sharply disagree. They say that they're simply engaged in "reality testing," helping the parties conduct their own cost-benefit analysis to determine whether settlement on terms the parties can agree to will likely provide a better outcome than trial.

At the end of the day, however, whether the evaluative approach is truly mediation doesn't matter. Evaluative mediation is a legitimate way to help attorneys and their clients settle out of court and potentially save a significant amount of money. In addition, it's often what the market wants, so it's a service you may want to add to your menu.

Taking a Joint Session or Separate Caucus Approach

One of the biggest choices you need to make as a mediator is whether to gather participants around a table to hash out their differences (a *joint session*) or caucus with each party separately and then shuttle back and forth between them to convey demands, offers, and other information.

Though joint sessions are generally preferable for collaborative negotiation and problem-solving, each approach has its place. The following sections present the pros and cons of each approach, describe situations in which one approach may be preferable, and provide suggestions and tips on how to use each strategy most effectively.

Mediating in joint session or separate caucuses isn't necessarily an either/ or proposition. For example, you may want to begin a mediation session by caucusing separately with each party and then gather around a table for collaborative problem-solving.

Conducting a joint session

Whether you choose to mediate primarily in joint session or separate caucus, to be a great mediator you need to know how to successfully facilitate a joint session mediation. Mediators who don't like to begin negotiations in joint session often justify their aversion by citing their desire to avoid a polarizing set of zealously adversarial presentations. The joint session, however, was never meant to be a mini-trial or reiteration of the parties' adversarial positions. The purpose of the joint session is to give participants the opportunity to brainstorm mutually acceptable solutions to their undeniably mutual problem: the sinkhole of litigation or painful stalemate of unresolved conflict.

Start your mediation in joint session and engage the parties and their attorneys in small talk. When engaged in small talk, the parties get to know each other as people and start thinking about something other than the money they stand to lose or gain.

Joint session offers some additional benefits:

- ✔ By observing how the participants interact with each other, you gain insight into factors that may be contributing to impasse.
- ✔ Interaction between the parties (and lawyers) may suggest paths to consensus that aren't apparent when speaking to just one side.
- ✔ You have the opportunity to set an appropriate tone, build trust, demonstrate evenhandedness, and model polite behavior.

✔ The parties have an opportunity to *speak directly* to their adversaries, satisfying their desire to be heard and understood.

✔ The parties have the opportunity to *hear and evaluate* the experience expressed by their adversary, permitting them, at long last, to gain insight into why the dispute arose.

✔ All participants have the opportunity to evaluate the emotional disposition of decision-makers, the credibility of those who may give evidence if the matter goes to trial, and the positions and interests the participants need to negotiate during the mediation.

Conducting separate caucuses

In some of the largest mediation markets today, nearly all mediations begin and end in separate caucus. Separate caucus mediation can be effective if the mediator can bring the parties together when necessary.

The primary drawback of mediating in separate caucuses is that you can't reap the benefits of joint session mediation, which I describe in the preceding section. Parties don't have a chance to air their grievances, and they don't engage in collaborative problem-solving. And although they may resolve the dispute, they may do so with such bitterness and resentment that they later challenge the settlement in court, creating a new dispute that arises from the injustice created by the mediation process.

A joint-session success story

I once mediated a lawsuit that arose from a three-car traffic accident. Only one of five injured parties had an insurance policy, and that policy precluded anyone from being fully compensated. Just before declaring the mediation a failure, I asked the parties to gather in a single conference room. I put a jar in the center of the table and asked them to imagine that it was filled with cash equal to the available insurance proceeds. I then asked the parties to take turns describing their injuries without exaggeration and to say how much of the money they felt entitled to take out of the jar for themselves.

You can imagine the result. The parties bonded over their shared experience and the injuries

each of them suffered, talking together about how frightened they'd been at the time, how lucky they all were to be alive, and what friends and family had done to help them recover from their injuries. When asked to "remove money from the jar of joint resources," all the parties asked for less than they'd previously demanded, and at least one person said that her adversary should receive the bulk of the proceeds.

I never could have achieved this result in separate caucus, where each party would justify his own need in the absence of the context in which his need might be satisfied — the community of people injured in the same accident.

Still, separate caucus mediation has its benefits, including

✔ Parties don't have the opportunity to exchange hostilities that often cause them to terminate the mediation prematurely.

✔ You can soften hard positions when you deliver a high demand or low offer. You can pitch the proposal not as an ultimatum but as the opponent's willingness to move into a reasonable range, assuming his adversary is sincerely willing to make concessions.

✔ The parties feel less pressure to respond immediately. They have time to ponder in private and consider the possible benefits of redefining their interests, clarifying their positions, identifying new structures for a deal, weighing the other party's proposals, and seeking the mediator's advice on process or substance.

✔ You and each party can discuss openly the risks of failing to reach agreement and the weaknesses in the party's case that the party can't freely share in a joint session.

✔ You can engage each party in problem-solving without the pressure of the other side's presence, which often feels like negotiating at gunpoint.

✔ You can directly challenge each party's assumptions and positions to expand the bargaining range. If you challenge assumptions and positions in joint session, you're more likely to narrow the bargaining range.

If you conduct mediation in separate caucuses because you're too conflict-averse to deal with the parties in a joint session, you're doing your clients a grave disservice. As I explain in the preceding section, joint session mediation can accomplish what no separate caucus mediation is capable of — a truly collaborative resolution based on the parties' shared or diverging interests. If the parties are conflict-averse themselves, you should be prepared to assist them in transitioning to more collaborative interactions.

Sharpening your caucusing skills

To caucus most effectively, you need to adhere to certain caucusing do's and don'ts. The do's include

✔ Assuring both parties that unless they expressly authorize it, nothing said in separate caucus will be communicated to the party in the other room.

✔ Fully utilizing the caucus to find out the following:

• Whether the party is troubled by anything happening in the joint session that you're capable of resolving, such as power imbalances and procedural aspects of the mediation (who speaks first, the tenor of a party's comments, your neutrality as a mediator, and the like).

- How the caucusing party views the adversary's interests and positions and whether that view is overly influenced by cognitive biases, such as reactive devaluation or demonization. (See Chapter 8 for more about cognitive biases.)

- How the caucusing party genuinely views the benefits and detriments of any proposed resolutions with an eye toward increasing the number of options available to settle the dispute.

- Whether you understand what the caucusing party believes the parties have communicated and how each party perceives those communications.

- Whether the party has concerns he feels unable to raise in joint session but is willing to communicate to you in an effort to narrow the bargaining range or increase negotiation options.

✔ Closing the caucus by reminding the party about the confidentiality of the caucus and seeking permission to communicate whatever he believes will best serve his interests at this stage of the mediation.

✔ Holding a caucus with the other party to keep the process balanced and prevent feelings of distrust or suspicion regarding what went on in the first caucus.

Caucusing don'ts include

✔ Never demonize or ridicule the opposition to ingratiate yourself to the party you're caucusing with. This escalates rather than de-escalates conflict.

✔ Never ask the party for her "genuine" or "real" or "absolute" bottom line. Doing so tends to lock the party into a position that's difficult to alter if the negotiation reaches a point when changing that bottom line seems necessary.

✔ Never tell a party what the other party is likely to offer or accept, unless you've been expressly authorized to do so. For example, if one party is demanding $1 million and you're almost certain she'd accept $750,000, don't divulge that fact to the other party. Doing so undermines the strength of the $1 million anchor and likely breaches your obligation to retain the offering party's confidence.

✔ Never lie to a party in separate caucus. For example, never say, "This is your adversary's best, last, and final offer," unless that party has authorized you to do so *and* has assured you that it *is* in fact her best, last, and final offer. If you *know* the party is bluffing and you communicate the bluff, you become an accomplice to a ruse, are acting unethically, and have lost your neutrality as you help one side attempt to fool the other.

Chapter 7

Honing Essential Mediation Skills

ertain skills are essential to effective mediation. Above all else, you need to maintain confidentiality and neutrality throughout the mediation process, so the parties have confidence and trust in both you and the process. In addition, you have to master certain techniques, including anchoring, framing, logrolling, and distributive bargaining. You also need to get in the habit of answering questions with questions and know how to appeal to the parties' higher values. I deem all these essential mediation skills. This chapter assists you in developing and sharpening these abilities.

Maintaining Confidentiality in Separate Caucuses

When the parties are in a joint session, you don't need to fret about keeping track of the information you're allowed to communicate among the parties, because everyone speaks out in the open. In contrast, the more time you spend in separate caucus, the more you risk damaging the parties' perception of procedural fairness, calling into question your own neutrality, and inadvertently breaching caucus confidentiality. To avoid breaching caucus confidentiality, follow these suggestions:

✔ Tell the parties you don't want to know what their true bottom lines are so you don't inadvertently reveal them to the other side.

✔ Never disclose what you believe to be the parties' bargaining weaknesses or strengths based on what you discover in separate caucus.

✔ Never suggest that a party is willing to accept less or pay more than the party currently has on the table.

✔ Never predict what the other party is willing to settle for.

✔ Never base a mediator's proposal on confidential information the parties provide in separate caucuses. Instead, use the parties' most recent offer and counteroffer.

✔ Never answer the question, "What's the mood in the other room?" or any other inquiry that calls on you to disclose or characterize what's going on in the other room.

Your credibility is one of your greatest assets in helping parties resolve a dispute and in securing future business. If you disclose confidential information to a party, she has every reason to suspect that you're disclosing her confidential information to the other party. As the old saying goes, "If he does it with you, he'll do it to you." If either party loses trust in you, your ability to resolve the dispute — and your reputation in the community — can be severely compromised.

Confidentiality extends beyond the mediation. Though the parties may be free to discuss the mediation and what they ultimately decided, as the mediator, you need to remain mum or at least keep the parties' identities under wraps.

Keeping a Neutral Position

Maintaining neutrality in the midst of conflict is essential in resolving disputes, but you're a human being, not a human Switzerland. You have feelings, opinions, and prejudices that cause you to like one party better than another, can impair your judgment, and may mislead you about the parties' true intentions.

Being neutral doesn't mean you have no opinions or feelings. It means you have no stake in the outcome. Being neutral doesn't require you to suppress conflict that may arise between you and your clients. It does, however, demand that you don't express opinions that favor one party over the other. The following sections explain techniques to help you maintain neutrality.

Staying neutral in tough situations

When parties ask you for an assessment or your opinion, present you with dubious facts or suppositions, or have a history of using your services, maintaining neutrality is even more difficult than it usually is. Read on for suggestions on how to stay neutral in these difficult situations.

Maintaining neutrality when asked for your opinion

When parties ask you for your opinions regarding their chances for victory, turn their questions back on them to encourage and assist them in performing their own assessments. Answering questions with questions, such as the following, gives you something to say instead of your opinion:

- ✔ You've asked for my opinion about your chances of victory. Is there a problem with the case that makes you doubt your own valuation?

- ✔ Are you concerned about anything in particular that may harm your chances for success?

- ✔ Is there anything the other party doesn't know now but may find out in the future that could harm your chances for success?

- ✔ Assuming everything goes your way — the jury believes and likes your witnesses, the judge sustains your objections and overrules the other side's, you win the pretrial motions, and so on — what do you believe are your chances for success?

- ✔ Assuming everything goes your way, what do you think is the likely range of damages or other relief a jury may award for or against you?

- ✔ What's likely to happen if you fail to settle the dispute today?

- ✔ How would you feel if you woke up tomorrow morning and no longer had to worry about a third party deciding against you?

- ✔ What would accepting the other party's proposal for resolving this dispute mean to you?

- ✔ What outcome do you believe would be fair to you? And to the other party?

- ✔ If you were in the other party's shoes, what would you most want to know about the weaknesses in your case? And what strengths would concern you?

These questions are just a few of the innumerable inquiries you can make to help the parties evaluate the probable consequences of their failure to resolve the dispute or their acceptance of an unsatisfactory outcome. By asking the parties tough questions, you can avoid injecting your opinions into the decision-making process and thereby maintain your neutrality. Many of these questions can be answered only in separate caucus. You may raise them for both parties in joint session as matters to be concerned with. One or more of the parties may want to discuss these matters in separate caucus with you if you raise them in joint session.

Don't conduct and communicate your own independent risk analysis. Instead, help the parties conduct a risk analysis by asking them reality-testing questions such as, "What do you believe your chances of victory are if the judge overrules your objection to the other party's smoking gun evidence?"

Doubting a party's version of events without showing it

When you doubt one party's version of events, your first impulse may be to consider the person a liar or a lunatic, and you may be more inclined to believe what the other party tells you. However, if you telegraph your own doubts about the story, you lose your neutrality in the eyes of the disputants. Suspend your disbelief and apply the UFO reality test.

Assume the party whose version of events you doubt firmly believes he was abducted by aliens. Listen to his story, ask him for details, and make an effort to understand how his belief may be interfering with resolution or serve as the key to breaking impasse. After giving the party an opportunity to describe his experience, perhaps for the first time, to someone willing to listen without judgment, gently reality-test his version of events. You don't have to believe or disbelieve the story. You can, however, suggest that not everyone is as understanding as you are.

Ask whether he's told this story to other people and what their responses were. Follow up by asking whether he has any reason to believe that a judge or jury may be more likely to believe this narrative of events than his mother, sister, cousin, wife, or best friend.

By engaging in gentle reality-testing, you shrewdly and effectively negotiate between the rock of understanding and the hard place of consensual reality. You also neatly avoid the problem of engaging in a futile argument with someone whose mind is made up.

Working for repeat clients

Small town or large, you inevitably have repeat clients who value your services as a mediator. Mediation has no hard and fast rules about disclosing prior contact with a party, but before you accept a mediation assignment, you should disclose to the other party any prior relationship you've had with his bargaining partner.

Consider asking the party with whom you've done business before whether she wants to disclose your relationship to the other party. She may have done so already. If she'd rather you handle the disclosure, call the other party, describe your relationship, and ask whether the party has any questions, concerns, or objections. Don't answer any questions that call on you to disclose confidential information; you're better off losing a gig than compromising your integrity.

If you don't disclose a friendly relationship (an existing personal or professional connection) with a party and the other party finds out about it in the course of the mediation, your neutrality is immediately called into question, and your effectiveness is damaged. Your failure to be open about prior relationships may also damage your reputation in the community, where members regularly share their opinions of mediators.

Resisting the urge to pressure a party

When a party refuses to budge or the weaker of the two parties digs in, resist the urge to pressure that party to achieve settlement. Remember that your job is to help the parties make a decision, not to make the decision for them. When you know your job is not to settle the matter, pressuring the parties to do so becomes less of a temptation.

If a dispute settles with your assistance, you can't chalk up a victory. If the parties don't settle, you shouldn't hang your head in defeat. Assist the parties in assessing their better and worse alternatives to a negotiated agreement (their BATNA and WATNA). If a party concludes that he has a better alternative to the last offer on the table, that's not a failure, and it's certainly not your failure. Pursuing a more attractive option is logical and often a wise move.

Don't sell out your neutrality to achieve settlement. When you feel yourself going for the jugular of the weaker or more inflexible party, remind yourself that your job is to help the parties make a difficult decision, not to make that decision for them. Check out Chapter 11 for more on how to treat the weaker party.

Probing with Diagnostic Questions

You mediate disputes in which parties make demands based on legal or moral positions. The plaintiff essentially says, "I'm right and he's wrong, so I'm entitled to such and such." The defense says, "I'm right and she's wrong, so she's not entitled to receive what she's asking for." To help each party get the best deal possible, you need more than bargaining tactics that influence or coerce compromise. You need to identify the motivations behind each party's position. The most effective way to reveal underlying motivations is to ask diagnostic questions.

Diagnostic questions are open-ended questions geared toward discovering what the parties need, want, fear, prefer, or prioritize. Only by understanding the parties' motivations goals are you able to diagnose and help them solve the problem that's the basis of their dispute. (*Open-ended questions* are like essay questions that require the parties to draw on their knowledge and experience to formulate a unique response. In contrast, *closed-ended questions* have yes/no/maybe, true/false, or multiple choice answers.)

Interrogating like a journalist

Diagnostic questions elicit information, which is why they're the initial questions that journalists ask when they're investigating a story: Who? What?

When? Where? Why? and How? Following are just a few diagnostic questions you can ask parties in a dispute over money:

- ✔ **Who** else may benefit from the resolution of this dispute?
- ✔ **Who** else may be harmed if this dispute isn't resolved in the way you want it to be?
- ✔ **What** do you want to accomplish by requiring your bargaining partner to pay you $X?
- ✔ **What** else besides money may enable you to accomplish your goals?
- ✔ **When** would you like this dispute to be resolved?
- ✔ **Where** else can you find the resources to achieve the desired outcome?
- ✔ **Why** should your bargaining partner pay you $X to resolve the dispute?
- ✔ **Why** should your bargaining partner be satisfied with $Y to resolve the dispute?
- ✔ **How** will $X help you accomplish that goal?

When the parties reach an impasse, diagnostic questions can help uncover what's at the root of that impasse, as I explain in Chapter 13.

Fearlessly asking follow-up questions

Everyone makes assumptions about what people mean when they say something that's not crystal clear. People are often afraid to ask questions for numerous reasons — they don't want to appear dumb or come across as "badgering the witness," or they fear that too many questions will reveal information or opinions they don't want to deal with. Instead of filling the gaps of misunderstanding with answers, they fill those gaps with assumptions, most of which are false.

To further compound the problem, people involved in an active dispute often stop speaking to each other, and they usually start telling themselves stories about why their opponent is behaving in a certain manner. Rarely are such stories accurate because people can't read minds.

The take-home lesson here is that if you don't fully understand an answer with a fair degree of certainty, ask a follow-up question — in most cases, another open-ended question. See the nearby sidebar for an example of one follow-up question that broke through an impasse in a malpractice dispute.

The mediator's job is to help the parties freely exchange information with each other so that they have the greatest array of opportunities to resolve their conflict. Relentlessly explore all avenues of information before ending your inquiries. Failure to do so only adds to the parties' communication problems.

One question that led to a malpractice settlement

Once, while I was mediating a medical malpractice action, the defendant physician said, "I can't do that" when his own attorney suggested that his insurance carrier pay $250,000 to settle a legal claim for the death of a child. The attorney was content to end the conversation there.

"May I ask your client why he can't authorize a settlement in that sum?" I asked his attorney.

"Sure."

The physician became quite grim and softly said, "If I paid her $250,000, that would mean I killed her child."

This question and answer commenced a longer conversation about why people bring lawsuits against their physicians, how juries respond to medical malpractice claims, and what a jury verdict against the doctor would mean to him. When the doctor realized that settling the case wouldn't alter what he knew to be true — that he had provided his patient with the best care possible — he was able to authorize the settlement of a case he stood a good chance of losing.

Whenever you sense that you're about to tread in emotional territory, you're onto something important. The question you're afraid to ask, out of concern that it will elicit an emotional response, is often the best question available, as illustrated in the nearby sidebar. Helping people deal with the emotions that arise as a result of conflict is your job and often leads to resolution.

Anchoring a Dispute

If you're negotiating a dispute in which the end result will consist of one party paying money to the other, be aware that the way the parties respond to a monetary offer or demand is strongly influenced by an *anchor* — any relevant number that enters the negotiation environment. You can use anchors strategically to help resolve a dispute by first recognizing the proven effects that anchors have in negotiations:

- ✔ The first offer or demand strongly influences the outcome of the negotiation.

- ✔ The greater the uncertainty about the value of a thing, the stronger the anchoring effect of the first offer or demand.

- ✔ People who deny that opening offers or demands influence their behavior are repeatedly found to be strongly influenced by them.

- ✔ High anchors selectively direct a person's attention toward an item's positive attributes, whereas low anchors direct attention to its flaws. (Items being negotiated have both positive and negative attributes — qualities that suggest a higher price and qualities that suggest a lower price.)

✔ An offer or demand that's too close to a party's bottom line limits his options, requiring him to make small concessions or stand by his original demand or offer.

✔ By making an aggressive first offer or demand (setting a high or low anchor), the offerer can "extract" more concessions from his bargaining partner. One of the best predictors of party satisfaction with an outcome is the number and size of the concessions extracted from an opponent.

If you see yourself as a *facilitative mediator* — one who helps the parties understand and use best bargaining practices (see Chapter 6 for info on the different styles of mediation) — you may want to share some of this information with the parties. For example, you can tell both parties that they're more likely to reach agreement if they give themselves enough bargaining room to make three or four concessions. If neither party is willing to go first, you might tell them that the first offer or demand strongly influences the negotiation's outcome.

Just as anchors may be used, they may also be abused. Adhere to the following guidelines to use anchors without abusing them:

✔ Beware of anchoring the negotiation yourself by making premature mediator's proposals. Let the parties reach an impasse before you put your own thumb on the scale of the bargaining range. If the parties ask you to suggest an opening offer, ask them to explain why they feel uncomfortable coming up with that number themselves. This sparks a conversation that can help you identify and address whatever issue is inhibiting each party from making an offer or demand.

✔ If you think an offer, demand, or concession may cause the negotiation to break down, ask any of the following questions to determine whether the party's negotiation strategy is too aggressive:

- If you were in the other party's shoes, how do you think the party would respond to that number?

- What's your thinking behind that number?

- What reasons would you give the other party to justify that number?

- Do you worry that making that offer/demand/concession may result in an impasse? If so, would you like me to present it as a soft offer/demand/concession?

If the dispute has a history of litigation, help the parties resist the effects of *abandoned anchors* — offers or demands from the past that don't account for subsequent damages and expenses. Past offers and demands are one of the most common causes for impasse, exerting a strong influence on the parties' subsequent bargaining behavior. Abandoned anchors may increase a party's sense of injustice, particularly when one party was once willing to accept far less and is now adding in the cost of litigation, arbitration, and mediation, even though the party's not eligible to recover those costs.

When parties get hung up on an abandoned anchor, you may be able to get them past it by explaining the concept of *sunk costs* — business funds already spent that are permanently lost. The term originated in the oil industry, where the decision to abandon or operate an oil well hinges on the well's expected production and not on how much money was spent to drill it. An oil company doesn't continue to pour money into a dry well. Explain that sometimes cutting your losses is the best business decision.

Framing and Reframing

Most disputes are framed as contests between good and evil, right and wrong. Master mediators help the parties *reframe* the dispute in a way that encourages them to find fresh solutions to old problems, move from anger to understanding, and shift from victimization to empowerment. Reframing consists of presenting an issue in a more optimistic, hopeful light and characterizing the dispute as a mutual problem, more often based on miscommunication than intentional misdeeds. Following are some common ways to reframe a dispute:

- **From fighting to problem-solving:** When parties engage in conflict, summarize their narratives, shift their focus from the people to the problem, and engage them in collaborative problem-solving.

- **From right to happy:** If one or both parties are stuck on being right, shift the focus to addressing their interests. Say something like, "Well, we're going to have to agree to disagree on this point, but what exactly does each of you want? What would you be willing to accept and give up to get past this issue?"

- **From intractable to cooperative:** If one party is willing to make concessions, you may be able to reframe the situation by saying something like, "Now we're getting somewhere. If the other party is willing to do this, what would you be willing to do?"

- **From past to future:** When one party is stuck in the past, remind the parties that what happened in the past stays in the past, and they can do nothing to change it. All they can control is the outcome, so looking forward, not back, behooves them.

- **From potential gain to potential loss:** Potential loss is a greater motivator than potential gain, so shift the parties' focus from the potential gain of a jury verdict in their favor to the expense, time, frustration, and unpredictability of litigation. Framing the adversarial process as a lose-lose proposition resolves more disputes than framing a successful mediation as a win-win.

Why framing works

A frame focuses the viewer's attention on what's inside the frame and excludes anything outside of it. If a photographer snaps a shot of all the medium-height students in a fifth grade class, you're unlikely to think about how tall or short they are. If he includes the shortest or the tallest, your attention focuses on height. If he includes one girl, you focus on gender.

Framing studies show that when people are asked to say how tall someone is, they estimate the height to be greater than when they're asked to guess how short someone is. The same is true for questions about duration, quantity, and other qualitative differences — attractive or unattractive; light or dark; gay or straight. Framing not only refocuses attention but also influences judgments. It organizes a person's thoughts around a specific category, and the person tends to unconsciously tailor his responses to fit the frame.

Engaging in Interest-Based Negotiation

In *competitive distributive bargaining,* the parties' goal is to divide and distribute a fixed sum of benefits, attempting to take the largest piece of the fixed sum pie for themselves. When the parties engage in *interest-based negotiation,* they seek to expand the pie of benefits in an attempt to satisfy as many of their interests (needs, desires, preferences, and priorities) as possible. The following sections highlight the limitations of distributive bargaining and persuasion in resolving disputes and reveal a better way — interest-based negotiation.

Recognizing the limitations of persuasion

When you try to persuade people to change their minds or behavior or accept less than they believe they're entitled to, they experience discomfort. In the face of information that challenges ingrained thoughts and behaviors, the brain sends out powerful messages that something's wrong. The painful distraction compromises a person's ability to think clearly.

The good news is that you don't have to change anyone's mind to resolve a dispute. Nor do the parties have to grudgingly accept half of the fixed mediation pie. In most disputes, unbeknownst to each other, the parties have a half dozen other items of value they'd be happy to exchange. By laying these items out on the bargaining table, you instantly expand the pie, so the parties have plenty to satisfy all their interests.

Identifying issues: What the parties really want and why they want it

Before the parties begin to suggest ways to resolve a dispute, encourage them to explore what they really want out of the deal. Saying they want money is easy, but people rarely want just money. Rather, they want what money buys — peace of mind, financial security, a trip around the world, a gift for their aging parents, or a down payment on a house. People also want money to have their adversaries pay for what they've done, in which case the money serves as a proxy for an apology, a sense of justice, or revenge.

After creating an atmosphere of hope and safety, as explained in Chapter 9, your next job as mediator is to lead the parties through the following five-step process, from grievance to identifying and prioritizing underlying interests:

1. **Encourage the parties to express their grievances.**

   Ask diagnostic questions to get the ball rolling, as I explain in the section "Probing with Diagnostic Questions" earlier in this chapter. The parties inevitably want to first air their grievances and be acknowledged for having them. Listen actively, empathize, and clarify statements you find ambiguous or confusing. Also make certain that both parties understand what's been said and acknowledge having heard the full story of their conflict partners' complaints.

2. **Help the parties identify their positions.**

   In the course of explaining their grievance, the parties focus on positions: I'm right and he's wrong; I was careful and she was negligent; I performed my duties under the contract and he breached his; I may have failed to warn her, but she didn't suffer any injuries as a result.

3. **Acknowledge the parties' stated interests.**

   Stated interests naturally follow as the parties identify and argue for their positions in an attempt to convince you to persuade the other party to do what they want them to do. This is a contentious negotiation tactic and not a very effective one, so you need to nudge the parties into the final stage of identifying and prioritizing their hidden interests.

4. **Explore each party's hidden interests.**

   An interest is what a party wants; a hidden interest is why the party wants it. When a party expresses an interest, usually in the form of a demand, ask what the party plans to do if that interest is met. For example, if the party receives $100,000 in a settlement, what does she plan to spend it on?

   If a party expresses the need for justice, explore with the parties precisely what the other did that leaves them feeling abused. You often find that all parties have made untested and often erroneous assumptions about their dispute partners' motivations. Defendants in litigation, for instance, are often aggrieved by the language used in a complaint that accuses them of fraud, not knowing that it was the lawyer's idea, not the plaintiff's, to allege a cause of action for intentional misrepresentation.

5. Help the parties prioritize their interests.

Prioritizing interests enables the parties to identify opportunities for exchanges that are mutually beneficial. The parties can then engage in logrolling so each party has the opportunity to bargain for what he values most by giving up what he values least. (See the section "Logrolling for Low-Cost, High-Value Concessions" later in the chapter for more on logrolling.)

Here's an example of how a party moves from grievance to underlying issues:

Grievance: That dirty contract breaker refused to rent me the apartment he promised, and I had to find another place to live in a worse location paying $75 a month more in rent!

Position: He breached his agreement to rent an apartment to me.

Stated interest: I want/deserve damages for the difference between the rent he quoted to me and the rent I now have to pay.

Underlying interests:

- ✔ **Saving face:** I told my wife I'd found the perfect apartment at a great cost, and now she doesn't believe me, and it's humiliating.

- ✔ **Seeking revenge:** The difference in rent is small, but I want to teach the landlord a lesson.

- ✔ **Concern for the larger community/justice:** I want the landlord to pay me so that he never does this to anyone else ever again.

- ✔ **Idiosyncratic interests:**

  - The landlord is my wife's brother, and he's been lying to us for years. I want to prove to my wife that he's a liar, and I never want to have to see him again.

  - I've been renting all my life, and I've never had an honest landlord. I want this landlord to understand that landlords can't treat people this way.

  - This was the only apartment available that was close enough to my workplace so that I could walk to work (I have no car) and keep my dog. I had to give my dog away because this landlord broke his promise to me.

You can't guess what drives other people's actions, motivates their demands, or may satisfy their interests. You must engage them in conversations that are fairly wide-ranging to encourage them to tell you what they're really after.

Listen for both conflicting and shared interests, because items of low cost to one party and high value to the other can be profitably exchanged, with neither party compromising as much as she believed might be necessary. For instance, if someone needs a certain amount of money right away to pay medical bills, one party may be willing to pay more now to address that immediate need in exchange for paying less overall.

Often, a party's perception that the other side is greedy, controlling, or bent on causing harm prevents the party from entering into an agreement to settle the dispute. By helping the parties understand each other's interests, these misperceptions evaporate and are replaced with a cooperative desire to help meet each other's needs.

Discovering ways to serve each party's interests

Creative problem-solving is the key to serving each party's interests. After identifying and defining the underlying interest as specifically as possible, ask the parties to brainstorm possible ways of satisfying that interest. For more about problem-solving strategies, check out Chapter 12.

Avoid the four major obstacles to brainstorming solutions:

- ✔ Prematurely terminating the negotiation
- ✔ Searching for a single answer
- ✔ Assuming the pie is fixed
- ✔ Believing that the other party is solely responsible for solving the problem

Slicing the Pie with Distributive Bargaining

No matter how much win-win value the parties create, they must still haggle over the portion of the pie they feel entitled to. They do this through distributive bargaining (also referred to as *distributive negotiation*). *Distributive bargaining* is "value claiming" negotiation in which the parties compete to get most of the fixed pie of apparently limited resources. It's *distributive* because the parties try to *distribute* between them the total resources they've placed on the bargaining table.

Understanding the principles

Every mediator must understand the basic principles of distributive bargaining tactics and strategy because most people bargain this way — it's a descriptive rather than a prescriptive process.

Following are the eight principles of successful competitive distributive bargaining:

- ✔ Start high.
- ✔ Concede slowly.
- ✔ Exaggerate the value of your concessions.
- ✔ Minimize the benefits of your opponent's concessions.
- ✔ Conceal information while encouraging or demanding the other party to share information.
- ✔ Argue forcefully on behalf of principles that imply favorable settlements to yourself.
- ✔ Make commitments to accept only agreements highly favorable to yourself.
- ✔ Patiently outwait your bargaining partner.

Putting the principles into practice

Understanding the principles of distributive bargaining is helpful, but even more useful is seeing these principles in practice. Distributive bargainers often do the following:

- ✔ Make an aggressive but reasonable first offer or demand and support it with good reasons. As I explain in the section "Anchoring a Dispute" earlier in the chapter, the person who goes first can gain the upper hand, especially by making an aggressive move.
- ✔ Listen carefully to the reasons that the other party gives to support his valuation of the item or service being discussed.
- ✔ Make counteroffers that acknowledge the bargaining partner's rationale for the previous offer or demand. For example:

  "I understand your need for a lower settlement payout. . . ."

  "You make a good point about the fees my client is seeking to recover from you being high. . . ."
- ✔ Keep their aspirations high and don't allow the other party to manipulate them into reducing their demand or raising their offer.

✔ Draw their bargaining partner's attention back to the value of what they're offering. For example:

"I understand your need for a lower settlement payout, but it's less than you'll pay your attorney to take this case to trial."

"You make a good point about my client's hourly rate being high, but it's the fee you agreed to pay when she agreed to represent you."

✔ Make concessions while acknowledging the other party's needs for those concessions, asserting the difficulty of making those concessions, and expressing a willingness to do so.

✔ Stress the fairness of their own proposals.

✔ Keep the parties at the table as long as possible, because the more time a negotiator has invested in a bargaining session, the less willing he is to give up any gains.

✔ Solicit as much information as possible from all participants.

✔ Be friendly, charming, interested, compassionate, and firm.

✔ Express their willingness to walk away if their aspirations can't be satisfied, while warning the other party against making threats and offering ultimatums.

Applying your knowledge of distributive bargaining to help resolve disputes

Understanding the dynamics of distributive bargaining helps you assist the parties when those tactics no longer work or when one party doesn't understand that distributive bargaining is standard practice and assumes that his opponent is trying to swindle him. In separate caucus, you can explain the other party's tactics by telling the offended party the following:

✔ I know the opening offer seems unreasonably high to you, but it's simply his first, not his last, offer.

✔ As long as you're both moving in the direction of each other, staying in the process makes sense, because you may find that your actual bottom lines overlap and that you're moving toward an agreement you simply don't yet know you have.

✔ If you don't feel comfortable responding to an offer that low, you can suggest a bracket; that is, you'd be willing to limit your demand to $X if she'd be willing to increase her offer to $Y.

✔ Most Americans buy retail and rarely engage in negotiations over price. In our retail culture, parties begin to get uncomfortable after an exchange of three offers and counters, but this isn't a retail situation, so extended haggling is to be expected.

Normalizing parties' bargaining behavior helps them get over their strong emotional reactions and return to a pragmatic and problem-solving state of mind.

Assigning a Monetary Value to a Loss

People use different metrics to determine what they consider to be fair compensation. Most people believe that government benefits should be based on need, not merit; that rewards in the marketplace should be based on what you do, not who you know; and that, in the absence of rules, customs, or laws, equitable principles should govern the distribution of resources.

When helping the parties decide what a just resolution of a dispute should be, ask them what measuring stick they're using to determine the fair division of resources. Often, the parties will tell you without asking. Following are some common metrics, along with examples:

- **Need:** "She doesn't need that much money to compensate her for her claim."
- **Merit:** "He deserves to be punished for what he did."
- **Equity:** "I've already paid $100,000 to clean up contamination on the property. The defendant should pay the next $100,000 before I'm asked to contribute more."

A party's measuring stick may be a valuable tool in assigning a monetary value to a loss. If a defendant claims that the plaintiff doesn't need that much money as compensation, for example, the plaintiff may respond by explaining what she needs the money for and how much it costs or by shifting the conversation to equity; that is, an injured party's need isn't the entirety of what she's being compensated for — she also wants to see justice done and the scales balanced. If a plaintiff wants to see the defendant punished, this can spark a discussion of just how much money the defendant would need to pay to suffer accordingly or to reevaluate punishment in light of the trust built between the parties during the mediation.

You can often shift the discussion from a knee-jerk metric toward a risk analysis to enable a party to change perspective and become more receptive to the other party's demand or offer. If a party objects that her bargaining partner doesn't *need* as much money as she demanded, for example, you can explain that need doesn't necessarily reflect what a court would award a plaintiff in litigation. The same is true for merit. Unless the alleged offender has acted intentionally or maliciously, the law won't punish him for carelessly causing the claimant damage. In that case, the risk analysis shows that the claimant is probably better off resolving the dispute in mediation than engaging in lengthy and costly litigation, at the end of which she probably won't get what she wants.

A transformative mediator (see Chapter 6 for the scoop on different media-tion styles) would likely steer parties from talking about needs and punish-ment deeper into their emotional responses to help the parties repair a relationship damaged by the injurious event. Often, parties who want to see someone punished don't believe that their conflict partner has experienced or expressed remorse for the injurious behavior. Often, all the claimant wants is a sincere expression of accountability ("I knew I could cause you harm and didn't assign as much priority to that risk as I did to my gain") and an apology ("I am truly regretful both that I acted irresponsibly and that my actions caused you harm, and I'd like to make amends for my careless behav-ior"). After the alleged offender expresses remorse, the injured party's desire to punish her opponent often recedes.

In some cases, people recoil from exchanging money for losses that have no price or for things that shouldn't be monetized, including human life, health, freedom, self-expression, sex, and friendship. But parents who've lost a child because of a physician's malpractice may seek money for something the law would forbid them to sell — their own child.

In litigation, the law is forced to place value on such incommensurables. When mediating personal injury cases, the mediator often needs to help the parties overcome their resistance to placing a value on these intimate losses. Following are some ways to help parties place a monetary value on a personal loss:

- ✔ Remind the parties how much money they're willing to spend to avoid pain, such as how much money they spend on prescription and over-the-counter medication. When the party causing another harm realizes the monetary value he places on avoiding pain, his willingness to com-pensate an injured party for her pain begins to make sense.

- ✔ If the pain-relief analogy isn't successful, remind the parties how much money they're willing to spend to feel pleasure, including vacations, movies, foreign travel, and shopping. Once again, this permits people to place a monetary value on feeling states they're unaccustomed to monetizing.

- ✔ Compare the price people place on inanimate objects to the price of the personal injury. For example, if a Picasso painting instead of the plain-tiff's child had been in the back seat of the car, you'd have no trouble placing a price of tens of millions of dollars on it. Why are you reluctant to place a similar value on the loss of a child's life?

Logrolling for Low-Cost, High-Value Concessions

Logrolling consists of exchanging items of unlike value with a bargaining partner. By engaging in logrolling, one party may be able to get something he values highly by giving up something that's relatively worthless to him but valued highly by the other party. The parties essentially buy what they want from the other party without giving up very much to get it. Logrolling is a great technique for moving the parties forward when they've reached an impasse, as I explain in Chapter 13. To help the parties identify and place a value on their *tangible* interests, ask each party the following questions:

- ✔ Do you have anything of value you might exchange with the other party that isn't yet on the table?
- ✔ Are you able to place a dollar value on that item?
- ✔ What is giving up (or keeping) that item worth to you?
- ✔ If your opponent were willing to give you that item, would you be willing to (for example) accept less money to resolve the dispute than you first suggested you would?

The parties may also have *intangible* interests, including receiving from the other party an apology or an explanation of the circumstances that led to the problem at the root of the dispute. These intangibles may do more to satisfy a party than the party's stated bottom line. The parties don't need to place a dollar value on intangibles, but they do need to identify them. You can help by asking the following questions:

- ✔ Is there anything the other party can do that would satisfy you, other than simply paying you the money you seek? What might that be? If the other party did that, would you be willing to reduce your monetary demand?
- ✔ You each have quite a different view of the potential for this shared business opportunity to produce income over the next few years. X expects it to bring in $100,000 per year, and Y expects it to bring in $50,000 per year. If X strongly believes the business will make $100,000 next year, is he willing to buy Y's interest, based on X's valuation?
- ✔ X has a great distribution network for her line of cosmetics, and Y has an inferior network but a better product. Would trading X's network for Y's trade secret lead to a potential resolution? Would you both do better by negotiating a partnership than either of you could do separately as competitors?

Suppose Dad has the opportunity to spend this coming summer in Alaska. He'd like to increase his summer visitation from two weeks to one month. He's willing to give up two Christmases in exchange. Are two Christmases with the kids valuable enough to Mom to justify her giving up two weeks during the summer? The actual number of days may not be equal. What's important is the relative value the parties place on those days.

Forming Contingent Agreements to Calm the Fears of an Uncertain Future

Parties often fear giving up something that may be significantly more valuable in the future. They don't want to lose out to their adversary. Situations like this often arise in commercial deals, especially in the sale of a business that the parties value differently. Trying to convince the buyer to pay a higher price, the seller is often more optimistic about prospective profits. The buyer, however, is almost always worried about overly optimistic projections, because if profits fall short, the buyer suffers the loss.

You can often bridge the gap between pessimism and optimism by asking the parties to consider a *contingency agreement* — a deal that ties the fortunes of both parties to future events. The seller can put his own skin in the game by agreeing to sell the business for the fixed sum the buyer is willing to pay but for less than the seller is willing to accept, on condition that the buyer pays the seller a percentage of future profits over a certain period of time. Suggesting that the parties enter into a conditional agreement has three positive effects:

- ✔ It satisfies the parties' concerns about price and the prospect of future value.

- ✔ It tests the seller's sunny projections, so if he knows his projections are overly optimistic, he's more receptive to dropping the asking price, or if he believes profits have a good chance of exceeding his projections, he has an incentive to accept less now to possibly earn more in the future.

- ✔ It tests the buyer's valuation, so if she knows her valuation is low and is expecting solid profits, she's more receptive to raising her offer, or if she believes that the profits are likely to fall short of the seller's rosy expectations, she's willing to give the buyer a percentage of future profits for a limited period of time in exchange for a lower price.

Appealing to Higher Values

Often, disputants are motivated by principles that are higher than material rewards or punishments could be. People value autonomy, freedom of choice, respect, generosity, accountability, and fairness as much or more than they value money or the goods and services that money can buy. They want what's best for their families and consistent with their systems of belief, and they often want to do the right thing.

Exploring these nonmaterial motivations expands the opportunities to help the parties resolve their disputes in ways that are not only in line with their interests but also with their values. In the following sections, I offer guidance on how to discover each party's core values and use shared values to help resolve disputes.

Discovering each party's core values

Discovering what core values may have brought the parties into dispute in the first instance is often the key to resolution. Once again, diagnostic questions are the order of the day, this time in an effort to ascertain what higher principles may be motivating a party to cling to his factual, legal, or moral position. Here are just a few such questions:

✔ What offended you about your opponent's behavior?

✔ If your opponent could learn something as a result of this dispute, what would you hope she learns?

✔ Why did you file this lawsuit (or fall into a dispute with your opponent)?

✔ Aside from money, what else, if anything, would you like to see happen, either by way of compensation or a change in your opponent's behavior?

Appealing to shared standards and principles

Disputants often have a great deal in common. Businesspeople, for example, are often in the same industry and share the drive to maintain profitable businesses. Disputants within a church or religious group may share a dedication to a higher power or a life of self-sacrifice. And divorced parents share the common concern of their children's well-being.

Find out what the parties have in common. After you discover their shared values or goals, help them develop potential solutions that align with what they both can agree on. You can do this through frequent reminders of what's really at stake here — keeping the focus, for example, on the kids or what would be best for each party's business or the community. You may also want to remind the parties of the goal of developing solutions consistent with those values.

This approach works. When helping businesspeople settle litigation, I refer early and often to their mutual interest in future commercial opportunities, their common understanding that deals can't be reached based on sunk costs, and the pragmatism they bring to bear on their other commercial dilemmas. I've also helped people from the same religious backgrounds apply mutually held spiritual values to resolve material disputes.

Chapter 8

Employing Conflict Dynamics to Resolve Any Dispute

. . . .

In This Chapter

▶ Understanding the causes of disputes

▶ Recognizing productive and counterproductive conflict resolution styles

▶ Escalating and de-escalating conflict to resolve disputes

▶ Overcoming stereotypes and cognitive biases that hinder conflict resolution

. . . .

Coming up with a solution that's satisfactory to everyone involved in a dispute typically requires more than a fair financial settlement. By exploring *conflict dynamics* — the underlying causes of conflict and the methods, both productive and counterproductive, that parties typically engage in to resolve a dispute — you can often help the parties address the underlying issues of their conflict more effectively to achieve a more satisfactory and durable outcome.

This chapter explores the nature of conflict, describes productive and counterproductive conflict resolution styles and strategies, provides guidance on how to escalate and de-escalate conflict to resolve disputes, and offers insight on how to deal with cognitive biases that deepen misunderstandings.

Examining the Nature of Conflict and How Disputes Arise from It

Understanding the nature of conflict and some of the reasons why conflicts often lead to disputes enables all participants to engage more productively in conflict resolution and better understand what the dispute is really about, which may be very different from what it appears to be about. The following sections shed light on the nature of conflict and explain how to identify and use the causes of disputes to help solve problems.

Grasping the nature of conflict

Conflict is neither good nor bad. It simply is. How people respond to it is what matters most. Conflict occurs at the intersection of unresolved problems and undeveloped skills. At this junction, adversaries have a golden opportunity to grow and develop a better understanding of each other. With each problem they solve, they mature and transcend the conflict with new skills that help them resolve and avoid future conflicts.

Conflict over scarce resources and intangibles such as self-determination, respect, and self-expression has caused incalculable loss and suffering. But it has also opened the way for people to stand up for human rights, self-governance, peaceful dispute resolution, independence, and tolerance of differences.

If people avoid and suppress conflict, they deprive themselves of opportunities to grow. If they learn how to effectively resolve their disputes, they become not only more sociable but also more content and productive. If they use conflict to transform their experience of the world and their value in it, conflict can open new vistas and enrich their lives. When people transcend conflict, they can move on to new experiences and new challenges that enliven and embolden themselves and their fellow human beings.

Identifying and addressing the underlying causes of conflict and dispute

Conflict exists whenever one person believes that his needs or desires can't be satisfied at the same time as other people's can. For example, say you go to your local grocery store to buy a watermelon but the store is sold out. You can't satisfy your desire for a watermelon, but no conflict exists until you see someone else with a watermelon in his shopping cart. Now you've been deprived of something that someone else has. That's a conflict.

As frustrated as you may be, you're not angry with the guy who bought the last juicy melon. That's just how life is. You may be in competition with others for scarce resources, but nothing wrong or unfair has happened to you. You have no one to name as the source of your deprivation, no one to blame for your empty cart, and no one from whom to claim the right to a watermelon right now. In the absence of name, blame, and claim, conflict may exist, but dispute doesn't.

Now, if the store had promised that any customer who shopped there on such and such a day would receive a watermelon, and you shopped there on that day, then the store owes you a watermelon. You have a valid claim against the store and can blame the store for not having a watermelon to give you. If you want to press the issue and the store can't or won't provide you with a watermelon, you're not only in conflict with the store, but that conflict has ripened into an active dispute.

In addition to scarce resources, disputes also arise out of differences in power, status, values, and other intangibles. By understanding the psychology that transforms a conflict into a dispute, you can often identify what triggered the dispute, explore that trigger with the parties, and use their resulting insight to help them resolve it, as I explain in the following sections.

Differences in perception

Disputes typically arise because two people perceive a situation differently. Generally, the problem isn't because resources are scarce but because people have different ideas about how to distribute those resources. For example, the 9/11 Commission's attempt to provide compensation to families who lost breadwinners raised classic disputes over the metric that should be used to distribute government funds. People who had the foresight to purchase life insurance argued that they shouldn't be penalized by having their compensation reduced by the sum of money they were already receiving for their loved one's death. Families whose breadwinners made less money than others (janitors versus investment bankers, for example) argued that compensation shouldn't be based on the wages earned by the deceased because that placed a higher value on the lives of the wealthy than on the lives of the working poor.

By exploring such differences in perception with the parties, you can help them gain insight into their own definitions of fairness and stimulate brainstorming to satisfy all parties' fairness needs. The party with the greater resources, for instance, is often willing to share more of her benefits with people who have suffered similar *personal* losses but different financial losses. When high earners in law firms realize that lower-earning attorneys are considering a move to another law firm over compensation issues, the high earners are often willing to sacrifice a portion of their income to preserve the well-being of the entire firm.

Differences in beliefs or values

Differences in beliefs or values often cause differences of opinion on how to solve a problem, as in the case of most political disputes. In the debate over the federal income tax, for example, some people believe that having the wealthy pay a greater percentage of their earnings in taxes because they can afford to pay more is a fair and just policy. Others believe that everyone should pay the same percentage and that graduated taxes punish the most productive members of society and discourage investment that leads to economic growth. To help parties who are engaged in a dispute that's based on beliefs and values, try the following techniques:

✔ Explore the bases of each party's beliefs and values. For example, mediators who volunteered to referee a dispute between drummers within the Occupy Wall Street encampment and the majority of Occupy Wall Street inhabitants were faced with a dispute not simply about noise while both protestors and neighbors were trying to sleep, but also about values relating to free expression and the decision-making process. The drummers considered it their universal human right to express themselves through their drumming when and in the manner they chose, regardless of whether their activities caused other people harm. The majority of protestors wanted the drummers to restrict their activities to certain hours of the day.

When the mediators cut to the heart of the conflict, they found that the drummers did acknowledge the right of others to be free from the sound of incessant drumming but disagreed about how the protestors had given themselves the authority to impose time, place, and manner restrictions on drumming. The mediators helped the parties understand one another's values, encouraged all parties to move from helplessness to empowerment and from self-concern to acceptance of community needs. As a result, the drummers agreed to voluntarily limit the time and duration of their drumming.

✔ Use stories, analogies, or hypothetical situations to gently challenge the underlying belief or value to determine whether the party may agree to exceptions in certain situations. The probing done in the Occupy Wall Street mediation found that the dispute was not about the drummers' right to drum, but the manner in which the encampment made decisions for the group. When both sides of the dispute demonstrated their willingness to listen to the other, to empathize, and to consider a point of view other than their own, the drummers were freed up to express their true concern, over the governing process, and to reach an agreement that satisfied all parties' needs rather than tussling over a conflict Occupy Wall Street may never resolve — when your demands include the dismantling of authority, who has the right to represent the interests of one group against another?

✔ Lead the parties through a process of identifying their goals. What is each party trying to achieve? The goal of finding an ideal system of governance, for instance, turned out to be irrelevant to the resolution of the drumming dispute at Occupy Wall Street.

✔ Encourage the parties to explore other solutions that may enable them to achieve their goals. People often feel as though they have only two choices and must choose between them, even when numerous options are available. In the Occupy Wall Street mediation, saving face played a large role in resolving the dispute. In fact, it was only when the mediators told the drummers that they gave up trying to find a solution that the drummers approached their negotiation partners with the same solution that had previously been suggested. It was clear that they simply wanted to feel that they had the freedom to do what they wanted.

Once that freedom seemed guaranteed, they had no problem compromising for the mutual benefit of the community.

Resistance to change

Some people are more change-averse than others, and disputes often arise out of differences between people's desire to live with a bad situation or risk that situation getting worse. Many personal disputes among intimate family members revolve around different attitudes toward change, including such things as marriage, a move to a new city, children growing up, or parents growing older. For instance, adult children may encourage their elderly mother to move to an assisted living home, but the mother may resist that change because she'd rather stay in the home she knows well.

Following are some suggestions to help alleviate the fear of change:

- ✔ **Create an atmosphere of hope and safety.** Project an air of confidence, model the respectful behavior you expect from the participants, and use an agenda to structure the mediation so that all participants know what to expect. You may even want to help the parties establish mutually agreed upon ground rules so they feel safe in openly discussing their dispute. See Chapter 4 for additional guidance on setting ground rules and establishing an atmosphere in which the parties feel safe and hopeful.

- ✔ **Question the basis for the fear.** Ask what, precisely, the party believes would result as a consequence of the change. Ask why the party feels that specific consequence is something to fear. Sometimes, exploring the fear is enough to make the party realize that what he fears isn't so scary after all.

  Don't dismiss or argue against what someone feels. Demonstrate empathy and express your understanding by repeating, in your own words, the person's concern and that you understand why he feels that way. Feelings can never be wrong, even when they may cause problems if allowed to prevent the parties from engaging in productive, collaborative problem-solving.

- ✔ **Explore ways that the person can implement the change without causing the scary consequence.** Engage in problem-solving to help the party develop possible solutions. People often have an all-or-nothing attitude; they reject an option based on a single issue. By helping the party resolve that issue, you transform an unworkable option into an acceptable one. (See Chapter 12 for more about problem-solving.)

Failure to recognize common ground

When people come to you with a dispute, they're focusing on what divides them, and they've usually spent a fair amount of time creating arguments to convince each other that their proposed solution to the problem is right, good, and just. In the process of sharpening their differences and justifying their point of view, the parties invariably fail to recognize and build on common ground. Help the parties recognize how much they have in common:

✔ Neither one has found a way to resolve the dispute.

✔ They both decided to bring their dispute to the bargaining table in the hope that a third party could help them brainstorm a mutually satisfactory solution.

✔ If they're business people, they're probably pragmatists who believe that creating a productive future is better than arguing about an unproductive past.

✔ If they're parents, they have children in common.

✔ If they're neighbors, they share their concern for the neighborhood's well-being and the safety and security of their homes.

You can often find common ground in common goals. Each party wants to resolve the conflict. Business people want to reduce costs and boost future profits. Parents want the best for their children. Employers and employees both have a stake in maintaining a profitable business and productive workplace.

Exploring Conflict Management Strategies and Tactics

Most people learn how to respond to conflict and resolve disputes as children from behaviors modeled by their parents, teachers, siblings, and others. Many people never consider that better, more effective ways of dealing with conflict are available. As you help people resolve their disputes, you begin to notice their conflict resolution styles. When those styles fail them, you can help them develop new, more effective strategies and skills for dealing with conflict and resolving disputes.

The following sections introduce the five primary conflict management strategies — effective and ineffective — along with some competitive tactics that negotiators often use to defeat their adversaries.

Recognizing conflict management strategies

When responding to conflict, people generally use one or more of the five primary conflict management strategies: suppression, avoidance, anger and blame, transformation, and transcendence.

Don't think of conflict management strategies in terms of which style is best. Each style's effectiveness depends on the situation. For example, avoiding conflict may be best in a hostage situation. Suppression may be called for when a family member is ill and shouldn't be drawn into a dispute with other family members.

Suppression

Suppression consists of denying that the issue exists and actively trying to keep others from talking about it. Though suppression may be helpful in keeping everyone calm in a critical situation, it's rarely useful for resolving the underlying issues. You'll recognize suppression at work whenever you hear a party instruct someone in the room not to talk about something or express a feeling, such as anger, sadness, irritation, or frustration. People who suppress conflict never get to the heart of the matter. They're never clear about why they're having a dispute in the first place or how they can possibly solve the problem because they're too busy pretending it doesn't exist.

Here are some questions you can ask conflict suppressors to help them move from suppression to resolution:

- ✓ I heard you say that you don't want to talk about how Johnny was hurt on the playground. Why is that?

- ✓ I understand that reliving these events must be painful. How can I help you talk about them with the least amount of discomfort?

- ✓ I heard you tell your client that his concerns are "irrelevant" to the resolution of the dispute. That may be true in court, but I'm wondering whether discussing this irrelevant detail may help us all better understand the dispute and help us resolve it.

Avoidance

Like conflict suppressors, conflict avoiders are often afraid that airing the dispute will cause them or their opponent to lose control, shout, hurl insults, or cause shame and humiliation. They don't actively try to shut down discussion about the issue, but they refuse to talk about it. Conflict avoidance is often useful when one party is apt to react in an extreme way if confronted. In negotiation, however, you eventually need to get past conflict avoidance to resolve underlying issues.

Conflict avoidance isn't as hard to break through as the active suppression of conflict, but it still requires gentle probing to help the conflict-averse individual discuss the dispute in enough detail to solve the problem. Questions to ask the conflict avoider are similar to those you pose to the conflict suppressor:

- ✓ Have you talked to anyone about this dispute before? If so, what permitted you to do so in relative comfort?

- ✓ Have you talked to your opponent here today about this dispute?

✔ What do you worry will happen if both you and your opponent are given the opportunity to discuss the dispute with each other?

✔ What can I do to help you feel safe discussing these matters during the mediation?

Anger and blame

When parties are able to freely talk about their problems, they often begin with blame, recounting only those facts that paint them in a positive light and paint their opponent in a negative manner. Instead of explaining how they feel about the conflict, many people act out their feelings by shouting or crying. This is the primary reason most people avoid and suppress conflict. It raises emotions that people don't want to feel and don't want directed at themselves.

To help people move from emotional outbursts to a problem-solving state of mind, ask the following questions:

✔ I hear that you're angry about what happened. Can you explain to your opponent what makes you angry enough to shout?

✔ I see how sad discussing this topic makes you. I'm sorry it's so difficult. Are you able to explain your unhappiness to your opponent with your words as well as your tears?

✔ Now that you've told your opponent everything that's made you angry and sad, would you like to say anything about your contribution to the dispute?

✔ Now that you've both had the opportunity to express your feelings to each other about this matter, would you be willing to work together to find a resolution that's satisfactory to both of you?

Transformation

Confronting conflict head-on sometimes helps people gain new insights into their own behavior and that of others. By engaging in the process of give and take, many people become willing, sometimes for the first time ever, to be fully accountable for the part they've played in causing their own harm or injuring someone else. Instead of feeling powerless and humiliated, taking responsibility for one's part in causing a dispute often puts people in greater control of their own lives and permits them to forgive themselves, as well as others, for their common human foibles.

When you mediate, look for opportunities to help people transform their relationships with themselves and others through conflict. Discovering how to peacefully resolve conflict with people they once believed were their enemies lightens their spirit and helps them create better personal relationships, not only with their conflict partner but also with others.

The following questions are helpful to lead a married couple to a transformative moment in their responses to conflict and their relationships with others:

- ✔ You've said several times that this is the type of problem that you and your spouse have never been able to solve. What makes it different from the problems you *are* able to solve?

- ✔ What type of problem-solving tactics did you use to solve that problem?

- ✔ Do you think you could use that tactic here?

- ✔ When you say that you and your spouse are incapable of solving problems like these, are you making any assumptions about what your spouse's response to your problem-solving efforts might be?

- ✔ (to the other spouse): Do you agree that you'd likely respond in the way your spouse describes if he tried that problem-solving technique on this problem?

If Uncle Sam and Saddam had hired a mediator

Consider the bombing of Baghdad. Assuming the only reason the United States went to war with Iraq was Iraq's refusal to turn over its weapons of mass destruction, the parties had one quite obvious solution to the impasse: Find out the real reason Saddam Hussein was willing to risk an American attack rather than turn over his WMDs or admit that he had none.

After attacking Baghdad, the U.S. learned that Iraq didn't possess any WMDs. People scratched their heads, wondering why Hussein would all but invite an American military intervention rather than acknowledge his lack of WMDs. The answer came quickly and, in hindsight, was obvious. For Hussein, having the enemies on his borders believe that Iraq possessed WMDs weighed more heavily than the chance that Americans would follow through on their threat to launch a preemptive war against Iraq, particularly because the Americans had never before mounted a preemptive strike.

In international affairs, mediation is called *diplomacy.* One of America's great diplomats, Colin Powell, has said that the most important information an international diplomat can know is "the other guy's decision cycle." In this case, Hussein's decision cycle required him to undertake a risk analysis. Was it more likely that he'd be attacked by his local enemies if they knew he didn't possess WMDs or that the Americans would attack him if he refused to acknowledge that he didn't possess WMDs?

Had a neutral third party been capable of establishing a relationship of trust and confidence with Hussein, the neutral party may have helped both the U.S. and Iraq solve the WMD problem instead of using violence to resolve it. The U.S. may have been willing, for instance, to pledge to use its own military resources if a neighboring country launched a war against Iraq. At the same time, the U.S. may have conditioned that promise on the commencement of peace negotiations between Iraq and the neighboring countries it feared might attack it. The two countries had an infinite number of options for resolving the real problem between them other than engaging their militaries in conflict.

This is a small sample of the dozens of questions you could ask to diagnose the cause of chronic impasse. The goal is to identify why these same issues keep coming up, why they're never resolved, and what resources the parties already possess that may successfully transform their relationship to the problem at hand.

Transcendence

Adversaries transcend conflict when they've learned all they have to learn from any given dispute. Family relations offer the best examples of conflict transcendence, although transcendence can occur in any setting, including during the resolution of a commercial transaction gone bad. I have a recurring conflict with my husband about losing my keys. He tells me to put them in the same place every day, and I tell him to stop trying to control me. From my point of view, my autonomy is at stake. From his point of view, he's simply trying to help me live my busy life more efficiently.

As soon as I give up my resistance to being controlled by another human being by realizing that no one can make me do anything I don't want to do, I can transcend the "where are my keys" argument with my husband, and we can move on to more productive disputes, like how to resolve the very different ways in which we deal with money. The keys argument may also be a proxy for a deeper issue in my relationship with my husband. In fact, our conflict may really be over the different ways we deal with money. Just as I feel as if I'm being controlled when my husband tells me to put my keys back on the hook, I may be feeling restricted by our differing attitudes toward the spending and saving of money.

Identifying contentious conflict resolution tactics

People commonly use ineffective and even counterproductive tactics in their attempts to resolve conflict. You need to be able to identify these tactics so you can intervene before they cause too much damage. Following are the most common contentious conflict resolution tactics:

- ✔ **Ingratiation:** Getting what you want through charm or flattery. "Honey, you've been working so hard. Instead of cooking, why don't we just go out for dinner?"

- ✔ **Gamesmanship:** Getting what you want by manipulating your bargaining partner. "If I have to give you ten-days notice, I'll give it to you at 5 p.m. on the Wednesday before Thanksgiving."

- ✔ **Promises:** Getting what you want now by promising you'll do something later. "I'll deliver the goods to you on an expedited basis but only if you pay me my normal charge upfront and a bonus of $250 at the time of delivery."

✔ **Threats:** Getting what you want now by threatening harm if your adversary doesn't comply. "If you don't comply with my demands, I'll sue you and your company in federal court, seek every document remotely relevant to the dispute, take deposition testimony from all your executives, and tie up your business operation in knots for years."

✔ **Shaming:** Expressions of dismay, shock, or disapproval of another's behavior, usually on moral grounds. "If you don't apologize to your sister today, I'll be disappointed in you. You won't be behaving like the considerate son I raised."

✔ **Physical force:** War, terrorism, hitting, pushing, shoving, or taking.

When you notice a party employing these tactics, gently but firmly suggest that the parties return to a more collaborative approach to resolving their differences. You may say something like, "Let's get back to where we were in trying to solve the problem." Check out the nearby sidebar for an example of world powers engaging in some contentious conflict-resolution tactics.

Harnessing the power of persuasion

Ideally, you want the parties to work out their differences on their own, but persuasion is a powerful tool that comes in handy if one party needs a gentle nudge in the right direction. To make effective use of persuasion, familiarize yourself with the primary principles of persuasion, as articulated by author Robert Cialdini:

✔ **Reciprocity:** People feel obliged to return favors. You may be able to convince an inflexible party to give a little by having the other party make the first move.

✔ **Commitment and consistency:** Most people feel a need to honor their commitments and express consistent beliefs. They don't want to be flip-floppers. In certain situations, reminding a party of what she said on an earlier occasion may be sufficient to put her back on track toward resolving an issue.

✔ **Social proof:** People tend to want to fit in and follow the crowd. Consider people who watch the news or popular TV shows. They don't do so solely for information or entertainment; many people want to know what's happening in the world around them and on TV so they can talk about those subjects with friends and co-workers. Getting one party to buy into a solution may be stimulus enough to get the other party to follow.

✔ **Authority:** People tend to obey authority figures. In my opening statement, I often point to my lapel pin and say that I'm a settlement officer with the federal court. I immediately feel the increased respect from the parties, which I can use later when they need a nudge to help them make a pragmatic decision.

✔ **Liking:** Liking follows liking. When clients in a mediation feel valued, respected, heard, and validated, they sense that you like them, and they'll like you back for that. There's no secret to likeability other than genuinely caring about and treating with respect the people who come to you for assistance.

✔ **Scarcity:** Perceived scarcity generates demand. In mediation, the scarcity created is usually time. You have only two months before trial and only one day to conclude a settlement that's probably better than any result the parties can get at trial. Let the parties know that the clock is ticking.

Discouraging Competitive Tactics

Competitive tactics, including stonewalling, posturing, and delivering ultimatums, are all excellent ways to ensure that the parties reach and fail to overcome an impasse:

✔ **Stonewalling** is any refusal to cooperate by making concessions, answering questions, or providing information. The party essentially "goes dark," rendering the other party powerless.

✔ **Posturing** is any behavior intended to convince the other party that you'll do something you may well *not* do, such as notice 20 depositions of the party's top-level management if the case doesn't. A party may also posture by demanding more than he really wants, offering less than he's willing to pay, or pretending he has the upper hand if the dispute goes to trial.

✔ **Delivering ultimatums** consists of giving the other party an either/or choice, usually in the form of a take-it-or-leave-it deal.

Use every tool in your toolbox to prevent these strategies from derailing a negotiation — tools you acquire primarily in Chapters 7 to 13.

Strategically Escalating and De-Escalating Conflict

Conflict is uncomfortable, but suppressing or avoiding it doesn't resolve it, so you may have to escalate the conflict to move the parties forward in negotiation. Of course, an overly heated dispute isn't conducive to resolving conflict either, so you need to know when and how to de-escalate conflict. The following sections explain how to engage the parties in conflict and stabilize the tone.

Using conflict escalation as a tool for resolving disputes

In your role as mediator, you sometimes need to help a party escalate the conflict to get the other party's attention or to impress on one or both parties the serious consequences of their failure to resolve their mutual problem. Of course, if one party obstinately refuses to engage in problem-solving discussions or insists on a solution that's satisfactory to him but not to his bargaining partner, the parties may intentionally or unintentionally escalate the conflict themselves.

The most effective way to escalate conflict is to highlight the potential for adverse consequences that may result if negotiations break down. Consequences may include the following:

✔ Termination of the mediation, along with diminished hope of reaching a peaceful resolution

✔ A return to litigation, leading to more time, money, and aggravation being invested in the dispute

✔ One party taking adverse action against the other, such as dissolving a partnership or terminating a relationship

While you escalate the conflict, encourage the parties to engage in positive ways and to communicate effectively. Following are a few ground rules you may want to review with the parties:

✔ Talk about the situation and the problem without avoiding or suppressing either the dispute or the emotions that accompany it.

✔ Listen carefully to each other.

✔ Reflect on what you've heard your negotiating partner say, try to empathize, and then state the problem from her point of view.

✔ Work cooperatively to find mutually beneficial solutions.

✔ If you don't come up with a solution, table it for another day, agree to seek advice, or research possible solutions that you haven't considered.

As conflict escalates, monitor the situation closely for any signs that one or both parties are becoming overly agitated. If someone appears to be losing it, you may need to de-escalate the conflict, as I explain in the next section. People who lack rudimentary communication skills may throw an adult tantrum by screaming and crying, or they may engage in physical force, shoving or pushing the other party, pounding on walls, slamming doors, or storming out of the room. Part of your job as a mediator is to ensure the parties' safety, so you need to assess the situation when it appears as if it may spin out of control and separate the parties if necessary to prevent harm.

You can often bring a noncooperative person back to the negotiation table by reminding her of the consequences of ending the mediation.

De-escalating conflict to resolve disputes

In heated disputes, you may need to crank down the thermostat. Here are some techniques to help the parties de-escalate the conflict:

- ✔ Speak softer and more slowly while maintaining eye contact.

- ✔ Suggest that the parties take a break, walk around the block, or have something to eat or drink.

- ✔ Remind the parties of the commitments they made at the mediation's commencement to listen to each other without interruption and treat each other with respect.

- ✔ Remind the parties what they agreed to accomplish and why they said it's important to them to do so.

- ✔ Refocus the discussion on party interests.

- ✔ Remind the parties of any agreements they've reached, congratulate them on their progress, and assure them of your faith in their ability to resolve the matters under discussion without emotional outbursts that may prematurely terminate the negotiation.

- ✔ Ask the parties to describe what precisely was said or done that triggered the escalating behavior and help them explore how things spun out of control and why.

- ✔ Remind the parties to speak only about their own knowledge and not to speculate about the motives of their conflict partner.

- ✔ Help the parties clarify their communications; for example, you may say something like, "I believe I heard you say X and then John said Y. I could have misheard both of you. Could you explain that to me again?"

- ✔ When speaking, use words that de-escalate conflict, including "maybe," "what if," "I feel," "it seems like," "I think," "sometimes," "perhaps," and "I wonder."

- ✔ Affirm and acknowledge each party's position and needs using phrases like "I can appreciate your situation," "It sounds hard for you too," and "Thank you for your. . . ." With practice, everyone can understand and/or appreciate another person's point of view or needs.

Dealing with Stereotypes

As much as most people like to believe they're fully in control of their attitudes and preconceptions, nobody really is. Whenever you make assumptions about other people (everyone does this), you usually apply social and cultural stereotypes to explain their behavior. These stereotypes or biases are *implicit* (subconscious), not *explicit* (directly expressed), so people often treat others according to a stereotype without even realizing it.

As a mediator, you have to deal with your market's implicit biases about you, the parties' implicit biases about each other, and your own implicit biases about the people who come to you for help. The following sections explain how to become more aware of your own biases, overcome your own prejudgments, and help others overcome theirs.

Taking Harvard's Project Implicit test

The geniuses at Harvard University have devised a collection of online tests to assess implicit biases in more than 90 different topic areas, including race, gender, political issues, pets, and music styles. I encourage you to take a few of the tests to get more in tune with your own biases. Each test session lasts 10 to 15 minutes. To register and engage in a session, go to https:// implicit.harvard.edu/implicit/research.

Challenging your own bias

Bias exists in the area between what you know and don't know about someone. People often form opinions about others without the information they need to form an accurate and sensible opinion. To overcome any bias you may have, ask questions to get to know the person better. Don't assume anything, and don't let first impressions, good or bad, govern your opinions. The deeper your understanding of someone, the less room exists for bias to creep in.

All people have preexisting attitudes about people whose backgrounds differ from theirs. That's nothing to be ashamed of. But don't let your prejudgments hinder your efforts to get to know someone as an individual.

Dealing with bias

During a mediation, everyone's biased for or against one another. That's just human nature. Your job is to discover whether any of those biases (including your own) are interfering with the process and take steps to eliminate bias. Following are some suggestions:

- **Engage in small talk.** Whether you commence your mediations in separate caucus or joint session, at some point in the mediation, introduce the parties to each other and let them engage in small talk, as I discuss in Chapter 11.

- **Ask how a person would prefer to be described.** If one person refers to another as belonging to a certain racial or ethnic group, ask how the person would like to be described. Some prefer Hispanic, for instance, while others identify with Latino/a or their national origin (Cuban, Mexican, Colombian, and so on).

- **Don't collude with one group in stereotyping the other group.** For example, avoid saying something like, "She's a woman so she's being overly emotional about this." Be especially careful of doing this in separate caucus.

- **Avoid humor related to a particular group.** Humor is always risky, but using humor based on racial, national, religious, or other stereotypes is always dangerous, even if no member of the group you're referring to is present. You have no way of knowing, for example, whether a litigant from France is married to a man from Mali or to a person of the same sex.

- **Avoid "positive" stereotypes.** "Positive" stereotypes, such as Jews are good with money and black men are good at sports, can be just as offensive as negative stereotypes.

- **Remain sensitive to nonverbal signs of bias.** Facial expressions, body language, and tone of voice can subtly express bias.

- **Familiarize yourself with cultural differences in your community.** In an urban, cosmopolitan area such as mine, I work with ultra-Orthodox Jews (whose men won't shake a woman's hand, a religious restriction that I mention and normalize on our first meeting), Persians (most of whom don't like to be referred to as Iranians), people whom I perceive to be African-American (many of whom don't consider themselves black but rather Dominican, Afro-Cuban, or Asian); and Asians (Japanese, South Korean, Chinese) who don't appreciate being all lumped together as Asians. Don't be ashamed to ask about a person's nationality.

- **Acknowledge and gently challenge suspected bias.** If you believe that biases are preventing the parties from resolving their dispute, don't hesitate to raise the issue by saying something like, "Do you believe race/gender/religion has anything to do with this?" If someone uses a derogatory term to refer to someone, consider asking that person why he used that particular term, and then gently challenge whether the term is really an accurate label for that person.

How not to deal with bias

Dealing with bias is never easy, but some ways are worse than others. I once mediated a police-citizen dispute that arose out of a gun battle between police and a local gang. The grandmother of a gang member was injured in the crossfire. In a separate caucus with the police officer and his attorney, the attorney called the grandmother a "skank."

I reacted angrily, accusing the attorney of racial bias and seriously damaging my neutrality and trustworthiness in the process. I should have asked the attorney why he used that term until I understood the basis for the insult.

You may also want to combat bias by using micro-affirmations to strengthen bonds among disputants and mitigate any of your own biases. *Micro-affirmations* are barely perceptible gestures of inclusion and caring, such as actively listening, acknowledging a concession's value, stepping in when you notice that a party feels threatened, or even asking a party what he thinks. Micro-affirmations often help overcome bias by shifting focus from the individual to what that person says or does.

Although you may consciously give micro-affirmations, they should appear to be subtle, unconscious gestures. Make sure they're specific, consistent, clear, fair, and timed appropriately.

Understanding, Avoiding, and Leveraging Cognitive Biases

Cognitive biases are universal human tendencies to process information in ways that often lead to erroneous judgments of others. These judgments usually arise from false assumptions about a person's motivations in the absence of knowledge about the person's true intentions. Someone who has a cognitive bias is usually either afraid to ask the person about her true motivations or doesn't trust the person's answer. Cognitive biases are one of the primary instigators of active disputes and often cause negotiations to reach an impasse and break down.

The following sections discuss the most common cognitive biases you can expect to encounter in mediation, including fundamental attribution error, confirmation bias, demonization, anchoring, and clustering error.

Fundamental attribution error

Fundamental attribution error is a natural human tendency to perceive other people's injurious actions as malicious while excusing one's own behavior because of uncontrollable circumstances. This tendency is called *fundamental* because everyone commits these errors, and it's an *error* because it often leads to misunderstanding.

Attribution is fairly easy to recognize. What's difficult at times is determining whether the attribution is an error. Regardless of whether you believe that the attribution is valid, help the parties understand each other's motives by encouraging them to talk about what led to the incident. More often than not, the injuries sustained and losses incurred are the results of accident, miscommunication, and circumstance. As soon as the parties realize that the other party intended no harm, they're in a far better state of mind to problem solve their dispute than to seek a pound of flesh from their opponent.

Of course, in some cases, one party really did intend to harm the other, in which case the discussion should lead to some sort of disclosure and an excuse or apology for behaving in such a way. Sometimes, one party may attribute his own malicious behavior to what he perceived, accurately or not, as malicious behavior on behalf of the other party, so be prepared to peel the layers of the onion until you reach the incident that triggered the series of injurious behaviors.

Confirmation bias and the silent treatment

Confirmation bias is the universal human tendency to seek out and accept as true information anything that confirms existing beliefs and to filter out or distrust information that challenges those beliefs. After all, no one likes to be wrong, and *cognitive dissonance* — the state of uncertainty about one's view of the world and place in it — is painful for everyone.

Add the silent treatment to confirmation bias and fundamental attribution error and you have a state of mind on both sides of a dispute where the parties have diametrically opposed views of what happened, how it happened, who made it happen, and why what happened isn't their fault but the other guy's. Even worse is that the parties mired in this morass have no way to test their negative assumptions because confirmation bias blocks the information necessary to challenge those assumptions, and the silent treatment shuts down communications. These two cognitive biases together make mediators tell the parties every day of the week that they haven't simply failed to get on the same page but that they're not even in the same solar system.

To overcome these overwhelming forces, you often must act as the conduit through which the parties communicate. Here's what you do:

1. **Listen actively as a party speaks, carefully attending to his recitation of events and opinions.**

2. **Repeat your understanding of what the speaker said back to the speaker to confirm that you heard it correctly.**

3. **Ask the speaker if your understanding is correct.**

   If you misunderstood the speaker, go back to Step 1 until you fully understand what the speaker has said.

4. **Ask the other party to repeat what he heard from both his conflict partner and you.**

This may be a time-consuming process, but it's well worth the investment in clarifying communication and combating confirmation bias and the silent treatment.

Demonization

When characterizing someone as an opponent, people often begin the process of *demonization:* rejecting as untrue, unworkable, or downright evil everything the adversary says, even when what the adversary says should be good news for the person hearing it. Demonization is an effect of fundamental attribution error, confirmation bias, and the silent treatment. To help the parties stop demonizing each other, try the following strategies:

- ✔ **Normalize the demonized party's behavior.** Normalizing someone's behavior consists of making unthinkable, inconceivable behavior sound reasonable. You can often normalize someone's behavior by asking questions to elicit information that explains that behavior and asking the other party what she'd do if she were in the same situation.

- ✔ **Model empathic rather than hostile responses.** Instead of challenging what someone says, start by saying something like, "I understand why you may have thought that," or, "If I were in that same situation, I might do the same thing."

- ✔ **Remain neutral.** Treat everyone's statements as valid until they can be empirically contradicted.

Anchoring and framing

Anchoring and framing are also cognitive biases that take advantage of how easily people are influenced by the way in which information is presented. As I explain in Chapter 7, *frames* focus our attention on only those facts or qualities inside the frame, and *anchors* influence negotiating behavior by calling attention to an item's or idea's benefits or detriments and then assigning a number that confirms those detriments or benefits.

Guard against anchoring and framing when helping the parties brainstorm solutions outside the "frame" and beyond the "anchor." Anchoring and framing can lead to an impasse and limit the number of options available to the parties to break through the impasse. Typically, the best approach is to expand the pie, not limit its size.

Clustering error

Clustering error is a natural human tendency to assume that one thing caused another simply because the things are in close proximity in time or space. Clustering errors result in endless disputes as people make the effort to relate unrelated events for the purpose of intuiting cause. In this regard, everyone's a born conspiracy theorist.

Rarely do people engage in clustering unrelated events for the purpose of painting a favorable picture of another's intentions. They cluster to avoid danger, not to amuse themselves on a sunny summer afternoon. Clustering error interferes with disputants' ability to profitably brainstorm solutions because it exacerbates suspicion, fear, and anger — emotions that actively interfere with the brain's ability to process complex information.

The prehistory of clustering error

Prehistoric people's ability to survive in the wild despite the predatory nature of creatures stronger and faster than them depended on their ability to make sense of their environment, plan how to avoid its dangers, express those dangers to their families, and communicate that plan to their tribes. If they saw tigers drinking in a shallow pond near two banyan trees in the early evening, they needed to take note so they could recognize and avoid similar dangerous situations in the future. So they'd remember the configuration of danger: two trees + pond + setting sun = tigers. The pond may well have been the reason the tigers congregated by the banyan trees that day. Then again, the tigers may have stumbled upon the pond on their way to new hunting grounds and may never return. In that case, the pond didn't cause the presence of tigers nearby any more than did the two trees or the setting sun. Nevertheless, the people would have given meaning to the combination, believed it to be causal, and forever after avoided ponds beside trees in the late afternoon.

Of course, prehistoric people may have been smarter than that, but you get the idea — clustering error is hardwired into the human psyche as a survival tool, but it's not always the most useful tool, especially when dealing with the complexity of human interactions.

To move the parties past clustering error, ask diagnostic and reality-testing questions that help the parties recognize the low probability of the suspected malicious intent. For instance, the likelihood that the presidents of five companies met secretly for the sole purpose of crafting a plan to drive a smaller company out of business is slight. Ask questions to reveal holes in the conspiracy theory, such as: What did these five presidents hope to gain? What kind of trouble would the presidents have gotten into with the SEC had they been caught? With so many people involved, how could they have kept it a secret? How much time and effort would be required to coordinate and execute such a plan? In probing, the conspiracy theory typically unravels under scrutiny and problem solving can begin. In some cases, however, the "paranoid" party has sufficient facts to prove his suspicions.

In a recent mediation concerning the transportation of goods from one city to another, the president of the defendant moving company expressed his belief that the plaintiff and his attorney weren't simply seeking damages for lost goods but were engaged in a conspiracy to drive him out of business. The facts were not in dispute. The plaintiff's attorney also represented the interests of a well-known brand-name moving company. The goods that the plaintiff claimed had been damaged were unusually pricey — a couple of museum quality sculptures. The defendant was a small, struggling moving company on the verge of bankruptcy.

Its president put together *unusually high cost goods + attorney for major moving company + unrelated marketplace losses in a tough economy* and concluded that all three parties — the plaintiff, the plaintiff's attorney, and the major moving company — were conspiring to drive him out of business. This is the common type of clustering error that mediators routinely encounter and that often creates an impasse. In this case, I helped the defendant understand that even were he able to prove his theory (difficult at best), he didn't have a lawyer and hadn't made a legal claim based on the alleged conspiracy. Doing so would be expensive and difficult to prove. On the other hand, the legal claim that *was* being made was far easier to defend based on his contention that he had simply withheld the sculptures for nonpayment and was willing to return them in exchange for full payment of his modest moving fee.

Part III
Improving Your Success Rate

The 5th Wave   By Rich Tennant

"In your complaint, you said you felt you were being manipulated by Mr. Prabhakar. Can you be more specific?"

In this part . . .

Understanding techniques and skills is only half of what it takes to become a master mediator. The other half is the ability to apply those skills to resolve disputes. You must be able to establish and maintain control; help the parties distinguish the differences among rights, remedies, issues, and interests; use your people skills to build an atmosphere of trust and collaboration; and identify opportunities in the most bewildering of problems. The chapters in this part present approaches to achieve these goals.

Ultimately, mediation leads to *impasse* — the chasm that neither party believes can be crossed. To be successful, you need to be able to encourage and facilitate the collaborative process of bridging the gap and achieving a durable resolution. Chapters 13 and 14 in this part present techniques to help the parties break through impasse and achieve closure.

Chapter 9

Establishing and Maintaining Control

In This Chapter

▶ Establishing an atmosphere that's conducive to mediation

▶ Working with angry, uncooperative, or deceptive parties

▶ Exposing hidden interests to help resolve a dispute

▶ Guiding the parties to impasse so the bargaining can begin

*P*arties need to engage in disputes to resolve underlying conflicts, but stonewalling, angry outbursts, bullying, and other such behaviors are counterproductive. The goal is to have a controlled blast, one that enables each party to express his emotions and grievances in a way that doesn't injure or threaten the other party or undermine the mediation process.

This chapter explains how to establish and maintain a suitable atmosphere for mediation and to deal effectively with difficult situations and people.

Setting the Tone

Early on in every mediation, you need to create an atmosphere of hope and safety — hope that the problem can be resolved and safety from physical or psychological harm and fear of the unknown. Without hope, the parties won't sit together long enough to brainstorm solutions. And without a sense of safety, they won't open up about the issues that need to be resolved.

The following sections explain various methods for creating and maintaining an atmosphere of hope and safety.

Preparing the participants for joint session mediation

If you're planning to help the parties resolve the dispute primarily through joint session mediation, in which the parties collaborate to reach a resolution that serves everyone's interests, contact them in advance to let them know that the game has changed. Adversarial litigation has ended, and mediation — and collaborative problem-solving — is about to commence.

Call the parties or their attorneys a day or two before the mediation to discuss the process, ask for and understand their greatest concerns, allay their worst fears, and get them to agree to a collaborative process. Recent research shows that these introductory phone calls improve outcomes in part by building trust between the mediator and the parties in advance of the mediation.

Making the parties active participants

One of the best ways to instill a sense of hope and safety is to treat the mediation as a collaborative effort among partners. Start by having the participants introduce themselves and describe their expectations for the mediation. Simple introductions make the parties feel like active participants in the process and boost their confidence to speak up later when they feel uncomfortable, need a break, or want to ask a clarifying question.

Encourage the parties to speak to each other directly, rather than to and through you, so they can engage in a conversation that may lead to a mutually satisfactory agreement. Remind the parties that the problem is theirs to solve and that they can solve it best by dealing directly with each other.

Because people in conflict tend to be angry and afraid, ask the parties to propose rules and procedures that will make them feel more comfortable with the process. Standard rules and procedures tend to calm fears and prevent outbursts. See Chapter 4 for recommended ground rules.

Structuring the mediation with an agenda

Parties often fear the mediation process because they don't know what to expect. Structure is a source of comfort, making the process more understandable and predictable. To establish a structure, collaborate with the parties to develop an agenda with the ultimate goal of revealing sources of value that can help the parties reach an agreement.

Value is anything one or more parties care strongly about — some aspect of the process or outcome. Value may include an attractive business opportunity, restored relationships, improved reputations, the appearance of propriety, the delivery of a fair result, or even a sense of accomplishment in overcoming a major challenge.

Although agendas vary depending on how the parties envision the process, they usually look something like this:

1. **Each party tells her story.**

   Tactfully remind the parties to take turns talking and not to interrupt each other. Provide the parties with paper and a pen or pencil so they can take notes about what they want to say when their turn comes around.

2. **You, as mediator, clarify areas of misunderstanding and confirm with the parties that nothing has been left unsaid and that they understand — even if they don't agree — what the other party wants or needs.**

3. **You list all the issues that must be resolved and all the problems that must be dealt with in order for the parties to reach agreement.**

   In a dispute with neighbors about noise pollution, for example, issues may include control of children playing or dogs barking, communication methods between neighbors (e-mail, phone, knocking on a front door, or shouting over a fence), and possibly compensation of some sort for any harm either party has suffered as a result of the dispute.

4. **You list all areas of agreement and all areas of disagreement.**

5. **All participants work together to prioritize areas of disagreement — problems that need to be solved and issues that must be addressed.**

   For information about identifying, prioritizing, and solving problems, see Chapter 12.

6. **The parties brainstorm, suggesting ways to resolve the problems or address the issues, while you transcribe all the parties' solutions, preferably on a white board that all participants can see.**

   Instruct the parties not to judge any proposed solution until they finish listing all the possible ways to resolve the dispute.

Separating the people from the problem and feelings from facts

People in conflict are uneasy, angry, anxious, and irritable. They almost always demonize their opponent and tell themselves stories about their adversary's motivations — stories that are counterproductive to reaching a peaceful accord. Compounding the problem is people's natural tendency to dig in their heels when they believe that the other side is unwilling to compromise.

Distancing the people from the problem enables the parties to approach the problem more objectively. This separation clears the actors off the stage and shines the spotlight squarely on the issues that need to be resolved. To distance the people from the problem, take the following steps:

1. **Help the parties humanize their adversaries.**

   Engaging in small talk prior to the mediation and during breaks helps the parties see each other as fellow human beings with common interests and daily challenges. Also, find out what the parties have in common and then stress the similarities.

2. **Assist the parties in normalizing the behavior they've interpreted as being wrong, evil, manipulative, or in bad faith.**

   Behaviors that appear malicious on the surface may seem less so when you understand what the person was thinking or going through at the time. Ascertain through open-ended questions why one party may have acted in a way that caused problems for the other party. Help him frame his behavior in a manner that makes his actions seem more reasonable and acceptable.

3. **Acknowledge the parties' right to continue to believe that their adversary is a bad person.**

   Remind the parties that there's a little bad in the best of us and a little good in the worst of us and that the problem can be solved without having to change their opinion about their adversary's character.

Never suppress a party's desire to share with you how evil or malicious his adversary is. Empathize without adopting his characterization, and then move him back to problem-solving instead of dwelling on personalities.

Feelings aren't facts. Many people favor their own emotional responses, even over their own best interests. If someone's so stuck on his own feelings that he overlooks the facts, remind him of the differences between feelings and facts by providing a few examples:

   ✔ I sometimes *feel* like it's raining only on me (laughing). But, of course, it's raining on *everyone*.

   ✔ I sometimes *feel* as though I'm the only honest businessperson left in America. But I know that other businesspeople have as much integrity as I do. I often form opinions about other people too quickly. When I examine the facts, I often find that my negative feelings about people don't necessarily align with the facts.

✔ Most people *feel* that their adversary in litigation will never behave in a reasonable manner. That feeling is strong, and I often have it too. But I've learned as a mediator that most people eventually make an offer or demand that's reasonable enough for the parties to negotiate a solution that's satisfactory to both of them.

Maintaining an atmosphere of hope and safety

As the mediation progresses, monitor and maintain the atmosphere of hope and safety by doing all or some of the following:

✔ After the parties introduce themselves and share their accounts of what led to the current predicament, ask them whether there's more to the problem that they believe has been omitted or neglected.

✔ Ask the parties to take a moment to consider whether they feel dissatisfied with anything they've said so far, assuring them that they'll have plenty of opportunity to clarify what they mean.

✔ Tell the parties that their input will significantly influence the outcome. Ask whether you can do anything to assure them that the process won't go so fast that they'll feel the decision was made for them.

✔ If you're engaging in joint session mediation, tell the parties that they can and should ask for a separate caucus anytime they feel uncomfortable or want to discuss something with you privately.

✔ State a zero-tolerance policy for bullying and point out any instances of bullying when it arises. (Many people don't know they're engaging in bullying behavior and need to understand examples of their own coercive conduct.)

Remaining positive and objective

Project confidence and composure. Assure the parties that they'll be protected from emotional bullying and physical harm, and express your own expectation that the problem, while complex and challenging, is not insurmountable.

Don't form a personal attachment to a particular outcome. Following are a couple of suggestions to help you monitor your inner reactions and self-correct so you don't lose your objectivity:

✔ If you notice that you're feeling disdain or contempt for a certain participant, ask yourself why and try to find a part of yourself, however small, in the other person.

✔ If you feel a need to protect your interests from attack, consider whether you really have something to worry about or you're reacting to something that's been triggered in your subconscious, such as pride or defensiveness over your competence. If the issue is yours, it's personal and inappropriate to bring into the room.

Dealing with Difficult Parties

Sometimes people are annoying. They're difficult. They're negative. They hurl insults at the other side and sometimes even at you. They whine and complain. They craft elaborate conspiracy theories to which they're unalterably attached. They've so demonized the other side that they continue to paint her reasonable and even generous proposals as filled with cunning, unseen traps, into which they're determined not to fall victim.

But difficult people shouldn't be allowed to bully the other participants; part of your job is to rein them in. In the following sections, I offer guidance on how to deal with difficult parties, whether they're uncooperative, stubborn, or bullying.

Getting an uncooperative party involved

In some cases, parties may refuse to play a role in resolving their issues. Perhaps they're so accustomed to their lawyers fighting it out and advising them not to say anything that they're conditioned to play a passive role. Or maybe they have a "my way or the highway" attitude and have convinced themselves that unless the settlement is 100 percent in their favor, it's unacceptable.

To make an uncooperative party cooperative, take the tit-for-tat approach:

1. **Open cooperatively.**

   Create an atmosphere of collaboration, as I explain earlier in this chapter.

2. **Punish proportionally for resistance.**

   Your disapproval is usually sufficient to bring an uncooperative party back into a cooperative endeavor. The parties are very attuned to your moods and want to stay on your good side. A frown and a shake of your head is usually sufficient punishment to bring an uncooperative party back into a collaborative process.

3. **Forgive quickly.**

4. **Return to cooperation as soon as the intractable party signals her willingness to be cooperative again.**

Don't let a party remain uncooperative. If one party continues to cooperate with a stonewaller, the cooperative party eventually enters into a cycle of victimization. If both parties refuse to cooperate, the negotiation between them escalates the conflict, creating more rather than fewer issues to be resolved.

Sometimes, you need to snap disputants out of their stupor of denial, their thinking that the problem will magically solve itself without their participation. If you feel your positive demeanor fraying at the edges, you're always better off speaking your mind than trying to suppress your frustration. If you let irritation and resentment build up, you risk acting out your anger and frustration rather than putting it out there as an issue that needs to be resolved before the process can move forward. Here are some ways to deal with difficult disputants:

✔ Be a realist while acknowledging as quite normal and permissible the disputant's own reasonable fears, anger, and frustration. Here are some examples of what you may want to say when frustration or anger hinders progress:

- I hear your frustration, and it's perfectly understandable. I feel frustrated myself. You have the opportunity to engage in a process that, more often than not, leads to a resolution satisfactory to both parties. The ultimate solution may not be at the top of your list right now. It may be better than what you imagine or it may be the second or third best way to avoid a much worse outcome if the matter isn't settled today. Are you willing to set aside your anger for a few hours in an attempt to resolve the dispute in a manner that may be surprisingly satisfactory to you?

- I know how angry impasse can make all the parties, but I also understand that both of you are committed to resolving this today if at all possible. If you can talk to me about your anger instead of shouting at me, I believe we may well be able to break through impasse and resolve the dispute today.

- I have to admit that I feel angry myself and a little disappointed with the lack of progress we've made today. I've been mediating for six years now, however, so I know that this *feeling* is not a *fact*. If I let my feelings drive my actions, I wouldn't have helped thousands of people settle thousands of disputes. I know you're feeling pessimistic, but I hold enough optimism in the process for all of us. I'd like to know, however, that you're willing to stay in the process too. Can I have your commitment on that?

✔ Go ahead and express your own irritation. For example:

- You know we've been negotiating for three hours now. The other party has put money on the table in an effort to resolve your joint problem. You've offered nothing. I can tell you from my communications with the other party that the dispute won't be settled today unless you put some money on the table. I don't care how small a sum it is, but now is the time. If you're not willing to do so, I think it's probably best to return to litigation.

- It's been three hours now, and everyone continues to bargain in the stratosphere. None of the demands or offers are within a reasonable range. It's time for someone to step up to the line of impasse, and frankly, I think the only one with the courage to do that today is you. (**Note:** I use this technique sparingly, always in separate caucus, and only when I believe deep in my heart that I'm giving this message to the right party. It has never, ever failed.)

✔ Acknowledge that you're out of solutions. Here are a couple of examples that, again, I use sparingly and that have never failed:

- I may be missing something important here. Both parties say they want to resolve the case, but no one has made an offer or demand that he reasonably believes the other side will accept. Frankly, I'm out of ideas. Do you have any?

- We've been at this for eight hours, and I've believed since hour two that we'd close this deal today, but that's looking more and more unlikely. Is there something you'd like me to do that I haven't done for you yet?

Relinquishing control to overcome resistance

When parties resist working with someone they believe is the enemy, your natural inclination may be to resist that resistance — to force the person to cooperate. When you have a knee-jerk reaction to battle a party's resistance, remember this: *That which you resist persists.*

People don't resist the satisfactory resolution of a dispute. They resist resolution for a reason, and your job is to let that reason (or reasons) emerge so the parties can examine it, address it, and let it go. That which people resist persists because, as long as they don't know or admit what's causing their resistance, they can't deal with it and move past it.

Tossing an aphorism at you is easy. Explaining how to overcome your own resistance to a party's resistance and how to help parties overcome their resistance is more involved. You must ask, listen, acknowledge, ask the other party to acknowledge, rinse, and repeat. In the following sections, I provide guidance on how to perform these steps.

You don't settle or fail to settle people's disputes; *they* do. You simply provide and facilitate a process proven to help resolve conflict. When you feel responsible for settling a dispute, you tend to try harder to control the process and lead the parties to the resolution *you* deem best. Control, however, is counterproductive and exhausting. Only the parties know what sparked the dispute, how nobly or ignobly they've behaved toward each other since then, which details of the dispute are important to them and which aren't, and what resources they have to resolve the dispute. Only the parties know what hidden constraints they're operating under and what hidden interests they're serving. If you're mediating litigated cases, you soon discover that even the parties' attorneys don't know enough to find the key to unlock impasse. If they did, they wouldn't have hired you to help them.

Ask

Ask diagnostic, open-ended, reality-testing questions that call for narrative responses rather than yes/no answers. These questions allow the parties to surrender control of the process and of their responses. Narrative responses bring new information to light, which generates discussion that leads to fresh insight and new solutions to old problems. See Chapter 7 for additional guidance on how to ask diagnostic questions.

Listen

Some people won't agree to resolve a problem until they're permitted to explain what happened, what they lost, and how badly they feel as a result. They refuse to make concessions until someone listens to and validates their story and how they feel as a result of what happened.

Validation doesn't mean believing that a person's version of events is correct or accurate. It simply means acknowledging that the version is true for that person. The story may sound absurd, but it's the way the storyteller experienced the events. That's what you listen for and validate — perceived, not objective truth.

Acknowledge

People in dispute have told their story to their spouses, children, parents, friends, and co-workers. They've tried to tell the story to their adversary, but their adversary has usually interrupted their narrative to discredit it, ridicule it, or disrespect it. You're likely the first person *ever* to hear the version of the story that the parties want to tell each other. When you acknowledge the story of a dispute in the presence of the disputants, you model interest, caring, understanding, and respect.

Ask the other party to acknowledge

By acknowledging a party's story as true from that person's perspective rather than the story's objective truth or falsity, you enable the other party to acknowledge that truth. Why? Because that truth doesn't need to be disputed — a perceived truth doesn't threaten to invalidate the truth of the speaker's opponent. You can help the other party acknowledge the story by summarizing it in your own words and asking whether you understood it correctly. Here's an example:

> I heard Louise say that she's already paid $50,000 to clean up her share of the contamination at the property; that she believes your company is at least partially responsible for that contamination; that she doesn't understand why your company hasn't agreed to do its share of the work; and that she got so frustrated trying to get a response from your company that she sought out legal advice and filed a lawsuit. Is that what you heard her say as well?

> Did you hear Louise say anything else that I missed?

Dealing with deception

My husband the attorney says, "The mediator lies to the parties, and everyone knows it." I respond, "Everyone lies to the mediator, and the parties know that the mediator knows it." Then we laugh and move on to the next conversation because he and I are now living in two different legal worlds. I live in a world where the mediator doesn't lie to the parties, shouldn't lie to the parties, and doesn't really care whether the parties believe she's lying to them.

So, what do the parties lie to the mediator about? Here are some common ways that parties hide or misrepresent the truth, along with suggestions on how to get at the truth:

✔ **They misrepresent their bottom line.**

Manipulative negotiation tactics about a party's "real" bottom line aren't facts subject to verification, nor would you want to try to verify them. As I explain in Chapter 7, you don't want to know either party's real bottom line, because that knowledge may limit the parties' options, especially if a party's bottom line were accidentally disclosed.

✔ **They disclaim the weaknesses or exaggerate the strengths of their positions.**

To test a party's claims, ask diagnostic questions, such as, "What is it about this case that makes your defense particularly strong?" and "What were the facts of some of the other cases that made your defense weaker?" These questions lead the person to engage in a deeper level of analysis that you can then use to engage the person in risk analysis.

✔ **They omit facts that would paint them in a bad light or weaken their position.**

To fill in the blanks, ask follow-up diagnostic questions, such as, "Why do you think the other party acted in that way?" You may also want to point out discrepancies that the other party's narrative revealed by saying something like, "So you didn't actually do what she said you did?"

✔ **They exaggerate what people did and said in an effort to increase the coherence and credibility of their narrative.**

To get a more realistic version, try repeating the details that seem to be exaggerated and ask the person whether your understanding is correct or sounds a little out there.

✔ **They misrepresent decision-making authority, often feigning the need to obtain permission to settle a matter on certain terms or for a certain sum.**

To test this "fact," ask follow-up questions, such as

- Who does have the authority to settle for that sum or on those terms?

- Is that person available by telephone?

- Will you please call that person and ask him to join the discussion by conference call?

- Will you please call that person and ask him for more authority?

As you explore the parties' statements respectfully and in-depth, you discover what you need to know to help them move away from positioning and toward problem-solving. More important, they discover what they need to know to do that themselves.

Differentiating puffery and fraud

Most negotiation deception falls under the legal category of puffery. *Puffing* is what salespeople do when they exaggerate a product's benefits and minimize its shortcomings. The law doesn't bother itself with puffing; people who puff aren't legally liable for fraud or misrepresentation. Good, better, and best are opinions of quality, not statements of fact. A company that claims it makes the best toothpaste or its detergent will get your clothes the whitest isn't engaged in fraud but in puffing.

Legal lying (actionable fraud) requires misstatements of fact. If a seller falsely represents that an independent lab has concluded that the seller's laundry detergent gets dirty clothes whiter than 20 of its competitors, the seller would be liable to consumers for fraud, because whether the lab was independent or did the testing or drew the stated conclusion are all facts subject to verification, not opinions subject to dispute.

Uncovering Hidden Interests, Secret Constraints, and Absent Stakeholders

Demonizing someone is easy when you don't have the whole story because you can fill in the blanks to make the person look more sinister. Sometimes, simply letting the party who's doing the demonizing know that the other party may be serving hidden interests, operating under undisclosed constraints, or answering to absent stakeholders helps that party stop demonizing his adversary and start collaborating to resolve the dispute, serve the hidden interests, and work around the secret constraints.

My favorite diagnostic question to flush out hidden interests, secret constraints, and absent stakeholders from corporate parties is, "What would you have to have in your file to justify changing your existing evaluation of the value of this case?" This is a wide open diagnostic question that corporate representatives are usually happy to answer but that they rarely reveal on their own. Some of the answers I've gotten to this question include

- ✔ Something that would convince my superiors that the plaintiff is more credible than they presumed she would be.

- ✔ Some fact we don't yet know that would tend to strengthen their case or weaken ours.

- ✔ A more believable story than the one we've heard so far.

These answers and others tell you exactly what the other party needs in order to overcome the obstacles preventing her from agreeing to a resolution. You can then go back to the other party to explore additional facts to shore up the claim or defense or to develop a story that more effectively expresses the value of her claim or the weakness of her opponent's defense.

Here's a list of some of the hidden interests and secret restraints revealed in mediation that helped settle a dispute:

- ✔ A doctor who believed that settlement would lower his estimation of his competence in his own eyes.

- ✔ A businessman who had the authority to reach any settlement he wanted but whose wife had told him she wouldn't respect him if he settled the dispute for less than a certain sum of money.

- ✔ A mother who wanted her child to be remembered, which led to an agreement by the other party to pay for a memorial in a local park.

✔ A neighbor who wanted his complaints about his neighbor's dog's loud and frequent barking to be taken seriously.

✔ An insurance claims representative who believed she'd be given a bad review if she settled the case for more than her superiors had originally valued it.

✔ A company that entered into a contract with a third party, promising not to settle any claims about the matter at hand on better terms than those given in the contract.

✔ An agent who was told he could settle the matter for $100,000 but that he should settle it for $50,000.

Mediation has also revealed hidden stakeholders, the knowledge of whom has helped settle a dispute:

✔ The revelation that a party needed a precise sum of money to pay over-due bills unrelated to the dispute.

✔ The revelation that other identical claims may be brought as lawsuits if the public became aware that the dispute was settled along the lines the claimant proposed.

✔ The existence of a greedy adult child who was more interested in the money than in a less costly solution that would make his elderly parent more comfortable in her current residence.

Leading the Parties to the Inevitable Impasse

Early in my mediation career, I heard mediators say, "The mediation doesn't really start until the parties have reached impasse." I wondered how that could be. I had always assumed that impasse meant the end, but as I gained experience, I discovered that in mediation, impasse is actually the beginning of the end. Until the parties reach impasse, they're merely jockeying for position outside the *zone of potential agreement* (ZOPA) in an attempt to get a better deal than they're actually willing to accept.

The ZOPA is the area where the parties' bottom lines overlap. For example, if you demand $100,000 in damages but you're willing to accept $50,000, and I offer $25,000 but I'm willing to pay as much as $75,000, our ZOPA is $50,000 to $75,000 (see Figure 9-1).

All you really need to do to lead the parties to impasse is to keep them at the negotiating table and keep them talking. As they trade concessions, they get closer and closer to their true bottom lines until they reach the zone of potential agreement, in which they're actually willing to compromise but are afraid to enter first. This is the point at which you start to earn your money. See Chapter 13 for guidance on how to break through impasse.

Figure 9-1:
The zone
of potential
agreement.

Chapter 10

Transitioning from Adversarial Negotiation to Collaborative Mediation

· ·

In This Chapter

▶ Leading the parties toward interest-based negotiation

▶ Encouraging and facilitating the free exchange of information

▶ Empowering the parties to resolve their issues together

· ·

Adversarial negotiation pits parties against each other and shuts down the free exchange of information. In an adversarial environment, each side needs to be careful about leaking information that the other side can use to its advantage, so the parties often "go dark." Unfortunately, you can't conduct effective mediation in the dark. Effective mediation requires disclosure, transparency, and collaboration so that the parties can explore the full range of possible solutions together.

In this chapter, I explain various strategies and techniques you can use to get the parties to open up (and have their attorneys permit them to participate), to encourage and facilitate the free exchange of information, and to coach the parties to work toward forming a more collaborative relationship. Here, you discover ways to help the parties let down their guard and work together to serve each of their interests.

Overcoming Strategic Barriers to Transparency of Interests

Strategies for winning the "game" of competitive negotiation often create barriers to the successful mediation of a dispute. Competitive negotiation requires the parties to open aggressively, maintain high aspirations for their own side throughout the negotiation, make small and grudging concessions, and seek information about the other party's interests while revealing little or nothing about their own interests. Mediation, on the other hand, seeks to reveal everyone's interests for the purpose of satisfying as many hidden desires, needs, preferences, and priorities as possible.

A large part of your job is to lead the parties out of the dark forest of competitive bargaining and into the sunlight of collaborative negotiation. The following sections explain how to help both the parties and their attorneys overcome the strategic barriers of competitive bargaining. First, I explain how to deal with the common tactic of opening with overly aggressive demands or low-ball offers, which tend to trigger competitive bargaining. I then offer guidance to help attorneys overcome their natural resistance to having their clients reveal more information than they're used to permitting.

Dealing with overly aggressive opening demands or low-ball offers

When a party makes an overly aggressive opening demand or tries to low-ball the other party, ask *diagnostic questions* (open-ended as opposed to yes/no) to unearth the party's underlying interests and bargaining strategies. Following are examples of questions you may want to ask the overly aggressive party in separate caucus:

- ✔ How do you believe your bargaining partner is likely to receive your demand?

- ✔ What do you hope to accomplish by starting the negotiation in that manner?

- ✔ How might you respond to that demand/proposal if you were in your bargaining partner's position?

- ✔ Do you believe your demand/proposal will be sufficiently attractive to your bargaining partner to generate a reasonable counter-proposal?

- ✔ Whose interests do you believe would best be served by resolving the dispute along those lines or in that range?

- ✔ Assuming we could resolve this dispute on terms similar to those you propose, how do you see them benefiting you; that is, how do you see yourself spending that money or using those resources?

Pose such questions to an overly aggressive party only in separate caucus so you don't embarrass the party into taking a defensive stance or force the party to reveal her strategy to the other side.

Your purpose in asking these questions is not only to learn the motivations behind seemingly aggressive opening proposals but also to make the party's bargaining strategies transparent to her (the parties are often unaware of the effect their own negotiation tactics may have on their negotiation partner). As soon as you know the party's strategy and she knows you know it, that strategy becomes less effective with you, and she begins to rely on it less.

Never encourage the parties to cut to the chase and put their bottom-line demand or offer on the table at the very beginning. The parties need room to bargain, even in an *interest-based negotiation* — an approach that seeks to ascertain what fears, desires, priorities, preferences, and the like are driving the parties' negotiation positions. Use the early stages of the mediation to model the type of open-ended diagnostic questions that reveal party interests.

After you discover the parties' interests and the strategy each is pursuing, you can help them open more realistically or soften their aggressive offers or demands. If you want to suggest that a party soften an opening offer, do so candidly. For example, you may say something like this:

> I'm concerned that opening the negotiation with a demand for more than you'd receive if your bargaining partner conceded every point may damage your opportunity to reach an agreement. I'd like to soften your demand by stressing to the other party that it's only an opening offer or that you remain flexible in seeking solutions but want to indicate your strong belief in the rectitude of your position.

Helping attorneys help their clients share information

Telling the parties and their attorneys that nothing they say in mediation can be used against them as evidence in a court of law is all well and good. Convincing them that the information they disclose won't come back to haunt them in an adversarial forum is the greater challenge. Attorneys are responsible for protecting their clients' legal positions. They understandably want to control what their clients disclose in mediation.

If you're mediating litigated cases, you must understand and respect the attorneys' reluctance to let their clients speak freely. If you don't, you may never earn their trust. Always acknowledge your understanding that the attorneys remain in control of the flow of information. Here are some suggestions on what to say to assure the attorneys that you're not trying to undermine their authority and that you're committed to teaming up with them to achieve the optimum outcome for their clients:

✔ Before I ask — or let your bargaining partner ask — your client questions, I'll ask your permission to do so.

✔ Before I suggest that the parties engage in an open-ended discussion with each other, I'll consult with you in private.

✔ If you consider an area of discussion to be off-limits, please let me know, and we can discuss whether opening up that area for problem-solving holds any advantage.

✔ Let's brainstorm some ways I can help you protect your client's litigation interests while at the same time exploring your client's bargaining interests.

✔ If you'd like, we can agree that you'll be given the opportunity to "object" to any questions that I or your bargaining partner would like to ask your client.

Telling an attorney to relinquish control over the flow of information is like asking a surgeon to make an incision without applying an antiseptic. Any foreign matter that enters the surgical site has the potential to spread harmful bacteria throughout the patient's body. And any information known to one side and not the other can open up areas of inquiry that lead to the discovery of information that's harmful to the lawyer's client, as I explain in the nearby sidebar.

Understanding and respecting the attorneys' need to control the exchange of information doesn't mean allowing them to shut down the pipeline. It simply means that you must partner with the attorneys to find a way to permit wide-ranging discussions that reveal interests without doing more harm than good to the parties.

Beware the fruit of the poisonous tree

In criminal law, the *poisonous tree* represents evidence that the parties are barred from producing during trial for various reasons, primarily because the evidence has been illegally obtained and is therefore inadmissible against a defendant. When evidence of that type is excluded, so is all evidence that is "fruit" of the tree; that is, information gathered or revealed as a result of the evidence illegally obtained.

For example, if the police search a murder suspect's residence without a warrant or the suspect's permission, any evidence they discover as a result of that search is inadmissible. In addition, if the police discover evidence through that search that leads to other evidence, such as information about where the victim's body is buried, that evidence is inadmissible as well.

Civil law has no comparable rule. Even though a party's litigation opponent may not be permitted to introduce into evidence something said during the mediation, the disclosure of facts previously unknown to both parties can give them reason to explore those facts in greater depth, weakening one side's legal case and strengthening the other's.

When attorneys represent parties in mediation, the attorneys are always concerned about the adversarial "fruit" that disclosure of confidential information may produce. Attorneys are concerned about the endgame — what happens if mediation fails and the dispute ends up in litigation after all?

When you let the attorneys keep their hands on the reins, they often let go of them as soon as they see that the communication of party interests isn't likely to damage their client's legal position and is calculated to lead to the case's settlement in a way that's better for their clients than continued litigation.

Unlocking the Door to Information Exchange

When the doors of communication are sealed shut, you can't exactly pry them open, but you can motivate the parties to open the doors themselves. The following sections present three techniques to encourage the parties to open the doors for the free exchange of information.

Re-characterizing the issues

One way parties lock the doors to information exchange is to take a position from which they refuse to budge. Even if you've artfully reframed the issue, one or both parties may continue to try to drag you back to their original frame — their position on one or more of the issues.

You can change the rules of the game by re-characterizing the issues — shifting the parties' focus from issues and their respective positions on those issues to sub-issues, where the real problems, and hence their solutions, reside.

Here's an issue and its corresponding position from a real case:

Issue: Whether the mother of adult children would be permitted to introduce evidence at trial that she had been tricked into signing a grant deed transferring ownership of the family home to them.

Position: Even though the law presumes that people know what they're signing and are bound by it whether they've read a contract or not, in this case the adult children used the mother's sketchy knowledge of English to convince her she was signing a document that would transfer her property to her daughters only at the time of her death.

Here's how you might reframe the issue and the position to get the parties back on track:

Reframed issue: Whether the mother would have voluntarily signed away ownership of her property to her children under any circumstances.

Reframed position: The mother offers to enter into a contract to transfer the property to her daughters under the circumstances that she would have voluntarily signed her rights away.

In the following sections, I give you more ways to move the parties from issues to positions to interests in order to dislodge the parties from their positions and open the doors to communication.

Identifying the issues

Issues are questions generally related to the goal of dividing the bargaining pie. Disputes arise when the parties have conflicting answers to these questions. Here are some examples of issues that parties often disagree over:

- ✔ How should profits between partners be distributed when one contributed capital and the other contributed sweat equity?

- ✔ Should a surgeon's patient be permitted to recover his diminished earning capacity if the physician's negligence paralyzed the patient from the waist down?

- ✔ Who should have custody of the children of divorce?

- ✔ How much responsibility does a neighbor owe to the neighborhood to keep his dog from incessantly barking every time the owner leaves his house?

Identifying each party's position

When parties are in dispute over certain issues, they each take up a *position* (how they think the issue should be resolved). Then, they justify their proposed solution and end up getting more and more entrenched in their respective points of view and the narratives supporting those views. Following are positions that parties may take related to the issues I describe in the preceding section, along with justifications for each position:

- ✔ The profits of the partnership business should be split 50-50 because

  - • The value of my work is equal to the value of the capital that my partner contributed.

  - • The partnership contract says that my sweat equity is equal in value to my partner's capital contributions.

  - • My partner and I had a handshake agreement but never talked about how profits would be split. The law in my jurisdiction says that, under those circumstances, the profits should be split 50-50.

- ✔ I should be entitled to recover all the money I would have earned as a chef because

  - • The surgeon's negligence resulted in my inability to do my job.

  - • I can't secure employment with comparable pay and benefits that enables me to use my skills.

✔ I should have custody of my children because

- My spouse's work requires her to be on the road at least one week out of every month.

- The children need more stability than my spouse can provide.

✔ My neighbor must get rid of his dog because

- He has proven unable or unwilling to keep his dog from incessantly barking every time he leaves his house.

- My city has noise regulations that my neighbor's dog violates.

Probing to uncover sub-issues

To re-characterize issues as a means of reaching agreement, you have to dig deeper past the issues to party interests. One way to do that is to find sub-issues that can help you lead the parties toward an interest-based negotiation.

Use the same strategy for uncovering sub-issues that you use to uncover hidden interests, absent stakeholders, and secret constraints — ask open-ended questions, as I explain in Chapter 7.

Each major issue in any dispute has numerous sub-issues. Following are examples of sub-issues for the various issues I describe in the two preceding sections:

✔ **Sub-issues for how partnership profits should be divided:**

- How does the contract between the parties address that issue?

- Has anything changed since the parties signed the contract that may illuminate the reason the parties now have a dispute about something they agreed upon in the past? For example, how well have the partners been performing all their obligations under the contract? Has the business suffered losses as a result of one party's failure to fulfill his contractual obligations? Have outside economic circumstances changed so drastically that the plan laid out in the partnership agreement is no longer realistic for one or both parties?

✔ **Sub-issues for malpractice claim:**

- What other types of work might the chef pursue?

- Could some of the settlement monies be used for rehabilitation or to reconfigure the chef's kitchen to permit him to continue to ply his trade?

- How much would rehabilitation cost?

- How much would reconfiguring the chef's kitchen cost?

- What are the most cost-efficient options for replacing the chef's income within the next two years?

✔ **Sub-issues for custody battle:**

- How can stability for the children be built into the custody agreement, given each parent's different circumstances?

- Are the parents more concerned about their children's welfare or their own convenience?

- Why have the parents chosen to focus on this problem rather than others?

✔ **Sub-issues for the nuisance dog scenario:**

- Are any aids available to stop the dog barking (collars that deliver a slight shock, for instance) when his barking exceeds a certain amount of time — say, five minutes?

- Would the presence of another pet in the house keep the dog from barking while the people are gone — a cat, for instance?

- The dog seems only to start barking a few hours after the people have left the house. Would a dog walker midday decrease the barking?

Asking the parties to discuss these sub-issues inevitably reveals problems and possible solutions that neither party has yet raised or considered. Often, the parties haven't raised these sub-issues because they're trying to avoid conflict on other issues that are the true reason for the dispute or are harboring resentments that they don't feel comfortable discussing.

Putting all the sub-issues on the table for discussion and brainstorming can get the parties past their narrow focus on a single issue and dislodge them from their respective take-it-or-leave it positions. Following are examples of how sub-issues may reveal better solutions that the parties haven't considered:

✔ **Partnership profits:** Perhaps the business isn't profitable enough for either party to be satisfied with a 50-50 split. The real issue is what the parties can do to make their business more profitable or cut their losses.

✔ **Malpractice claim:** Maybe the real issue is one of choice — the patient wants to feel free to craft his new life in the manner he chooses, opening up for discussion what that would look like in a post-injury world.

✔ **Custody battle:** Perhaps the real issue is the parents' different child-rearing strategies.

✔ **Nuisance dog:** Maybe the real issue is a fight between the neighbors over a boundary line or even an encounter that one neighbor experienced as a slight and the other did not.

Re-humanizing the parties

At the very beginning of the mediation process, you humanize the parties by engaging in small talk and having the parties introduce themselves, as I explain in Chapter 4. When the parties move into different rooms for separate caucuses, however, the benefits of this initial humanizing process are often lost as the parties fall back into the trap of reading everything their opponents do or propose as sinister. The result is that the once open doors to communication are slammed shut. The fix is to re-humanize the parties, by doing one or more of the following:

- ✔ Reconvene the parties in a joint session. Demonizing someone is easier when the person is absent.

- ✔ Remind the parties of the common experiences they shared with each other earlier.

- ✔ Normalize their opponent's behavior. For example, you can say something like, "It's common in disputes for some people to make outrageous demands because they're afraid they'll be taken advantage of if they don't. That's part of your fear too, right? That your opponent is trying to take advantage of some presumed weakness in your negotiation strategy?"

The ways in which you can return the parties to a nonhostile (if not necessarily a trusting) state are nearly infinite and depend entirely on how you read the parties' unique emotional responses to the conflict. As my own mentor Ken Cloke always reminds me, "*You* are the technique." If you're sensitive to the parties' changing moods and knowledgeable about the social psychology of conflict, you'll find an effective way to humanize the parties to each other when demonization kicks in. Find some small part of yourself in every participant, and you'll know what do to.

Separating people problems from issues

Whether the disputants are engaged in competitive distributive bargaining or have entered into a collaborative interest-based negotiation, people problems always continue to dog their efforts to concentrate on and solve their mutual conflict problem. People problems often arise from emotional responses, unfounded fears, biases or assumptions that lead to defensiveness, hard bargaining tactics, and adversarial responses.

As a mediator, you walk the razor's edge of people problems: If you allow the people problems to persist, they continue to hinder progress and threaten to derail negotiations. If you try to suppress the people problems rather than separate them from the conflict problem, the people problems will continue to haunt the mediation and derail rational decision-making.

To walk this difficult line, you first have to ask enough diagnostic questions to separate unfounded from founded fears and assumptions and then explore the source of those fears and the basis for those assumptions that are pertinent to the dispute. (See Chapter 7 for more information about asking diagnostic questions.)

Understanding is the first step, but it's never the entire solution. After you understand the people problems and help the parties locate their dispute partner's motivations, fears, and desires, you still have to help them mend the relationship that their responses to the dispute have damaged. Following are some ways to deal with the people problems and help the parties mend their relationship:

✔ Treat the people problem and the problem to be solved as two separate tasks. Let the parties know that you see both as important and intertwined but that you believe the problem to be solved can more fruitfully be addressed by uncritically brainstorming all possible solutions after the people problem is aired, discussed, and put to bed.

✔ Encourage the disputants to attack the problem rather than each other. For example, suppose a married couple is arguing over whether to buy a new or used car. The wife argues that a new car is the better choice and that her husband has always been stingy. The husband wants a used car, blaming his wife's overspending for the fact that they can't afford a new car. The parties are attacking each other instead of the problem.

As a mediator, you can help the parties shift their focus back to the problem by encouraging them to discuss the pros and cons of each choice. A used car, for instance, may have mechanical problems and a shorter life span that would make the purchase of a new car a better choice. On the other hand, the husband might be an amateur mechanic who's able to affordably repair and maintain the used car. In addition, he may be secretly worried about his job security in the present economy and concerned about committing to monthly car payments.

You can see from this example how important separating the people from the problem is. After the parties are focused on the pros and cons of any decision, you can engage their problem-solving skills to reach a mutually agreeable decision. If you support the parties in proving each other wrong, the chance that any reasonable resolution will be reached is slim to none.

✔ Honor all emotional responses as understandable and normal while at the same time helping the parties talk about those responses. The goal is for all participants to gain a better understanding of the following:

• How each party may have contributed to the dispute in the first place.

• How each party's post-dispute behavior may have escalated the conflict and caused further harm to both parties.

- How the emotional responses are serving as obstacles to resolution.

- How the emotional responses can serve as a means to resolution instead.

✔ Encourage the parties to talk about their feelings and to own them by using "I" and "we" statements instead of "you" statements. For example, instead of the "bullied" party saying, "You bullied me into signing that contract," he may say, "I *felt* bullied when I signed that contract." Such "I" statements are less likely to put the other party on the defensive and can't be argued against. You can't argue against how someone feels; you can argue only whether that feeling is justified.

Don't encourage the parties to *vent* their feelings, because they're likely to hear your encouragement as permission to accuse and attack their perceived opponents. Listen, validate, and then get back to the issues. Eventually, the parties will get the message that they really need to focus on the problems and not on their perceived adversary.

Coaching to Empower and Guide the Parties

Parties in dispute come to you for help in effectively communicating their desires, fears, needs, priorities, and preferences without causing their dispute partner to react defensively. They expect you to play the role of coach and referee. To serve this role effectively, coach the parties to communicate effectively and non-threateningly in separate caucus, coach and referee in joint session to foster teamwork, and always cheer the parties on to mutual victory, as I explain in the following sections.

Strategically using the separate caucus: Exploring and coaching

Taking separate session breaks with the parties permits you to explore new interests that come to light during joint session. Doing so also allows you to investigate possible solutions and the strategies for achieving them and to coach the parties to communicate their responses and proposals for resolution.

Taking each party's pulse with diagnostic questions

Here are some wide-open diagnostic questions to use with parties in separate caucus after the joint session has proceeded for some time:

✔ How do you feel about the progress you're making?

✔ What, if anything, do you wish you could say to or ask of your bargaining partner that you haven't yet said or asked?

✔ Am I doing or not doing something you believe would be helpful in moving the negotiation forward in the direction you'd like it to go?

✔ Am I doing or not doing something you believe is unhelpful or harmful to the resolution process?

✔ Would you like to talk about that last proposal that your bargaining partner put on the table?

✔ I can see that you're angry. Can you tell me about that? Would you like to be able to explain your anger to your dispute partner in a way that she can hear it?

✔ Your bargaining partner has put an ultimatum on the table, saying, essentially, "My way or the highway." How would you prefer to respond to that?

✔ You put an ultimatum on the table. How do you think you'd respond to that if you were in the other party's shoes?

✔ I can tell that you're discouraged. Let's talk about a few ways we can get the discussion moving in a more productive direction for you.

✔ How do you feel about having blown up at the other side? How would you feel if she did that to you? Can you think of any way to mend the rift in the relationship that exists right now?

The questions you can pose in separate caucus to find out what each party is thinking and feeling and to reveal the issues that each party is wrestling with are infinite. Ask diagnostic questions such as these to get the problem-solving process back on track, to spark a brainstorming session with a party who doesn't feel comfortable brainstorming in a joint session, or to open a discussion about negotiation strategy and tactics. (For more about asking diagnostic questions, check out Chapter 7.)

Parties often try to vent their frustration and anger in separate caucus. Don't join an irritated party in a separate caucus session of "trash my opponent." Acknowledge the party's anger, normalize it, explore its sources, validate it as a permissible and entirely valid human response, discuss how the other party's statements or behavior can be explained by something less sinister, and discuss ways of getting the mediation back on track again.

Preserving the progress you made

Separate caucus work is sometimes like digging a hole in the sand. While you're making progress in one room, the other room returns to defensive, group-think posture, as both parties remind themselves why they're right and the other side is wrong. When you left the room, they were one move from resolution. When you return, they've taken five steps back.

The best way to avoid this problem is to give the room you leave a problem-solving task that keeps the parties moving forward toward resolution. Here are some problem-solving tasks you may want to assign to a party and the party's attorney before you leave the room:

- ✔ Write the other side's closing argument.

- ✔ Draw a decision tree or complete a tree that's already mapped out.

- ✔ Divide the probable trial outcomes into thirds, assigning to each third a percentage probability. Do the same for damages if the other side prevails on liability.

- ✔ Write an essay on what your life would be like if you woke up the next morning without having to deal with the dispute because it's been resolved.

- ✔ Discuss the issues we've been talking about among yourselves and be prepared to talk to me about your conclusions when I return.

If you find yourself spending more than 20 minutes in the other room, check back in with the other participants to ask them how they're doing, to explain in general terms why you've been gone so long, and to estimate when you'll be returning.

Working toward mutual respect and understanding

While in separate caucus, always model and work toward a greater degree of respect and understanding for the other side. The parties will follow your lead. Continue to model for all participants the highest values of peaceful dispute resolution. If you're faithful to your own principles, the parties will value what you do more than what you say.

Don't buddy up with one or both parties in separate caucus, increasing rather than decreasing demonization and putting your own fingerprints on probable future impasse. I've seen too many mediators try this, and the results are always detrimental. Remain positive, optimistic, and respectful of all participants.

In some cases, you use separate caucus to coach the parties for a first or final joint session. Coaching the parties is often quite personal. Some people need assistance to find a way to say what their concerns are without doing so in a manner that places all the blame for the problem on the other side. In such cases I may ask a party whether he feels comfortable acknowledging his part in the dispute's evolution or whether he can admit uncertainty about his own position while at the same time explaining what he wants and why he wants it.

I'm always surprised when my coaching feels unnecessary because the parties are more ready than I thought they'd be to treat each other with respect, to listen attentively, to reflect back what they've heard, and to make an effort to problem-solve rather than argue the merits of their position.

Rewarding small steps and encouraging progress

Everyone likes to be rewarded for doing a good job. When you reward people for even a small step toward the finish line, they make an effort to replicate the behavior that's been praised. Encourage and reward the parties often throughout the process as they progress. You must, of course, be honest with the parties about the progress of the mediation or lack thereof or they won't trust you. And when the parties begin to distrust you, your usefulness is over.

Let the parties know that you understand the difficulty of the obstacles they face. Normalize their fearful predictions. People don't pay a mediator to help them solve a conflict they're capable of resolving themselves. They've brought to you the thorniest dispute they've ever encountered. They're angry, afraid, and discouraged. Be honest. Their dispute is one that would stump you as well. What you have faith in and what you show fidelity to is the process of mediation. Collaborative, interest-based dispute resolution coupled with people dedicated to resolving conflict works. And it will work for them.

Preside over the process and celebrate progress. Impasse, not the other party, is the opposition. Everyone in the room has the identical stake in the identical problem — finding a way to serve both parties' interests at the same time. Be free with praise and clear-eyed about the challenge.

Chapter 11

Capitalizing on Your People Skills

*E*very dispute has two sides, and not necessarily the two sides most people think about — one party's side and the other's. The two sides I'm talking about are the people side and the problem side. Solve the problem and the dispute between the people often subsides. However, the people side often prevents the parties from addressing the problem in the first place, so one of your jobs is to capitalize on your people skills to help the parties get past the people side of the dispute. This chapter presents various ways to do just that.

Drawing On the Sources of Trust

Collaborative mediation requires that a certain level of trust be rebuilt between parties who stopped trusting each other long ago. The parties also need to develop trust in you and in the mediation process. Trust enables the parties to reveal the information necessary to create value where none appears to exist, to brainstorm outside-the-box resolutions, and to persist in negotiations in good faith when agreement seems hopeless.

The following sections describe three different sources of trust and explain how to tap these sources to foster an atmosphere of trust and overcome distrust.

You can't *make* one party trust another, but you can put certain protections in place to help the parties feel more secure. For example, setting ground rules helps the parties feel more comfortable knowing that certain bargaining tactics won't be tolerated during the mediation. Likewise, contingency agreements, as discussed in the following sections, can help alleviate a party's fear of signing on to an agreement.

Calculus-based trust

Calculus-based trust is a low-level form of trust that results when someone carefully calculates that he has more to gain than to lose. When two parties consent to mediation, they usually have calculus-based trust in you and in the process because they believe they have more to gain than lose by having the dispute resolved through mediation. If they adhere to the process and work patiently with you to achieve a desired result, the potential benefit in resolving the dispute is significant — the result satisfies their needs, solves a burdensome problem, and perhaps even mends a relationship. In a litigated dispute, a successful mediation also saves both parties considerable time and money.

To boost calculus-based trust, set ground rules, as I explain in Chapter 4, and enforce them. Ground rules remove some of the potential risk from the cost side of the cost/benefit equation. The promise of confidentiality also boosts the level of calculus-based trust by ensuring the parties that nothing they reveal in mediation can be used against them in a court of law or in an administrative proceeding. In other words, if either party considers the disclosure of information a potential cost of mediation, he can now remove that from the equation.

To reinforce calculus-based trust, enable the parties to trust but verify. For example, if one party makes representations during the mediation to convince the other party to accept a proposal and the other party doesn't trust those representations, consider suggesting that the agreement be made contingent upon proof of the representations. If the person making the representations is lying, this calls his bluff and may result in further negotiation. If the representations are valid, the contingency agreement allays the concerns of the dubious party.

You can significantly enhance calculus-based trust by erecting safeguards to anticipate and prevent breaches of trust. Those safeguards begin with the establishment and subtle enforcement of the ground rules and end with contingency agreements that enable the parties to trust but verify.

Knowledge-based trust

Knowledge-based trust is based on the information each party has that enables her to foresee the probable consequences of a proposed solution. If a party knows that the other party always keeps her word, for instance, then she's likely to trust that person when she makes a promise. If one party makes representations that the other party knows are true, trust is a given. Prior to mediation, knowledge-based trust is usually at a low point; the knowledge the two parties have of each other from past dealings usually works to undermine trust, not deepen it.

To test knowledge-based trust, ask questions about each party's knowledge and experience. For example, you may ask a party in private caucus, "Is this the type of agreement she has shown herself capable of abiding by in the past?" If the answer is no, you might follow up by asking, "Are there other inducements available to ensure that she'll abide by this agreement in the future?"

You may also use contingency agreements to offer assurance to a party who lacks the knowledge or certainty of the ostensible facts the other party presents. Making the agreement conditional upon proof of those facts is often an acceptable substitute for knowledge-based trust. (For more about using contingency agreements to address trust issues, see Chapter 7.)

Identification-based trust

Identification-based trust is the trust among people who share values and interests. As mediator, reminding the parties of their shared values and interests often helps them move forward with greater trust for each other. In business conflicts, for example, I often remind businesspeople of their shared values — the recognition that they can't recover sunk costs or factor them in to the value of any deal going forward; the principle of pragmatism that values rationality over emotionality (a sound business decision over revenge, for instance); and the shared view that planning for a productive future is better than fighting over the details of an unproductive past.

In disputes within religious organizations, identification-based trust is also often rooted in shared values — accountability, confession, forgiveness, and reconciliation, to name a few. Within ethnic communities, you have to discover the values that the parties share so you can remind them of the interests they have in common.

Using Mirroring to Empathize and Get the Parties to Follow Your Lead

Mirroring is a technique that capitalizes on the fact that people naturally tend to reflect what they observe. When you see someone in pain, you're likely to wince in empathy. When you witness other people pitching in to help someone, you're more likely to lend a hand. Mirroring enables mediators, in a very short period of time, to build trust between themselves and each of the parties and then to use that trust to help the parties inch their way toward trusting each other.

Mirroring is a two-way street, and you should take advantage of it in both directions. First, behave the way you want the parties in the mediation to behave so they can mirror your behavior. Second, use mirroring to reflect the empathy you feel for the distress that the parties physically manifest in their facial expressions, body language, and tone of voice.

To use mirroring to model behavior, be the person you want the participants to be more like:

- ✔ Be open-minded, authentic, and transparent.

- ✔ Be reliable. Explain how you do what you do and then do it the way you said you'd do it.

- ✔ Treat the parties with respect. Find some part of yourself, no matter how small, in each person at the table.

- ✔ Care genuinely about the parties and the problem they're trying to solve.

- ✔ Listen carefully and indicate not only that you understand but also that you empathize.

Don't try to fake empathy. Conscious efforts to empathize often come across as inauthentic. Try to put yourself in that person's shoes to really get a sense of what he's feeling. If you succeed, you'll feel and communicate a *genuine* sense of empathy.

- ✔ Be patient with the parties and persistent in your attempts to help them solve their problem.

- ✔ Demonstrate curiosity by asking nonthreatening, open-ended questions.

- ✔ Express how open and receptive you are to what each party is saying by relaxing your body and keeping your arms open. If you clasp your arms across your chest, frown, or fidget in your chair, you're experiencing underlying feelings that you need to acknowledge and deal with. Otherwise, the parties will sense your anxiety and mirror it.

The biological basis for mirroring

According to some neuroscientists, certain brain cells, called *mirror neurons,* replay in people's minds the actions of someone they're watching. These scientists speculate that this near simultaneous replay permits people to predict what someone is about to do. When you watch someone pull back his arm, for instance, the re-creation of the event in your mind allows you to imagine that he's about to throw something.

In a way, this simultaneous replay makes a person experience what the other person experiences — the very definition of empathy. In extreme cases, someone may even share symptoms of a loved one in distress, as when a husband of a pregnant wife experiences sympathy pains or morning sickness.

The fact that some people feel another person's joy, fear, or pain so intensely that they unconsciously mirror the other person's external manifestations of distress during intense conversation seems a likely effect of the activity of the mirror neurons in the brain.

Angry at the absence of anger

Recently, a client complained that I wasn't "getting angry" in response to his opponent's recalcitrance. I probed for the reasons he so badly wanted me to be angry. Did he believe my anger might pressure his opponent into being more rational — perhaps shame him into compliance?

No amount of explanation about my role and the circumstances satisfied my client, to whom I was speaking in separate caucus. Without giving it much thought, I began to describe a recent situation in which I'd lost my temper over a parking spot. We both laughed about my intemperance, and this had the surprising effect of calming my client and satisfying his desire for me to express anger.

Looking back on this interaction, I believe that what my client wanted was recognition that his own anger was legitimate — that it was neither unprofessional nor unreasonable for him to express anger. My client may also have perceived my failure to exhibit anger at his opponent's disrespectful treatment of the process as inauthentic. He probably thought that I was either incapable of this very human emotion or was faking temperance.

Whatever his reasons, telling my own story about my own anger (over a lost parking spot no less!) seemed to completely restore his faith in me and mend the break in our relationship. Together we laughed at our shared human foible and then proceeded to work together to solve the problem that his opponent's obstructionism was causing.

You'll most likely be liked by liking, be trusted by being trustworthy, and be empathic by truly feeling the other person's experience.

Attaining and Maintaining a State of Equanimity

As a mediator, you need to remain above the fray, or *in the balcony,* as some mediators like to describe it. From this detached perspective, you don't distinguish between friends and enemies, strangers and family, or good and evil. Buddhism refers to this as a state of *equanimity* — a clear and tranquil state of mind in which you treat everyone as equals.

Equanimity is somewhat of an unattainable ideal. You can aspire to it and strive for it, but rarely does anyone fully attain it. Still, you should try. And if you have trouble, remind yourself of how fallible human beings are and how little you really know about the myriad causes that result in the behaviors you're observing. When you realize how little you know about what motivates an individual's thoughts, emotions, and actions, you're less likely to judge those thoughts, emotions, and actions as something bad.

Equanimity, though without judgment, is not indifference. You must still play your role as umpire. You must continue to recognize selfishness, vengeance, bullying, and other counterproductive thoughts and actions and step in to ensure fair play and progress toward a mutually satisfactory solution. Equanimity just means that you do all this more objectively, without taking sides.

Tapping the Power of Persuasion to Keep the Process Rolling

You do a lot of persuading as a mediator. Perhaps you persuade both parties to refrain from delivering ultimatums, to soften their positions, or to stay in the process rather than storm out of the room. But you must develop people-friendly persuasion skills that don't rub the parties the wrong way or make you appear to be manipulative or dictatorial.

The following sections help you develop the persuasion skills you need to keep the mediation process on track.

Be very careful not to use the power of persuasion to coerce either party to do something she really doesn't want to do. When you overpower someone's will, any agreement reached tends to be unstable. Buyer's remorse inevitably sets in, and the parties find ways to attack the settlement directly or to undermine its performance indirectly, all of which can and does lead them back to the adversarial system from which mediation was supposed to deliver them.

Using your position of authority to ensure fair play

Never undervalue the authority of your position as mediator. Sure, you don't wear a black robe, but most people have never been in a courtroom. You're the closest they may ever come to someone akin to a judge, and you're definitely the authority figure everyone in the room is counting on to ensure justice.

Although you may represent justice, don't try to act like a judge. Your role doesn't call for handing down a decision or issuing a verdict. In mediation, the parties are actually the judge and jury; they ultimately decide the outcome. Your authority is more like that of a referee or umpire. Your responsibility is to ensure *procedural justice* — a sense of fair play. To create an atmosphere of fair play, do the following:

✔ Remain impartial in dealing with all participants. Cultivate a sense of self-awareness and monitor yourself for bias, as I explain in Chapter 8.

✔ Treat all participants with dignity and respect and require the parties to engage in conversation that treats everyone involved with dignity and respect.

✔ Establish and maintain a forum in which the parties have an equal opportunity to speak, listen, and respond to each other. Having a voice in the proceedings is particularly important for weaker parties who may have been marginalized or outgunned in terms of resources and access to power.

✔ Make sure the parties understand each other, especially when they disagree.

Employing commitment and consistency to control the process

Commitment and consistency are powerful tools for keeping a mediation on track and progressing in the right direction. When disputants make a commitment to the mediation process, they subject themselves to pressure, both internally and externally, to honor that commitment and remain consistent with the process. Likewise, the need for consistency can be very influential. When a person's thoughts, words, and deeds don't align, he typically feels uncomfortable in his own skin as well as in his community, where fellow community members expect him to keep his word and be consistent in words and actions. You can use these internal and external pressures to your advantage in keeping a mediation on track, as I explain in the following sections.

Leveraging the power of commitment

When the parties' patience is flagging, remind them that they agreed to stay in the process until it appears that no possible solution may be found. If they lose their temper and begin to interrupt the other party, forgive them their outburst but remind them that they agreed, as did their dispute partner, to listen respectfully and patiently until it was their turn to speak.

If you secured a commitment from the parties to find a reasonable solution that, while not entirely satisfactory, was good enough to satisfy both parties' essential needs, remind them of that fact when they reach the inevitable impasse. "What," you might ask, "is unreasonable about the solution on the table right now?" and then proceed to brainstorm that problem — and the next one, and the next one after that — until no "unreasonable" part of the proposed deal remains or the parties agree to new reasonable deal points.

Start small. In one study, a researcher went door to door asking homeowners to place a large and unattractive public service sign on their front lawn urging motorists to drive carefully. Only 17 percent agreed. When that request was preceded by a more attractive commitment — to place a small, nicely lettered *Be a Safe Driver* sign — compliance with the request to place the large and ugly sign rocketed from 17 percent to 76 percent. Small commitments often lead to larger ones later.

Use the power of small commitments to encourage larger ones. In a family mediation, obtaining a commitment by the divorced parents of small children to cooperate by setting the same bedtime in both houses can be followed by a larger request to cooperate in scheduling summer activities to meet both parents' work schedules. In a business mediation, obtaining a commitment to use a particular method to value the goodwill of the business can be followed by a larger commitment to use a single expert to value the entire business.

Harnessing the power of consistency

Consistency can be a powerful tool to persuade a party to look at an issue from a different perspective. If a party uses a certain line of reasoning, for example, to support an extreme demand, you may ask how he'd react if his bargaining partner followed the same line of reasoning to justify a low-ball offer.

Consistency isn't always beneficial. The greatest obstacle to innovation in business is the belief that because business "is always done that way," the old way is best. If a party insists on a foolish and unproductive consistency, acknowledge the power of consistency while bringing up Ralph Waldo Emerson's quote: "A foolish consistency is the hobgoblin of little minds."

Persuading through the power of reciprocity

You may not think of reciprocity as a tool of persuasion, but it's one of the most effective ways to persuade someone to be generous and, in a mediation, to offer concessions. People are hard-wired to reciprocate and actually return a gift or a favor with something of greater value.

When negotiations stall, use the power of reciprocity to kick-start negotiations by naming the concessions made by both parties throughout the day and stressing how difficult they were to make. By doing so, you remind the parties of their continuing obligation to reciprocate the concessions each party has made. (See Chapter 6 for more about harnessing the power of reciprocity.)

Persuading through social proof

Social proof is what your mother warned you against. "If all the other kids jumped off a cliff," you might recall her saying, "would you jump too?" Of course, this isn't the best question to ask teenagers in an era where bridge jumping has become a popular and dangerous pastime. But social proof can be a very effective tool for building hope and encouraging the parties to behave in a certain way.

As a mediator, you can use social proof to instill hope in the disputants and deepen their commitment to the process. You may, for example, tell your clients the percentage of the cases you've mediated in which the disputants have settled. "Ninety percent of all cases I handle settle," I've heard many a mediator say. Strictly speaking, that's probably true, because 90 percent of *all* litigation settles, and the mediator didn't say the dispute settled *because* he was mediating it. Strictly true or not, you can use statements about most of your cases settling (they *should*) not only to create an atmosphere of hope (cases like this settle all the time, so don't believe yours can't) but also to encourage certain behaviors (everyone else settles when they come to me, so you should too).

Exercising the power of likability

If you're like most people, the people you admire have more influence and persuasive power over you than those you dislike or don't really know. And you're far more likely to do favors for friends than for strangers. This is true of the disputants, as well. If they like you, they want to please you. They want to remain in your good graces and not disappoint you.

But how do you go about being more likable? The key is to find something to like in everyone — either something you find attractive or something you have in common. When you make someone feel liked, that person often reciprocates by looking for something to like about you. And when the disputants like you, they're more prone to reward you by their desire to not only resolve their conflict but also live up to your example and be liked by you.

Convincing with the cost of time

Scarcity thinking is usually counterproductive to mediation. It's the source of all conflict, leading people to believe that their needs and the needs of others can't be satisfied at the same time. When parties think that no resolution is possible, you often need to help them overcome scarcity thinking and look at the abundance of available solutions.

On the other hand, you can often use scarcity of time to your advantage in revving up progress. Occasionally remind the parties that the clock is ticking. If they're hung up over events that happened in the past, remind them of what a waste of their time it is to fight over the unproductive past and how little time they have to move confidently into the future. You may also want to mention that every ticking minute carries a price tag in the form of attorney fees, mediator fees, or both.

How I discovered the power of like

I learned the power of *like* early in my legal career during a *360 degree job review* — a review in which everyone you work with, whether closely or at a great distance, evaluates your work, up and down the corporate hierarchy. When my immediate superior asked me into his office to deliver the verdict, his brow was knitted as he tapped the paper in his hands.

"Strange," he said. "The people who work with you a lot like you quite well and believe your work is excellent. The people who work with you only a little are neutral. But the people who don't work with you at all have formed a very negative opinion of you and your work."

Ouch.

"Why do you think that is?" he asked.

"I have no idea," I responded. "How could they dislike me if they admit they don't know me?"

"The only advice I have for you," he said, "is to get to know everyone in the office better. Join the softball team."

I didn't join the softball team but I did think deeply about this stinging judgment. I realized that I tended to avoid the people I didn't know well.

I was in my mid-20s, and though I was already practicing law, I was insecure, and the older attorneys intimidated me. I also realized that I didn't like most of them either, even though I hadn't bothered to get to know any of them.

So I decided to make an effort to be cordial and learn something about the people I was avoiding. I soon discovered that we shared more interests than I expected and that I'd made some sweepingly negative judgments about many of them based on the type of law they practiced.

The following year, my superior once again gave me my 360 degree review. "You didn't join the softball team," he said, "but you must have done something because the opinion of the people you don't work with has changed dramatically. They think very highly of you, describe your reputation as sterling and your work product as excellent. What happened?"

"I realized," I said, "that I didn't like them. So I decided to see what would happen if I got to know them well enough to like them. Which is what I did. And I found that they liked me right back."

Don't try to pander your way to likeability by dressing the part and telling people what you think they want to hear. People demand authenticity in the people they like. Try hard to find something to like in everyone, but don't try too hard to be who you think others will like.

I often remind the parties of Henry David Thoreau's maxim about the cost of our decisions. "The cost of a thing," he said, "is the amount of life we are willing to exchange for it, now or in the long run." It's that last part, the long run, that moves the parties the most. It helps them reflect on what they value over money: time with their families. Time to lay the groundwork of their life's greatest work. Time to hike in the wilderness and listen to the sound of the wind in the leaves.

Don't use time as an endurance test to coerce the parties into settlement. "We'll stay here until three in the morning to get this done," I've heard many a mediator and settlement conference judge say. Tired and hungry, the parties often agree to anything just to get the matter resolved so they can have dinner or get some sleep. This ultimately leads to buyer's remorse, and the deal you made at 3 a.m. quickly returns to litigation.

Ensuring Fair Play

In most disputes, one party has more bargaining power than the other and may try to use it to her own advantage, but power plays can quickly undermine a mediation. When you notice a power imbalance and a party trying to leverage that power, you may need to step in as referee, but you must do so as a neutral. In the following sections, I explain how to deal with one party's attempted manipulation of the other and how to assist the weaker party without playing favorites.

Dealing with one party's attempted manipulation of the other

The more powerful of the two parties may try to use her power to manipulate or bully the weaker party into submission. When this happens, you have a choice. You can act as a moral authority, calling people to their higher angels, or you can step back and let the parties work it out.

Some mediators believe that neutrality means hands-off. Others believe, as I do, that the mediator should serve as a referee or umpire and, as such, has a duty to ensure fair play. Strong-arming a bargaining partner doesn't constitute fair play.

Because mediation is a voluntary, consensual process and because you're the umpire of that process, don't feel inhibited in calling a ball or a strike when you see one. Whether you do this in joint session or in separate caucus is a judgment call. You don't want to condemn or humiliate either party in the presence of the other, so you may want to talk to the offending party in separate caucus.

If you decide to address bullying in joint session and in a more direct manner, do so using open-ended, nonjudgmental "I" statements that authentically communicate your own discomfort. Here's an example:

> If I were in X's position, I'd be feeling a little intimidated right now. Is that what you intended, Y, or am I reading you incorrectly?

This type of inquiry gives the bully an "out" if he was behaving in a coercive manner. It permits him to bring his behavior back into compliance with the process of brainstorming without admitting that he was actually trying to force the other party to cave in to his pressure. On the other hand, you and the other party may be misreading the situation, in which case, you give the suspected bully the opportunity to clear up your misunderstanding.

In assessing the situation, pay attention to the body language of both parties. You know frightened facial expressions and defensive postures when you see them. Don't assume, however, that you're right. Always note your impressions and ask questions to verify whether in this particular case your assessment is accurate.

Assisting the party in the weaker position

Cheering for the underdog and wanting to assist a weaker party are natural inclinations. Opponents in battles between big business and consumers, employees and employers, landlords and tenants, and husbands and wives often seem mismatched. But assisting a party who appears to be in the weaker bargaining position would violate your neutrality. Following are some ways to level the playing field without compromising your neutrality:

✔ **Ask the apparently big bad stronger party questions that may reveal the people behind the power.** In a battle over an insurance claim, for example, the insured or injured party may view the claims examiner as the big bad insurance company. By asking the claims examiner questions about his life, you may reveal that the claims examiner is no better off (and perhaps worse off) than the insured or injured party. Here are some questions you can ask to humanize organizations:

  • How long have you worked at X Corp?

  • What are some of the most common on-the-job stressors at X Corp?

  • How much time do you spend handling claims against X Corp?

  • I imagine that your performance evaluations are based at least in part on how well you handle claims for X Corp, is that right?

✔ **Seek to understand and humanize the situation.** A claims examiner, for instance, labors under hidden constraints and serves hidden interests. Find out what those constraints and interests are so you can help the claims examiner serve those interests or escape from those constraints. You might ask the examiner, "What information would you need from the plaintiff to help you deal with his claim more effectively?"

✔ **Help the apparently "weaker" party humanize the apparently stronger party.** Encourage the two parties to share the personal or job-related interests they're attempting to serve in a joint session.

Don't make assumptions about relative bargaining power. A tenant who hasn't paid rent in three months but refuses to move out of a rental unit may have greater bargaining power than a landlord who has to hire an attorney to commence eviction proceedings.

Bridging Cross-Cultural Gaps

More conflict is caused by miscommunication than by intentional misdeeds, and miscommunication is most common among people from different cultures, particularly if they speak different languages. (The different languages may be actual languages, such as Russian and Spanish, or colloquial languages, such as production line versus boardroom language.)

The parties don't have to be raised in different countries or worship different gods to have miscommunication. A colleague of mine claims that all negotiation is cross-cultural because we're all raised in different families, each with its own attitudes toward airing and resolving disputes. You must understand each party's unique response to conflict to be able to help the parties bridge the distance created by their dispute.

Fortunately, as a master of people skills, you know that the secret to understanding a person's response to conflict is no secret at all: Ask. Assume nothing. Be curious. If a party doesn't seem receptive to a particular solution that's been offered, ask why and ask what may be more helpful. Continue the process until you hit upon a solution that's satisfactory to everyone involved.

The proper approach to mediating cross-cultural disputes varies and is subject to debate. Some mediators argue that mediating such disputes requires cultural competence — an understanding of the cultural differences between the two parties. Some clients may even inquire about your cultural competence. Certainly, a deeper understanding of the cultural differences between the parties is beneficial, and broadening your understanding of different cultures always makes you a better mediator. However, even without cultural competence, you can effectively mediate by respecting all parties, assuming nothing, and remaining open-minded.

This is particularly true in cosmopolitan areas where you're called upon to mediate among dozens of different cultures. In my own practice, I routinely see Korean, mainland Chinese, Vietnamese, Japanese, Russian, Ukrainian, Israeli, Iranian, Western European, South African, Australian, New Zealand, East Indian, Mexican, and Central and South American nationals, to name just a few. I also see U.S. citizens of all nationalities, races, gender identities, and sexual preferences. I frankly don't know anyone who could call herself "culturally competent" to handle mediations that involve two or more of any of these individuals. Learn as much as possible about everyone, err on the side of deference and respect for differences, and ask diagnostic cultural questions if you feel you're missing something based on race, nationality, religion, or sexual preference, and you'll do fine.

I married a man with children. Steve and I were both lawyers and baby boomers. We attended similar universities and studied many of the same subjects. He's Jewish and I am Protestant. He's from the Midwest, while I'm from Southern California. Nothing, however, prepared me to negotiate the presence of his family for his open heart surgery.

When the doctor told us that my husband needed open heart surgery, we asked, "Should the children be here?" The doctor responded by saying that if it were him, he'd want his family present. I asked my husband if he wanted his children and ex-wife present. He said, "If they want to be." I asked his ex-wife, and she said she wanted to be there if Steve wanted her there. I then called Steve's daughter, who said she wanted to be there if her mother and father wanted her there. I told my stepdaughter and her mother that Steve said he wanted them to do what they wanted to do. They repeated that they wanted to do what he wanted to do. I was at impasse.

I called my stepson, who was working for me as a legal assistant. I knew him better than any of the other family members. "What should I do?" I asked. "Everyone says they want what everybody else wants. How did your family ever make a decision about anything?" He told me that someone had to be the first to state a preference and that person may as well be me. He asked me what *I* wanted. "I want everyone to be here," I replied. "Then call and tell everyone that," he said, which is what I did, and they all came.

My husband's conflict resolution style is not Jewish or Midwestern. It's not male or lawyerish. It's a style that developed in his family over the course of decades, and I couldn't possibly intuit it. I had to *ask*. Whenever you encounter behavior that's unfamiliar, avoid the temptation to assume the motivation behind it. If you really want to know, ask.

Chapter 12

Problem-Solving Like a Pro

. . . .

In This Chapter

▶ Figuring out the real problems at the heart of a dispute

▶ Using various methods to find solutions

▶ Untangling a dispute to isolate overlooked factors

▶ Helping the parties build a bridge

▶ Assigning a monetary value to something priceless

▶ Packaging issues to help the parties move forward

. . . .

*T*he old saying "It's better to be happy than to be right" isn't completely true. After all, everyone should strive for the truth. But when parties are engaged in a lose-lose dispute over a difference of opinion, they're usually better off seeking a mutually satisfactory solution than trying to prove who's right and who's wrong. Seeking a common solution requires problem-solving strategies and skills, an analytical approach to break down complex issues into simpler problems, and a creative mind to identify potential solutions.

In this chapter, I explain problem-solving methods that enable you to help the parties identify the real issues at the center of their dispute, to brainstorm solutions, and to settle on solutions that satisfy both parties' interests.

Defining and Prioritizing Problems

Rarely does a dispute revolve around a single problem. Ask one of the disputants to define the problem and you'll likely hear a 15-minute rant about everything the other party did wrong — failed to uphold his end of the agreement; didn't return phone calls or offer an explanation or apology; was consistently unreliable, rude, and disrespectful; and so on. And that list represents only what the party can rattle off from the top of his head.

This problem avalanche can make beginners and intermediate mediators feel overwhelmed. The parties don't have a clear idea of how to solve their problems because they often can't differentiate between their emotional response to a perceived slight and the conflict at the heart of the dispute. So the first steps in problem-solving are to define and prioritize the problems while acknowledging and empathizing with all parties' emotional reactions to the conflict itself. The following sections lead you through the process of helping the parties define and prioritize their mutual problems.

Engaging the parties in storytelling

After the parties introduce themselves and exchange pleasantries, and after you review the ground rules for the mediation, have each complainant and thereafter each respondent tell her story in all its texture, dimension, and complexity. As each party relates her account of what led up to and caused the conflict, do the following:

- ✔ Take notes.
- ✔ Tune in to the nonverbal expressions of the parties who are listening. If they're grimacing, shaking their heads, sighing loudly, or being disrespectful in any way, remind them of their agreement to listen respectfully without ridiculing or dismissing what the other person says.

After each person finishes telling her story, ask open-ended questions to fully flesh out and clarify her account. (See Chapter 7 for details about asking open-ended questions.) Give the other parties the opportunity to ask questions, as well, but discourage argument over details, reminding all parties that they'll be entitled to tell their story in an atmosphere of mutual attention and respect.

Repeat the process for each party, allowing them to tell their version of events. If the parties are represented by attorneys, the attorneys often prohibit their clients from speaking and give the facts of the dispute themselves. Because the parties describing the dispute themselves is so much more effective, consider discussing ways that the attorneys' need to protect their clients can be met other than by sidelining them. Most attorneys feel comfortable with a question-and-answer process as long as they can object to their client answering any given question. You, of course, are the best person to lead a client through her story.

Summarizing the narrative

After both parties tell their stories and answer questions, retell the story in your own words in a way that harmonizes the similarities and starkly contrasts the differences between the two accounts. As you retell the story, do the following:

 ✔ Check back with the parties frequently to be sure you haven't misstated or omitted anything.

 ✔ Jot down problems as the parties identify them. Problems may be actual issues, differences of opinion over specific incidents, or unmet needs.

Write a list of problems on a white board or a large sheet of paper so both parties can see the list. Ask the parties whether you've omitted any problems, and add them to the list as directed by the parties. Make sure the list is comprehensive. Otherwise, you may end up with a solution that fails to address a key issue, which often results in impasse or the parties' entry into a grudging compromise that creates an unsustainable agreement.

Prioritizing the problems

After the parties develop a comprehensive list of problems, lead them through the process of ranking the problems from most to least important so they can deal with each problem in turn instead of trying to tackle them all at once.

Prioritizing issues is a judgment call. Sometimes, starting with easier issues is the best approach because you can build on the parties' success to solve bigger problems. In other situations, you may want to start with the most difficult issue, especially if the resolution of a certain issue is a prerequisite to solving other problems.

In pure money cases, consider encouraging the parties to defer issues such as payment plans and the due date for the first payment. The parties invest a lot of time and emotional energy to reach an agreement, and you don't want them to throw all that hard work away simply because they disagree over the timing of payments.

A potential drawback of deferring the discussion of payment issues is that the parties may express anger at you for doing so. Why? For three reasons:

 ✔ They're tired and they want closure.

 ✔ They feel blind-sided. The plaintiff may think he'll receive the payment immediately in one lump sum, whereas the defendant may think he'll pay it over time and perhaps not owe a payment for several weeks.

 ✔ They feel betrayed. If they demanded clarity of terms before agreeing to a settlement, but you responded by saying, "Let's deal with that issue after we reach agreement on a number," they may feel duped now that you're springing new terms on them. Explain why you deferred payment issues.

If the parties are angry, you may be able to defuse that anger by saying something like this:

I thought you might never reach agreement if we started talking timing issues before we had an agreement in principle on the substantive issues. I know it's disappointing to have to deal with these ancillary issues now, but we've demonstrated our ability to tackle the toughest disputes, so let's dig in together and solve these in the same manner.

Payment terms and timing then become an entirely new negotiation, and if the parties still harbor resentment about having to continue negotiations, they often try to take out their frustration on their opponent by being even more intractable. This is where your people skills come in (see Chapter 11). The devil is often in the details, and the details give the parties the opportunity to save the face they lost in the negotiation of the settlement amount.

To help the parties navigate lost face and buyer's remorse, try the following:

- ✔ Acknowledge how hard all parties have worked to reach a deal and how much everyone gave up to do so.

- ✔ Normalize a party's attempt to carve an ounce of flesh out of the final details in an effort to save face — not as an opportunity to demonize the opposition again.

- ✔ Let the parties know that you understand their feelings and, if possible, let them share those feelings with each other without acting them out. Sharing is often marked by the words "I feel," and acting out is often marked by "You did," sometimes punctuated with shouting or sarcasm. Ask the party who's creating impasse to explain his reasoning to the other party using words instead of emotional responses. Advise the other party to listen attentively, restate what his opponent has said, indicate that he understands it, and then explain what's motivating his request.

Discovering and Inventing Solutions

Most problems have numerous solutions. When people collaborate they can solve nearly any problem imaginable. All they need is the creativity to discover a viable solution and resources to execute it. Collaboration provides both.

The following sections present various ways to come up with creative solutions to meet each party's needs.

Negotiation itself is an effective problem-solving tool, especially when the problem is the parties' inability to divide a fixed mediation pie. So don't overlook negotiating strategies, including framing, anchoring, and logrolling, as I discuss in Chapter 7, and presenting reasons for the parties' demands and offers, as I discuss in Chapter 8. Check each item off the list as the negotiation proceeds. Although these negotiating strategies may not produce the desired outcome, the failure to engage in any one of them has the potential to undermine the entire effort by neglecting a party's concern or simply failing to pursue all available resolution pathways.

Probing problems for solutions

You can often discover a solution by digging deeper into a problem. For example, suppose a person who feels that her employer unjustly terminated her employment complains that she can't find a job. Upon further discussion, you discover that she's had several offers, but because she doesn't have transportation to and from work, she can't accept the offers. The problem suddenly shifts from not being able to find a job to not having transportation, and with the change in problem comes a change in solution. The solution now requires the parties to brainstorm the transportation problem, which can be solved by earmarking some of the settlement funds for the purchase of a used car, finding suitable public transportation, carpooling, telecommuting, or a combination of these solutions.

As the parties describe their problems, ask questions to find out what the underlying problems are. These underlying problems may offer clues that lead to additional solutions.

Crafting solutions using each party's social capital

Social capital is the intrinsic and intangible value of the parties' professional and social relationships, as well as their education, skills, and talents. Few people in conflict consider their own or their bargaining partner's social capital as the means for making a deal, but this social capital can significantly expand the available options beyond a pure-money solution.

To assess the parties' social capital, ask open-ended questions about what they do, where they work, which schools they've attended, what their hobbies and interests and family connections are, and so on. As you converse with people about their lives, you often uncover hidden gems of social capital that may include potential educational opportunities, job leads, unique skills and training, family businesses, and network connections. Any of these intangible assets may be something that one party needs and the other can give at little or no cost.

Social capital is often very useful in resolving employment disputes, especially when the parties' estimates of damages are impossible to bridge, as is often the case in alleged job discrimination. A dispute between an employer and an employee can become so bitter that re-employment isn't an option.

But the employer often has social capital that can substantially benefit the former employee and resolve the conflict.

An employer of a sheet metal worker, for instance, likely knows other employers in his industry that may need the services of just such a skilled worker. The employer may also be aware of training programs that can transform the worker's sheet metal experience into a skill that's in greater demand. The employer may be able and willing to make introductions or even procure special favors for the employee, such as allowing the employee to audit a retraining course offered by one of the employer's acquaintances.

In this era of growing social and commercial online networks, don't overlook the value of online networks and the relationships they contain as potential sources of added value to one or both parties.

A party may try to use his social capital to threaten or bully the other party. For example, he may say something like, "You'll never work in this town again!" How you deal with these bullying tactics is a judgment call. Personally, I don't tolerate them, but some mediators have a hands-off policy and let the parties hash it out. See Chapter 9 for guidance on how to deal with bullying and other tactics that are counterproductive to resolution.

Brainstorming solutions

Old-school brainstorming is a great way to come up with a list of possible solutions. Your job is to engage the parties in performing a preliminary analysis of each proposed solution to see how realistic and acceptable it's likely to be. Take the following steps to facilitate a problem-solving brainstorming session:

1. **Encourage the parties to suggest any solutions that pop into their heads.**

   Don't allow any analysis or criticism of these suggested solutions at this point because doing so can stifle creativity. Save the analysis for later. Write everything down on a white board or a large piece of paper (giant Post-it notepads that rest on inexpensive easels are very useful for this task).

2. **As the parties suggest solutions, jot them down.**

   If the parties are completely at a loss, feel free to suggest potential solutions. Some people need the brainstorming well primed to get their own creative juices flowing. Allow your own suggestions to be shot down with grace and good humor, modeling best brainstorming practices for the participants.

3. **Ask diagnostic questions to determine the viability of each proposed solution.**

Questions should elicit the following information:

- The proposal's pros and cons

- How the parties envision the proposal playing out

- Whether the other side is likely to be satisfied and, if not, why

- Whether any stakeholders whose permission is needed to approve any given proposal are absent

- Whether hidden constraints are tying the hands of any of the disputants

- Whether any concealed interests must be dealt with to implement any of the suggested solutions

   4. Cross unworkable or unacceptable solutions off the list.

Discovering solutions by searching for value

If you engage the parties in a search for value, you often help them discover creative solutions to their problems. *Value* is anything a party cares strongly enough about in the mediation process or outcome to change his mind about the parties' ability to solve their dispute:

- ✔ **Value in the process:** If the parties believe that the outcome was reached through a fair and equitable system, that's value. Likewise, the parties may find value in feeling good about the role they played in the process — that they acted with integrity, for example, or that they were open-minded and perhaps even generous. Some parties answer to higher authorities such as Biblical injunctions not to sue your neighbor or to seek peace wherever possible. Don't forget to explore these higher values with the parties. They often contain the key to resolution.

- ✔ **Value in the outcome:** The value of the outcome may take the form of a new business opportunity, a restored relationship, the appearance of propriety, time and money saved by avoiding litigation, an agreeable settlement sum on workable terms, an opportunity to save face, and so on.

Getting at the Heart of the Dispute

Though problem-solving often relies on inspired moments, inspiration is usually the result of *slow thinking*. Through aggressive and defensive posturing, the parties have collapsed all the factors that have contributed to the unpleasant state of affairs. Any one of these factors, often overlooked by parties and mediator alike, may be able to resolve the dispute. These factors include the following:

- **Rights:** Entitlements granted by law, custom, and agreement
- **Obligations:** Duties required by law, custom, and agreement
- **Remedies:** Legal solutions available in adversarial proceedings
- **Issues:** Questions or topics that give rise to disputes
- **Positions:** Opinions regarding an issue
- **Interests:** Needs, desires, fears, preferences, priorities, beliefs, and motivations for the positions that people take
- **Values:** Beliefs and principles that govern a person's behavior and choices
- **Identity:** Characteristics that define a person, including groups the person feels she belongs to, such as Christian, Democrat, or baby boomer
- **Power:** The need to win or at least feel that the outcome is fair

By carefully unpacking these issues from the tangled mess the dispute has become, you can often help the parties get to the heart of the matter, overcome obstacles that prevent them from moving forward, and begin to recognize possible solutions.

Think of a dispute as a tangled ball of different-colored string. Untangling it may seem overwhelming until you patiently begin working on, say, the green piece. After you manage to extract that thread, you may discover that it represents one of the party's legal rights or obligations in which neither party has an interest. Or you may strike it rich on the first try and identify the one interest that both parties are most concerned about.

Parties often get so tangled up in the various factors that contribute to their dispute that they lose sight of what really matters. In the following sections, I explain how you can better grasp what's going on so you're better able to help the parties extricate themselves from their entanglement and begin to see the problems clearly, to recognize solutions, and to overcome barriers to progress.

Exploring rights, obligations, remedies, issues, positions, and interests

Parties in dispute are often unaware of all the issues that have turned a conflict over scarce resources, pride, or identity into an active dispute. A party may be aware of his legal right to receive what the other party promised under their contract but totally unaware of his own obligations under that contract, such as his duty to mitigate any loss caused by the other party's breach. A plaintiff may be aware of the remedies to which he's entitled but unaware of legal limits on those remedies. Some people are so focused on their legal rights that they forget to ask themselves whether the enforcement of those rights would best serve their interests.

When a party is stuck on a single issue, one of the best solutions is to help him explore his rights and obligations, the available remedies for the perceived assault on his rights or over-estimation of his obligations, the legal restrictions on the available remedies, the issues being contested, each party's position on those issues, and whether the party is acting in his own best interest.

A party who takes a strong position on an issue relating to his rights sometimes forgets that his interests may be better served if he stopped fighting about the issues and concentrated on serving his interests instead.

Exploring values, identity, and power

When a party negotiates against her own interests, she usually places more importance on values, identity, and power than on her own narrow and immediate self-interest. This often occurs in politics when people vote against policies that would actually benefit them. Many people who can't afford health insurance or healthcare, for instance, prefer to remain uninsured and forgo healthcare than to be required to participate in a government-sponsored program.

In a mediation, basing decisions on values, identity, and power often leads to gridlock, but only if the mediator fails to ascertain and help the parties appreciate what's really standing in the way of resolution. Frequently, breaking the gridlock is simply a matter of letting a party know what she's doing and its effect — undermining her own interests. In other cases, focusing on values or identity creates an entirely new path to resolution.

Keeping an open mind to what motivates a party

As a mediator, don't assume what a party's motivation is or let other participants make that assumption. Until someone tells you what he's thinking, why he wants what he's seeking, or why he's unalterably opposed to satisfying any request made by his adversary, you don't know anything useful that may help the parties resolve their dispute.

A man seeking monetary damages for injuries he suffered in a traffic accident may be trying to get reimbursed for his out-of-pocket expenses, hoping to strike it rich, or asking for compensation because he knows of no other way a corporation can be held accountable. A husband may be suing a physician or hospital for the death of his spouse because he's never gotten an adequate explanation for why she died. A wife could be fighting over the custody of her children solely to make her former husband's life miserable because of his infidelities.

When helping people find the heart of their dispute, keep a mental checklist of what you learn about each party's positions, interests, constraints, rights, obligations, remedies, values, and identity. Also be prepared to help people express what they're really fighting about when they irrationally reject a reasonable, even generous, offer.

If the parties are stuck on money, explore their intangible interests. If they're stuck on their legal rights, explore tangible benefits that may not be available as remedies in litigation. If emotions seem to be preventing a party from making a pragmatic decision, explore the power or identity issues that may need resolution. The bottom line is to never give up and to make sure you explore every possible avenue of potential value or impasse, even if it seems unlikely to resolve the problem. Patience and persistence always pay off.

Building a Golden Bridge

Have you ever experienced a situation in which you were so focused on getting what you want that you completely lost the capacity to think rationally? Perhaps you tried for two hours to convince someone to come over to your place when you could've met the person at his place in 15 minutes. You wasted an hour and 45 minutes of your life because the other person took a hard-line position and you responded in kind.

When you're the mediator and the parties are stuck, you can help them build a *golden bridge* — instead of asking the party to move where she doesn't want to go, you begin at the point where she is right now and help her build a bridge that will take her where she's willing to end up. A golden bridge helps the parties avoid the waste and frustration created by posturing, positioning, and arguing about matters that may not even be the point.

Following are techniques to build a golden bridge:

- ✔ Start where the most recalcitrant party is.

- ✔ Bring the other party over.

- ✔ Build on the recalcitrant party's ideas but don't necessarily accept them.

- ✔ Select the most constructive proposals and move them in a direction that can benefit both parties. You may say something like, "Building on your idea, what if we. . . ."

- Ask for constructive feedback from one or both parties.
- Ask about the interests that the suggested approach fails to satisfy and in what ways it can be improved.
- Offer more than one choice.
- Continue asking diagnostic questions to ascertain how the proposal toward which you're building the bridge may more effectively satisfy unserved interests.
- Suggest that the parties make hypothetical offers, such as, "If John is willing to put $25,000 on the table, what would you be willing to lower your demand to?"

In building a golden bridge, you help the parties discover their own solutions and craft an agreement that satisfies them both. If one of the parties is stuck in a position, you walk right on over to that position and start building.

Suppose one party from a divorced couple takes the position that "I'll never let her take the kids for more than two weeks at a time, so her grand plan to take them to Europe for a month this summer is out of the question." You can help the parties start building their golden bridge right from the former husband's flat-out refusal:

1. **Start where Dad is but move the ball forward by reframing the negative in positive terms:**

   "So you're offering Mom two weeks with the kids this summer, right? That's good."

2. **Bring the other party (Mom, in this example) over to Dad's side of the bridge:**

   "Mom, you'd like to have at least two weeks with the kids this summer, right?"

3. **Ask the other party for constructive feedback:**

   "So, Mom, if two weeks in Europe this summer were the only option, would it be possible?"

   This open-ended question probes for Mom's interests and needs, both logistic and intangible. Mom may respond with something like this:

   "It's possible, of course it's possible, but the only reason I can afford the trip is because I have a week of business meetings in Milan. The kids want to see their grandmother in London, and our teenager, Jill, is dying to spend some time in Paris because she's thinking of doing a semester abroad there for her junior year of college. She was hoping to have at least a week there before we move on to London."

4. **Ask diagnostic questions and call for additional proposals:**

"Dad, what do you think about Jill's desire to spend a week in Paris? Can you think of a way that Mom and the kids could spend time with Grandma in London and do the Paris week as well?"

Dad may reply with something like the following:

"Why doesn't Mom leave the kids with her mother in London while she's in Milan? Then they can spend the following week in Paris."

This conversation can go in any number of directions. If expense turns out to be the real problem, Dad may offer to underwrite some of the trip later in the summer, after Mom's business trip. Or Mom may be able to convince her mother to take the kids for a week in London and then meet them in Paris.

Or, if the logistical problem-solving process gets too complicated, Dad may give up his "my way or the highway" position and agree to a third week or even a fourth. Nobody has questioned Dad about why he's adamant that the kids shouldn't be gone for an entire month. If his feelings aren't simply spite, you can invoke an entire problem-solving process for whatever obstacles Dad believes make Mom's proposal a nonstarter.

This kind of bridge-building also allows the recalcitrant party to save face. As he engages in brainstorming, he can quietly let go of his hard-line position as it slowly slips away in the process of finding solutions to logistical problems. This process is slow but sure as you guide the parties step-by-step across the bridge they build as their own.

Dealing with the Irrationality of Monetary Solutions

Although a monetary value may seem like an objective measure of something's value, people don't spend money objectively or rationally. Buyers tend to be frugal in spending the dollars they earn, for example, and more frivolous in spending dollars they've won or received as gifts. While you can find a good pair of shoes for under $100, some people routinely spend in excess of $1,000 for a designer brand. While some people eke out a living on $20,000 a year, others drop that much during an evening in Vegas.

Particularly when it's used to satisfy a person's desire for justice, money can and does convey social and psychological meaning. For example, the voluntary payment of money may demonstrate accountability, sympathy, or fulfillment of an obligation. Awarding punitive damages to victims shows them that the person or institution that has caused them harm has literally had to pay for its wrongdoing.

One of your primary jobs as a mediator is to help the parties understand the meaning of money in the context of the dispute. The following sections present a few techniques for overcoming the irrationality of monetary solutions and placing a price tag on something that's priceless.

Giving a reason for a demand or offer

Numbers sometimes feel as if they're the only objective reality in a universe of uncertainty and ambiguity. But numbers — particularly in dollars, euros, yen, or pounds — have unfathomable subjective meanings to everyone. A great mediator learns what those meanings are (or aids the parties in learning them from each other) and then assists the parties in using those "money meanings" to resolve disputes in a manner the parties accept as being just.

To give money meaning, the parties, with the aid of the mediator, need to provide reasons for every demand, every offer, every counteroffer, and every threat to walk away from the bargaining table.

Reason-giving is especially important when a party changes position. In the absence of a new rationale for an increased demand or decreased offer, the parties may react violently to a perceived injustice. Asking one party to alter his position for no reason at all violates the human sense of fairness. Most people fill the vacuum with their own imaginings, which usually leads to demonizing the position-changer and results in impasse.

 When a party makes an offer or demand or changes position, help the party think up as many reasons as possible to justify the demand or offer, but share only the top one or two reasons with the other party so you have a couple more reasons in reserve, just in case you need them.

How to successfully cut in line

In experiments on reason-giving, researchers have found that people are far more likely to accommodate someone if given a reason to do so, even if the reason makes no sense whatsoever. In one experiment, students were asked to cut in line at a copy shop. One group was instructed to give no reason. Another was told to give a good reason ("I'm late for class."). The last group was directed to give an irrational reason ("Because I need to.").

Unsurprisingly, those who provided no rationale at all were the least successful — only 60 percent of their requests were granted. Those who presented a logical reason got what they wanted 94 percent of the time. Here's the surprise: The students who presented a meaningless rationale racked up a 93 percent success rate, only 1 percent less than their logical peers.

The following sections explain how to discover the reason behind an offer, demand, or change in position and how to most effectively present that reason.

Finding the reason for a number

When a party presents a demand or offer, ask questions to determine how the party came up with that number. If a demand seems excessive, ask the party what she plans to do with that money. How will she use it to right the perceived wrong? Why does she feel she's entitled to that amount? If she were the party to whom that demand or offer was made, how would she respond to it? If an offer seems far too low, ask how the person calculated that offer. Is it based on what she can afford to pay, what she thinks the other party deserves, or something else entirely?

Don't try to assign a monetary value to human life, because the universal tendency is to view any attempt to do so as crass, coldhearted, or sinister. Instead, make the money talk. The money should say, "We're sorry for your loss, we acknowledge our responsibility for the harm, and we'll do everything possible to keep it from happening again."

Mastering different reason-giving styles

People fail to persuade when they talk past each other by using different *reasoning styles:*

- ✔ **Conventions:** These are the rules your mother and grade school teachers taught you. Don't be a tattletale. Share with your sister. Don't whine. Say "thank you" to the nice man for giving you an extra dollop of ice cream.

- ✔ **Stories:** This is what attorneys do for a living. They tell stories, read stories, make up stories, listen to stories, and then compare stories to determine whether the same rules of law that apply to one story should apply to the other.

- ✔ **Codes:** These are "high-level" conventions — the rules courts follow to resolve disputes. For example, in contract law, the code states that all real estate transactions must be in writing.

- ✔ **Technical accounts:** These are the equivalent of expert testimony; for example, an explanation of what blowing a .01 on a breathalyzer means.

If one person gives a technical account (the DNA samples found at the murder scene matched those of O.J. Simpson) and the other a convention (if the glove don't fit, you must acquit), the chances that a jury will weigh the two arguments equally are remote. They're apples and oranges. People simply pick the type of reasoning they're more likely to "get."

Look for the common signs of failure to persuade. The unconvinced person rolls her eyes, taps her foot, yawns, ignores what's being said, excuses herself, or walks away. When this happens in a mediation, take a deep breath, give yourself a moment to reflect, and ask yourself whether the parties are talking past each other. Then consider changing reasoning styles. As all mediators eventually discover, the failure of a single argument is never enough to sink a mediation. If the first reason doesn't work, encourage the person to try another reason of a different type.

Defusing the anger and discomfort caused by pricing the priceless

When putting a price tag on something that's priceless, such as a person's health and wellbeing or the life of a loved one, start by acknowledging the impossibility of the task. Admit the inadequacy of monetary compensation to the bereaved parents. Acknowledge that the parents would give everything they have if their child could be returned to them.

Point out, however, that the justice system can't perform miracles. It can't undo the harm that's been done. It can only try to deliver some form of justice, and the only remedy the law provides is the payment of money by the responsible party.

 A monetary award has no objective equivalent in such situations, but you can make the award seem more acceptable to the recipient by explaining its value in terms of accountability and perhaps helping to prevent a similar loss to someone else in the future. If a defendant is reluctant to pay damages because he sees it as an admission of guilt when he feels he has done no wrong, consider exploring with that party what it will mean to him if a jury finds him liable for wrongdoing. The jury verdict won't change the facts as he knows them — that he's innocent of wrongdoing. The same is true with the settlement of the case. Settlement doesn't mean he's in the wrong; it simply means that a trial is not worth the time, stress, and expense to possibly suffer an unjust verdict.

Pricing the priceless

Often, you may overcome a party's reluctance to place a price on something that's priceless by giving a reason, even if it's not a very good reason, for your estimate. (See Chapter 6 for details about the power of giving a reason.) Lawyers who benchmark the value of a life have hundreds of thousands of metrics they use to support pretty much any number they choose. Here are just a few:

✔ People suffering from impaired mental health such as mood and anxiety disorders earn at least 40 percent less every year than people in good mental health. Using that as an indicator and Mr. and Mrs. Toponah's joint income of $100,000 per year before their son's death, both stand to lose as much as $40,000 a year for the remainder of their working lives (35 years) for a total of $1.4 million.

✔ Raising a child through college in the United States costs approximately $1.1 million for parents. This is the value Americans place on a single child and only for that child's first 21 to 22 years. The Andersons have been deprived of their child for the remainder of their lives — the next 60 or 70 years. If you apply the $1.1 million value to the Anderson's lifetime loss, the most minimal damage award a jury should bring back is at least $3.3 million.

✔ Art appraisers would have no trouble telling you that had Mrs. Jones been carrying a Picasso instead of her priceless six-year old in her car, she would have been damaged in the sum of more than $100 million. Isn't Jonah's life worth as much as an old oil painting on cracked canvas?

✔ The average American household has approximately $24,000 in discretionary income every year. The Andersons would gladly pay all of that income to have their child back for the remainder of their lives, which is approximately an additional 65 years or $1.65 million.

When one or both parties complain that the other is trying to monetize something that money can't buy, help them move past impasse by talking about what money means and how it's used. People save money for retirement, for instance, to live comfortably in old age. Children also help ensure comfort in old age. The mother whose child has died because of someone else's negligence will be more reliant in her old age on money than on family. The yearly cost of residing in an assisted living facility as opposed to living with family in one's elderly years (which can be as many as 10 to 15 years) can run as high as $48,000 a year, or between $480,000 and $720,00 over the course of a person's final years, and that's just at life's end. Another way to assign a dollar value to the loss of something that's priceless is to consider the payment by the negligent party as a way to establish a standard of care in the community. Rationales for this measure of damages include the following:

✔ The sum the defendant would be required to spend to train its drivers better or make its cars safer or to test for contaminants in the food it packages.

✔ The sum the defendant would have had to spend to put up railings on curves in mountain roads.

Bundling and Unbundling Issues

You can often help parties solve their mutual problems by bundling or unbundling issues. In the following sections, I provide guidance on how to identify situations in which bundling or unbundling may help the parties move forward and how to apply these strategies.

Creating unexpected benefits with a package deal

You may be able to create unexpected benefits by helping the parties explore package deals that address several unrelated issues. Some disputes, including the following, lend themselves to package deals and global settlements better than others:

- Disputes between parties with multiple contracts spanning several months or years.

- In personal injury cases, where insurance carriers are faced with limited coverage for multiple claimants. A *global settlement mediation* enables the insurance carrier to offer claimants the opportunity to settle their claim within policy limits. This shifts the dispute so that it's no longer between the insurance carrier and each claimant but is now a dispute among the claimants who are fighting one another for the fixed mediation pie of a single policy.

The parties can build trades into larger packages that satisfy both parties' interests, and they can do so in two ways:

- **Incrementally:** By adding smaller trades into an increasingly large package.

- **Jigsaw approach:** By assembling already-complex trades, each of which is quite substantial in its own right.

Maximizing win-win resolutions by unbundling issues

Dispute resolution rarely ends in the resolution of a single issue. When money's involved, for example, the dispute is never solely about price. It's also about terms — when and how payments are to be made, penalties for nonpayment, and so on. Problems often arise when parties attempt to resolve all issues at the same time. When this occurs, you can often get the parties moving forward again by unbundling the issues.

For example, suppose two girls want the same orange. Mom asks each girl why she wants the orange. The first explains that she wants the peel to make candied orange peels. The second explains that she wants the juice. Mom has successfully unbundled the one issue (disagreement over who gets the orange) to create two separate issues (who gets the peel and who gets the juice). Each girl receives what she wants.

Emotional issues are often similar to this scenario. One party may refuse to budge from a $20,000 demand against a moving company for damage done to his furniture because he feels that the moving company treated him disrespectfully when he called to complain. The issue of disrespect prevents the parties from resolving the payment issue. By unbundling the issues and having the parties resolve them separately, perhaps resolving the issue of the indignity caused by the rude treatment first, the parties are more likely to overcome the obstacle that's getting in the way of resolving the payment issue.

Delivering two lousy offers

Sophisticated disputants often present two offers, equally beneficial to themselves, simultaneously as an either/or choice. This puts the other party in the undesirable position of choosing between two equally bad offers instead of making a counter to a single offer.

Savvy offerees who recognize this ploy generally choose one of the two offers and counter it, holding the other offer in reserve so they can commence an entirely different negotiation in the event that the first one fails to satisfy them. If the offeree isn't so savvy and is angered at having been given two offers equally beneficial to the offerer, you have two choices, depending on your mediation philosophy (whether to coach the parties or not):

✔ **Help the offeree strategize.** If your approach allows you to coach the parties, suggest that the offeree choose one of the two offers to respond to and hold the other offer in reserve.

✔ **Ask questions to reveal the source of the anger.** As a transformative mediator, you may simply ask questions about the source of the anger and then let the dispute play out in a manner that doesn't erupt into name calling, door slamming, or termination of the process.

Chapter 13

Breaking through Impasse

*I*mpasse occurs when neither party is willing to compromise any further on an issue. When parties reach impasse, they're likely to regard it as the end of negotiations. They may tell themselves that they tried their best and tell each other, "I'll see you in court!" As a mediator, however, you know this is just the beginning of negotiations. This is where you thrive.

Many techniques for breaking through impasse are fundamental negotiating skills — asking diagnostic questions, anchoring, framing, reframing, pitching offers and counteroffers, bracketing, making concessions, and asking for reciprocity. But you need to know how to apply these skills in the context of impasse. This chapter explains how.

To help you navigate this chapter, the following table lists various reasons for impasse and the sections in which I address those situations. That way you can quickly find information for the type of impasse you may be dealing with.

Reason for Impasse	See This Section
Not sure	"Asking Diagnostic Questions"
One or both parties are overly optimistic about the potential outcome of litigation	"Using a Decision Tree or Cost-Benefit Analysis"
One or both parties' perception or understanding is getting in the way	"Reframing to Readjust the Parties' Perspective"
The gap between what one party offers and the other is willing to accept seems insurmountable	"Reaching Compromise on Nonnegotiable Demands and Offers" and "Negotiating concessions with logrolling"
One party is bluffing or makes an exaggerated claim	"Calling a bluff with a contingent concession"

Asking Diagnostic Questions

To break through impasse, you must first ask each party diagnostic questions. Pretend that the parties are from Mars. Like hypothetical Martians, the parties are a complete and utter mystery to you until you find out more about them, their motivations, and the reasons underlying their dispute. You must ask questions to determine what they want and need, who they're afraid of, why they're so angry, how they got into this mess in the first place, where they're hoping the mediation leads them, what their preferred resolutions are, whether they'd be open to other solutions, and so on. *Diagnostic questions* extract all this valuable information from the parties so that you can begin to consider solutions that serve each party's interests and address each party's concerns.

Before looking at the questions, however, work through this exercise to experience the difference between powerful questions and the weak questions that most people, even experienced attorneys and mediators, typically ask:

> A man walks into a bar. The bartender pulls out a gun and points it at the man. The man thanks the bartender and leaves the bar.

What the heck happened here?

Most people try to figure out what happened by asking weak, *closed-ended questions* — yes/no questions that begin with "Did he" or "Was he" or "Might he have been." Here are some of the weak, closed-ended questions that partners in major national law firms, film studio executives, and managers of Fortune 500 companies have asked when performing this exercise:

✔ Did the bartender know the man? No.

✔ Did the man threaten the bartender? No.

✔ Did the man ask the bartender a question? Yes.

✔ Was the bartender afraid? No.

✔ Did the question make the bartender pull out a gun? Yes.

✔ Was the question whether the bartender had money in the cash register? No.

✔ Did the man match the description of a wanted criminal? No.

✔ Did the man look disturbed or angry? No.

✔ Did someone else warn the bartender that the man was about to rob him? No.

These questions assume the answer, extract no useful information, and leave the interrogator flustered. On the other hand, *open-ended questions* reveal additional details, including factors that motivate the parties to behave as they do. These are the same kind of open-ended questions all journalists are taught to ask in their first day of class — who, what, when, where, why, and how:

> Why did the bartender pull out a gun?
>
> Because the man who walked up to him had a bad case of hiccups.

> What did the man with the hiccups say to the bartender?
>
> He asked the bartender for a glass of water.

> Why did the bartender pull out the gun instead?
>
> Because the bartender believed that frightening people was a more effective way to cure hiccups.

> Why did the man thank the bartender?
>
> Because the gun ploy worked. The man's hiccups were cured.

As you can see, these open-ended diagnostic questions are much more effective in eliciting useful information about what each person was thinking and what motivated his actions. Master mediators begin the problem-solving process by asking diagnostic questions, and they keep on asking them until the parties run out of answers. Unfortunately, only about 7 percent of all negotiators ask diagnostic questions.

In mediation, you're working with individuals whose motivations may appear obvious on the surface but whose thinking is idiosyncratic, unpredictable, and often downright peculiar. You can't read minds, but you can ask questions. Ask probing, diagnostic questions to gather the information and insight you need to break impasse.

The following sections explain the four most powerful diagnostic questions that master mediators ask to break negotiation impasse.

Why?

A key rule for trial lawyers is to never ask *Why?* unless you already know the answer, because if you don't know, the person you're questioning may provide an answer that undermines your case. As a mediator, however, you get to be a rule-breaker. *Why?* is the first and perhaps most important question you need to ask. It's a question you can never ask too often, but it's asked far too seldom.

An attorney typically assumes she knows why her client wants to sue — money. And for an attorney who works in the world of rights and remedies, that assumption is fine.

For mediators, however, that same assumption is toxic. People don't really go to lawyers or mediators to get money. It's not an *economic* system. It's the *justice* system. People seek justice when they believe they've been wronged. Perhaps they want money, but they usually want more than that — to express outrage, get revenge, teach wrongdoers a lesson, or make sure that nobody else suffers this same injustice. Asking *Why?* helps you determine what the parties really want.

Give clients what they really need to make a final decision. When the time comes to settle a case, clients want to know that

- ✔ They're not being taken advantage of.
- ✔ They're not getting less than the defendant is willing to pay or paying more than the plaintiff would accept.
- ✔ They're making the decision. (Nobody's holding a gun to their head.)

Any one of these items can be a deal-breaker. Asking *Why?* is one of the best ways to diagnose which of these potential deal-breakers, if any, are influencing the parties.

Here's an example of a case in which the question *Why?* revealed the real reason why the person was suing and broke impasse:

Q. "Why do you want at least six figures in settlement of your malpractice suit against the dialysis center where your wife died?"

A. "Because I told my attorney when I hired him that I'd read in the paper about a veterinarian who paid $25,000 for the death of a dog. That's what the dialysis center offered me not to file suit. A dog! If the insurance carrier pays anything less than $100,000, they'll be treating my wife no better than a dog."

Q. "Why will $100,000 make you feel like justice has been done, though? Why do you envision yourself being satisfied with that figure?"

A. "Well, I'd like to make myself a photo studio. I used to be a professional photographer, but that was 40 years ago. Now that I'm retired and a widow, I need something productive to do. After paying attorneys' fees and expenses, I'd receive only $57,000, and I'm told that I'll have to pay taxes on that, so it'll all boil down to the price of that dog — $25,000 in my pocket. That's the absolute minimum amount I'd need to set up my photo studio. It may also allow me to contribute to my granddaughter's university fees. If I can't help her out with tuition, I'm afraid she's going to drop out."

After I learned what this man wanted to do with his settlement, we made numerous calculations to determine whether he could achieve his desires for less. But we needn't have bothered. Something about his concern for his granddaughter and his plans to make a better life for himself softened the insurance carrier to pay him $100,000 for his loss. She stopped feeling as though he was just trying to get money out of her pocket. His story moved her. She realized he had similar desires to her own. "I worry about my own daughter," she told me. "I had an ample college fund, but then the recession hit, my husband left me, and I had to invade her savings account to pay the mortgage or I would have lost the house."

But don't think emotion is the only path toward resolution. In what some mediators call a "pure money case" — the reimbursement of an overpayment by an insurance carrier to a physician — the two sides were stuck at a number I considered odd: $107,500 exactly. The defendant physician thought the insurance carrier (owned by doctors) was trying to chisel him. He saw no reason why he had to repay them the $250,000 they'd negligently credited to his account. He was willing to pay some of it back, but more than $50,000 seemed wrong to him.

After hours of bargaining, I pulled the insurance carrier and its attorney aside and asked, "Why $107,500 exactly?" In this case, the question *Why?* revealed one of the greatest contributors to impasse — the hidden constraint tying one of the party's hands. "We settled another case exactly like this one," said the insurance carrier. "We overpaid a lot of doctors, including some who are on our board of directors. In our settlement agreement with one of them, we promised that we wouldn't settle with anyone else for less than 43 percent of the total we overpaid. In this case, that's $107,500. We genuinely can't go under that number or we'd be in breach of contract."

"May I tell that to the plaintiff?" I asked. "I believe it will help break impasse."

Sure enough, as soon as the physician found out that a principle of basic fairness (everyone in the same situation should be treated the same) was underlying the offer, the justice issue underlying the money issue evaporated, and the case settled . . . for exactly $107,500.

What do you believe would be the best solution for everyone?

It's never too early to engage parties in the problem-solving process, but perhaps the best time is when the parties have effectively rejected every solution that's been proposed. Ask this very powerful diagnostic question:

> What do you believe would be the best solution for everyone?

This question accomplishes three goals:

- ✔ It moves the focus from the parties to the problem, removing some of the blame factor.
- ✔ It makes each party stand in the other party's shoes, switching their perspectives.
- ✔ It engages the parties in a mutual problem-solving process with the goal of developing win-win solutions.

Rex and Jane, board members of a local condominium homeowners' association (HOA), and tenants Brad and Lisa arrived at the West Hollywood Community Mediation Center one bright spring morning fighting mad.

Brad and Lisa had been bitterly complaining to the board for more than a year about their upstairs neighbors, the Coopers. The Coopers played their stereo loud and late into the night. They had two dogs who engaged in a nightly Pekinese rodeo at 3 a.m., complete with barking, thumping, and the incessant click-clacking of untrimmed nails on hardwood floors. If that wasn't enough, the Coopers' teenagers used the pool in the early morning hours after clubbing with friends. Sometimes they brought as many as a dozen of their friends back to their place to carouse, drink, and play Marco Polo at 2 a.m.

Brad and Lisa were threatening to sue the HOA if it didn't control these hijinks. The board had issued warnings but had no authorization to terminate the Coopers' tenancy for failure to abide by the rules.

I'd suggested several ways the parties might resolve the dispute, all of which they rejected. At the third hour, the parties were getting angrier and more entrenched, so I asked this one simple but powerful question:

> What do you think would be the best solution for all of the homeowners?

"Everyone who's obeying the condo rules should be able to evict anyone who isn't," Lisa offered.

"Great solution," said Rex, "but you've disobeyed the rules yourself. Just last week, the Gomez family complained that you were grilling hamburgers on your balcony. You know that's not allowed. Should I be able to evict you for that?"

As soon as the parties understood that sanctions for rule-breaking would apply to everyone, including themselves, their punitive views evaporated and they began to set reasonable limits on the board's power and reasonable sanctions for disobedience.

This dispute transitioned into a joint problem-solving session in which the parties drew up a new set of regulations. The rules provided for graduated sanctions based on the type of misconduct and number of repeat violations. Everyone at the negotiation table wanted to give violators notice of a hearing and the opportunity to explain themselves and bring their conduct into compliance. Eviction was the last resort.

When the parties left the Community Mediation Center that day, I was pleased that they'd provided the procedural due process the U.S. Constitution itself guarantees. And they had done so without my lawyerly insistence.

What could your opponent do to signal progress?

In disputes where feelings of animosity and distrust run particularly high, consider asking this question: What could [the other party] do that would be a sign of progress to you?

Asking the parties how their opponent can make a show of good faith allows them to come back down to reality and stop making demands motivated by anger and calculated to punish. The question generates clearheaded brainstorming geared to solve the mutual problem the parties' undeniably face — the expense, duration, and strain of the litigation itself.

Don't give up the fight if someone continues in a hostile vein, saying something like, "He could pay me everything I'm asking for!" or "She could dismiss her frivolous lawsuit." That's an occasion to inject a little levity. Say something like, "I'm sorry, I forgot to add the word *reasonable*. What could the other party *reasonably* do to signal his good faith and the potential for progress?"

Then be silent. Wait, wait, wait. Your patience will be rewarded. One of the parties is poised to divulge to you something that he really wants his adversary to do or say. Don't speak too quickly or you'll cut him off. If you're mediating a litigated case, remember that his attorney long ago monetized the injustice he suffered. He can barely recall what he really wanted in the first place. He's going back in time to consider how he was feeling before the dispute fossilized into a fight over dollars and cents — back when he would've been happy with an apology, or 20 percent of the profits, or something equally *reasonable*.

"They could at least offer . . . to pay my attorneys' fees, or begin the next round of negotiations in the six-figure range, or admit that they were partially at fault for the loss of my shipment of leather jackets from Hong Kong." Now you're getting somewhere.

Too many people walk out of a mediation not knowing that they're willing to accept just about the same amount of money their adversary is willing to pay. You just need to jiggle their brain cells to get them thinking.

What information does your file need to justify this payment?

When you're dealing with bureaucrats — the people who keep a corporate or public entity humming along on all cylinders — the parties are likely to reach impasse merely because the corporation's representative doesn't feel she has sufficient documentation to support the approval of a large payout. So ask:

> What information does your file need to justify this payment?

Claims representatives who work with insurance companies have told me that they need something in the file to justify a change in their original evaluation of the claim. The organization has a lot riding on that number. Claims managers or a committee of managers set *reserves* — an amount of money sufficient to pay all claims. They don't want to change that number for many reasons, not the least of which is not wanting to admit they were wrong. On the other hand, no insurance company representative wants to be caught with his pants down. If a verdict far in excess of the reserve is rendered, it's a bad day for managers and claims representatives alike. They need a good reason to bump up that number, and you need to supply it.

The same is true of the plaintiff. If the plaintiff's counsel has long been telling her that she should expect between $50,000 and $200,000 with a 70 percent chance of success, you must find and give the plaintiff information pertinent to the value of the claim or the likelihood of success that the plaintiff hasn't already considered.

A friend of mine who is in-house counsel to an insurance carrier tells me she always remembers what her dad told her as a child. All a cat wants to know is two things: Is it good for the cat or is it bad for the cat? You need to present sufficient proof that what you're proposing is good for the cat, whether that cat's the plaintiff or defendant.

Using a Decision Tree or Cost-Benefit Analysis

Parties in the middle of impasse are probably being too optimistic. They're stuck because, for months, they've had an idea in their heads that they're going to sue for, say, $500,000, and that's all they think of. They rarely consider the potential costs involved or the possibility that they may lose, even though their attorneys explain these facts of life to them over and over. They feel like they're walking away as losers if they settle for anything much less than their attorney originally suggested they may recover. To bring the parties back down to earth, present one or both parties with a decision tree, cost analysis, and/or the expected monetary value (EMV) of the possible outcomes.

Shaking the decision tree

A *decision tree* is a quick and graphic way to help clients analyze the potential costs and benefits of their choices when they're focused only on the best possible outcome. Perform a decision tree analysis with each party in separate caucus. At this stage of the mediation, your job is to bring both parties' high-flying expectations of success back down to earth by revealing the realistic merits of each party's position. If you do this in joint session, you defeat the purpose with both parties because they simply hear what supports their view one more time.

To create a decision tree, team up with each party in separate caucus and perform the following steps:

1. **Brainstorm to identify all possible outcomes.**

   Include good outcomes and bad, those that result from litigation and those that don't. Typical outcomes from litigation include winning a summary judgment motion, prevailing on any other pretrial proceeding, or "winning" through discovery (for instance, finding the "smoking gun") and obtaining a jury verdict. Of course, winning isn't always the final outcome. If enough money is at stake and the parties can afford to continue fighting, the appeals process can drag on for months or even years. Because the remedies available in court are limited, brainstorming outcomes that aren't available to the parties through litigation and trial are particularly useful chips to put on the bargaining table. Consider the status quo and any outcomes that may result from mediation.

2. **Determine the potential cost or benefit of each outcome.**

   For example, if the case goes to trial, how much money can the plaintiff expect to walk away with if she wins? How many months or years will it take? How much can she expect to pay in attorney's fees, and what chances does she have to recover those fees?

3. **For each option, jot down the likelihood that it'll occur based on your experience.**

   You may not know the chance of each outcome occurring, but you may know that the client has a 50/50 chance of winning a judgment or a 50 percent chance of recovering attorney fees. The results at trial are so uncertain that I personally would never estimate more than a 70 percent chance of winning.

4. **Draw your decision tree.**

   Start with a You Are Here box, with one line radiating out of it for each possible outcome. For each outcome, list the potential costs, benefits, and other pros and cons. Figure 13-1 shows a sample decision tree I used in a mediation between parents suing a school district about their disabled child's Individual Education Plan (IEP).

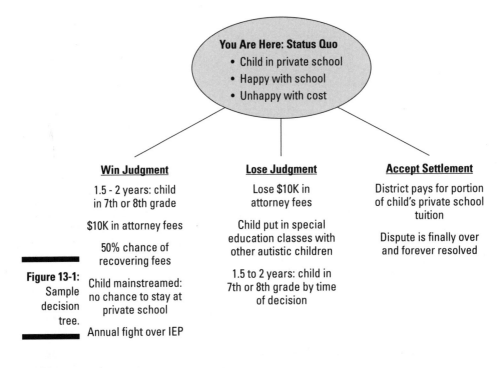

You Are Here: Status Quo
- Child in private school
- Happy with school
- Unhappy with cost

Win Judgment

1.5 - 2 years: child in 7th or 8th grade

$10K in attorney fees

50% chance of recovering fees

Child mainstreamed: no chance to stay at private school

Annual fight over IEP

Lose Judgment

Lose $10K in attorney fees

Child put in special education classes with other autistic children

1.5 to 2 years: child in 7th or 8th grade by time of decision

Accept Settlement

District pays for portion of child's private school tuition

Dispute is finally over and forever resolved

Figure 13-1: Sample decision tree.

In the case illustrated in Figure 13-1, the parents realized for the first time during mediation that "winning" wasn't something they wanted. Their child would be reevaluated and his IEP revised once a year. The parents didn't like any of the district's previous IEPs, and winning the litigation wouldn't assure them that the district's annual reevaluations would be a significant improvement over previous ones. The specter of yearly reevaluations with educational requirements the parents believed would be detrimental to their child was a major potential consequence of winning.

They also recognized that their continued fight with the school district was upsetting their 10-year-old son, who had to be evaluated and reevaluated, not only for the yearly IEP but also for court proceedings. When we built a timeline into the decision tree, the value of settling now became much more attractive than pursuing victory in the distant future.

Finally, the district's offer to underwrite a portion of the son's education in a private school wasn't a possibility under formal district rules, nor was it a possible litigation outcome, but it was an option in settlement. The settlement only required that the parents absolve the school district of its obligation to educate their son for as many years as the district was responsible for his education, which they were more than happy to do.

Walking the parties through this decision tree settled the case after a previous mediation had failed to do so. The previous mediator failed at impasse without constructing a decision tree. I believe the parties could have settled this matter much earlier and saved considerably on attorney fees had the first mediator used a decision tree.

Your job as a mediator is to help the parties consider all the upsides and downsides of going to trial and to make the most well-informed decision possible. Your job isn't to convince them to decide one way or the other.

Examining potential costs and benefits

Decision trees may become more complex and require a deeper cost-benefit analysis, especially if lots of numbers are involved. If you're working on a litigated case, each party's attorney usually has an informal decision tree in his head if not necessarily on paper. In all cases, I recommend that your cost-benefit analysis answer the following questions:

- ✔ What's the monetary value of what's in dispute, from each party's perspective? Each party may have an appraisal or at least a number and some reasoning to support its valuation.

- ✔ How much does each party stand to gain or lose in each possible outcome? Consider litigated and nonlitigated outcomes, and look at the best and worst possible outcomes, as well as everything in between.

- ✔ What's the chance of achieving each outcome in terms of a percentage?

> ✔ How much will each party spend on attorneys, expert witnesses, and other professional services to achieve each outcome?
>
> ✔ How much extra will each side spend if the other side files an appeal? Have each party monetize the cost of appeal and retrial in the event the appellant is successful on appeal.

A cost-benefit analysis with or without a decision tree provides a party with a clearer picture of what the client stands to lose or gain from each possible outcome. It enables the client to make a well-informed decision and often reveals that mediation is preferable to litigation.

Calculating expected monetary value (EMV)

Expected monetary value (EMV) is a ballpark figure that shows how much money a plaintiff can *reasonably* expect. Think of it as an average of the best- and worst-case scenarios. It accounts not only for the dollar figure assigned to each outcome but also for the likelihood of that outcome occurring. To calculate EMV, multiply the dollar value of each possible outcome by each outcome's chance of occurring (percentage), and total the results.

For example, if I bet $60 that I'll roll a die and it'll come up on the number 4, the EMV is –$40, because I have a 1 in 6 chance of winning $60 and a 5 in 6 chance of losing $60:

$$\left(\$60 \times \frac{1}{6}\right) + \left(-\$60 \times \frac{5}{6}\right) = \$10 + \left(-\$50\right) = -\$40$$

On the other hand, if I bet $60 that I'd flip a coin once and it would come up heads, I'd have a 50/50 chance of winning, so my EMV would look like this:

$$\left(\$60 \times \frac{1}{2}\right) + \left(-\$60 \times \frac{1}{2}\right) = \$30 - \$30 = \$0$$

If I had the choice of which bet to make, I'd be wise to listen to the EMVs and opt for the coin flip.

As you may expect, EMVs get more complicated when you toss in a string of multiple outcomes. Here's an example my colleague and good friend John DeGroote has shared with me and has agreed to share with you. It starts with the decision tree shown in Figure 13-2. (The values include attorney fees, and $124,000 represents the EMV for no settlement.)

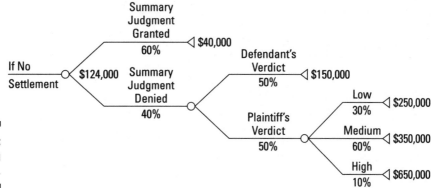

Summary
Judgment
Granted
◁ $40,000
60%

Defendant's
Verdict
◁ $150,000
50%

If No
Settlement   ○ $124,000   Summary
Judgment
Denied
40%

Low
30%   ◁ $250,000

Plaintiff's
Verdict   Medium   ◁ $350,000
50%   60%

High   ◁ $650,000
10%

Figure 13-2:
Calculating
the EMV.

A decision-tree program generated the tree and already calculated the EMV for the no settlement outcome, but you're probably wondering how it came up with that number. To calculate the EMV for the no settlement, start on the far right, where the plaintiff has a 30 percent chance of winning a $250,000 judgment, 60 percent chance for $350,000, and 10 percent chance for $650,000:

$$(.30 \times \$250,000) + (.60 \times \$350,000) + (.10 \times \$650,000) =$$

$$\$75,000 + \$210,000 + \$65,000 = \$350,000$$

Now, you must multiply that by the 50 percent chance that the plaintiff wins the verdict — half of $350,000 is $175,000.

The EMV for the defendant's verdict is 50 percent of $150,000, or $75,000.

Add the EMVs for the defendant and plaintiff: $175,000 for the plaintiff plus $75,000 for the defendant gives you $250,000. Because the summary judgment denied outcome has a 40 percent chance of occurring, multiply the $250,000 by .40 to get $100,000.

The EMV for summary judgment granted is 60 percent of $40,000, which comes to $24,000.

Total the EMV for summary judgment granted and summary judgment denied, and you get $100,000 + $24,000 = $124,000, which represents the EMV for no settlement.

This EMV is likely to give the client a new perspective, especially if the client is the plaintiff who's convinced of winning a settlement of $650,000. Compared to an EMV of $124,000, a much lower sure-thing settlement of, say, $300,000 looks much more attractive.

Reframing to Readjust the Parties' Perspectives

Framing and *reframing* are ways to put something into perspective for the one or both parties in a way that's likely to help them find new and more productive ways to view both the problem and the potential solutions to it. For example, someone sues you for $100,000 for damages suffered in a car accident that was your fault, that amount might sound excessive, but if the person shows you that she has medical bills of $50,000 and is likely to be facing a long recovery with additional procedures, that $100,000 looks much more reasonable.

As the difference between the parties' most recent offer and counteroffer narrows, framing, which I discuss in Chapter 7, becomes an effective technique in moving the parties closer to agreement. Framing enables you to accentuate the facts you want the parties to focus on, minimize the relevance of counterproductive facts, and present the current reality in a perspective that's more conducive to resolution.

The following sections explain how to use different framing techniques to resolve impasse.

Cheering on both sides

The parties may not be at agreement yet, but as they move closer, call their attention to how much progress they've made during the settlement negotiation and remind them of the potential benefits of resolution. If the parties were $1.2 million apart when mediation began and are only $200,000 apart now, call that to their attention. Praise the parties for their progress and serve as cheerleader for the deal as they approach the goal line.

As you're cheering the parties forward, ask them to imagine the benefits of resolution — less stress, more time for work and leisure activities, savings on attorneys' fees, the satisfaction of resolving a contentious issue, and more restful sleep, to name a few.

Making the money something more than it is

Although almost everyone dismisses the importance of money with phrases like "it's just money" or "money can't buy happiness," money is a huge hang-up for parties in negotiation. To prevent money from becoming a bigger issue than it needs to be, make it something more than just a number. Here are some techniques I've used:

- ✔ Pull a dollar out of your wallet and pantomime what it's *not.* You can't eat it, use it as a poultice on a wound, take it out to the country for a picnic, or rely on its continuing value to provide for your old age sometime in 2035. It's a symbol of value, not true value itself.

- ✔ Take money out of your wallet, tell the plaintiff it represents the sum being offered, and ask whether he's really ready to leave that money on the table.

- ✔ If the amount of insurance money available is insufficient to make all injured parties whole, create an imaginary hat into which you ask each party to place his hand and withdraw the sum of money he believes he's entitled to — physically depriving the other injured parties of the use of that money for their own injuries. This kicks in each party's own sense of fair play. It's much harder to literally grab more than your own share out of the hands of another deserving person.

- ✔ Have the litigants put a dollar bill into a cup in the middle of the table every time they notice that their response to the other side's offer or counteroffer is driven by anger or fear. Tell them the dollar represents, say, the $250 per hour their attorney is charging them in fees or the dollar loss to their business for every hour they spend fighting the other side in the litigation. How you explain the dollar they're losing when they let their emotions drive their decision-making process doesn't matter. It simply needs to reasonably relate to the dollar value of their case versus the expense of failing to settle it.

These are all ways of framing the parties' dispute and its resolution as something beneficial, concrete, immediately available, within the parties' control, satisfying, and (sometimes, if you're lucky) even fair or just. Reframing doesn't always resolve impasse, but it's worth trying when other options have failed. If the parties are still deadlocked, consider trying to move them closer through compromise and concessions, as I explain in the next section.

Reaching Compromise on Nonnegotiable Demands and Offers

Impasse often occurs when parties present exaggerated numbers or nonnegotiable offers hoping to gain an edge in negotiation. The plaintiff is usually willing to accept less, and the defendant is willing to pay more, so the gap is much smaller than the parties perceive it to be, but the apparent gap often becomes a huge obstacle to agreement. A hard, nonnegotiable offer has the same affect.

You can often help parties overcome these obstacles through the techniques I explain in the following sections.

Making hard offers soft

One of the mediator's primary jobs is to keep the parties negotiating. The more time they spend negotiating, the stronger their buy in to close the deal. Just think back to the last time you purchased a car. The car salesman probably did just about anything to keep you talking. The longer you stay, the more strongly the image of that car sitting in your driveway or making the trip to Aunt Jane's house becomes.

Unfortunately, a party may nearly shut down the negotiation by pitching a *hard offer* — an outrageous proposal that feels insulting to the other party and gives the other side no chance of winning. As mediator, your job is to soften that hard offer to keep the other party from walking away.

The first step is to ask diagnostic questions, as I explain near the beginning of this chapter, to find out where that outrageous offer came from and what motivated it. In your question-and-answer session, you're likely to find out one of the following:

- ✔ The offer or counteroffer isn't as outrageous as it first seemed. Sound reasoning and solid proof may be available to back it up. As a result, you may have a fighting chance to provide the other side with a reasonable argument in support of that position.

- ✔ The outrageous offer or counteroffer is part of a negotiation strategy or tactic. The party making it wants to appear unreasonable to gain an initial advantage or to simply send the message that he's angry.

To soften the blow of an unreasonable offer or counteroffer, explain the circumstances that motivated it or suggest that it's just the way the other side is opening the negotiation — that it's not an ultimatum or an insult, just an idiosyncratic or ineffective strategy or tactic. Here are some examples of how you can soften a hard offer:

- ✔ I know the plaintiff's opening demand of $3.2 million seems frivolous or insulting, but before you fly out of your chair, let me remind you that it's an *opening* offer.

- ✔ I know the plaintiff's move from $15 million to $14.9 million seems to be an outrageous and maddening negotiation strategy, but let me give you the plaintiff's thinking on that. (Try this only if the plaintiff has given you permission to convey his thinking.)

- ✔ The plaintiff's opening demand is $100 million. You and I both know that's not a serious way to open negotiations. I believe the attorney

> is trying to satisfy an unreasonable client. I'll be helping him bring his client back into the range of reason throughout the day.

> ✔ I know you don't want to hear this, but the defendant's opening offer is zero. I can see how angry that makes you. I believe the defense attorney may simply be making an effort to satisfy an angry client with whom I'll have several heart-to-heart talks during the course of the mediation.

> ✔ The defendant's opening offer is $1,000. I understand you think you'd be less insulted if he had offered nothing. I'd prefer to get a reasonable counter from you instead of an equally ridiculous response, because that will help me move them into the range of reason.

Reassure the parties. If they falter in their resolve to keep negotiating, tell them that as long as they're moving in the same direction, a deal is possible. Also consider telling them that you're not going to needlessly keep them in the room if you don't believe in the strong possibility that the parties' bottom lines already do, or will by session's end, overlap.

Rejecting an offer or demand without saying "No"

Impasse is common when you're confronting a take-it-or-leave-it offer or nonnegotiable demand that the other party's likely to reject. Instead of allowing the other party to reject the offer or demand outright, shift the focus from positions to underlying interests. Start by asking diagnostic questions to explore what the parties really want, as I explain in the section "Asking Diagnostic Questions" earlier in this chapter. After identifying each party's underlying interests, work with the parties to develop options that address those underlying interests instead of wasting time and effort on the much more difficult task of bringing their positions into alignment.

Suppose you're helping the parties settle a claim for a breach of a software contract. The plaintiff demands a broad *indemnity agreement* (legal protection against future loss) that amounts to an insurance policy. You know the type: "I want to be indemnified for all litigation arising from any breach of the settlement agreement and for our company's continuing use of your software in perpetuity (forever). It's nonnegotiable. We'll stop the mediation right now and pull out of the deal if you don't provide it to us."

Before making an effort to persuade the plaintiff to do something other than what he wants to do, make an effort to learn whether the party is being driven by need, desire, or fear (flip back to those diagnostic questions again). When any party asks to be indemnified, he's asking for protection from harm as the result of future unforeseeable events. In another words, the plaintiff's interest is his fear of potential liability. The defense can rest assured that the plaintiff isn't worried about what'll happen if an asteroid strikes his corporate offices. A specific danger is lurking in the back of his mind or the mind of his manager.

The diagnostic question is simple: *What type of potential liabilities are you worried about?* When the plaintiff answers that question, the parties can begin crafting a far narrower indemnity agreement than the plaintiff originally sought. Ideally, the agreement serves both parties' interests by protecting the defendant against unlimited liability for unknowable future catastrophes and by protecting the plaintiff from reasonably anticipated events.

If the parties can't come up with examples of their own, prime the pump by asking leading questions, such as:

> Would Software Services be willing to enter into an indemnity agreement that covers potential liabilities arising from software defects?

> Would you need to define what constitutes a defect?

Through suggestive questions such as these, you lead the parties into the process of problem-solving rather than simply saying "No" and remaining at the same roadblock.

Continually reframe disputes as opportunities to problem-solve. The key is to refocus the parties' attention on resolution and to slow down the negotiation process so they have time to brainstorm.

Bracketing the way to compromise

Bracketing is a technique for establishing a zone of potential agreement — an upper and lower limit between which the parties are willing to negotiate. Bracketing moves the parties closer to the true gap and makes bridging that divide seem far more attractive and possible. You "bracket" for the parties or solicit a bracketed offer or counteroffer by suggesting that Party A put $X on the table if Party B will agree to accept $Y in settlement. For example, if the parties are stuck at $100,000 (defendant) and $200,000 (plaintiff), a bracketed offer or proposal might look like this:

> If the defendant will offer $130,000, would the plaintiff be willing to reduce her demand to $170,000? If the parties are willing to do so, the gap is narrowed from $100,000 to only $40,000. The parties also have broken the barrier of round numbers beyond which they've previously pledged not to venture.

Through bracketing, you:

✔ Test the distance between the parties' true bottom lines without requiring them to reveal their bottom lines to each other.

✔ Encourage the parties to continue negotiating. You make the gap smaller and give them hope of bridging it.

✔ Protect the parties from anchoring the next round of negotiations too high or too low. When the parties have some idea of the actual range in which their negotiating partners are really in, they're far less likely to present extreme offers.

Try bracketing in any of the following ways:

✔ Ask the parties to suggest a bracket within which they'd be willing to continue negotiations. I like this method best because it encourages the parties to take ownership of the range. You can do this either in a joint session or in a separate caucus, but if you're using bracketing, the parties are likely to be negotiating in separate caucus, in which case you're usually better off seeking out these brackets separately, even if they're not yet negotiating in separate rooms.

✔ Tell the parties how far apart they really are. Based on their previous offer and counteroffer, they may think the gap is huge. If you know, through separate caucuses, each party's true bottom line, you can state the size of the gap (for example, "You're a hard $100,000 apart.") without revealing their bottom lines.

✔ Tell the parties that although both are willing to make further compromises, because they're so far apart, neither is willing to put another number on the table today. This alone often emboldens one party or the other to move down or up to a small degree to restart stalled negotiations.

✔ Suggest a hypothetical set of offers and counteroffers. For example, you might ask, "If the plaintiff came down to $X and the defendant came up to $Y, would you both be willing to negotiate in that range?"

When developing brackets, avoid these costly bottom line blunders:

✔ **Never ask for a party's true bottom line.** Knowing the bottom line *anchors* you and may tempt you to drive the negotiation toward that bottom line.

✔ **Never allow a party to tell you his bottom line if he seems poised to do so.** Revealing the true bottom line locks the party into a position from which he may not be able to extricate himself.

✔ **If you believe you may know one party's bottom line, never tell or signal to the other side what it is.** A bottom line is like blood in the water. The sharks sense it and move in for the kill.

First do no harm. Revealing a party's bottom line limits her bargaining range and her ability to change her mind. Your goal is to establish a range of reasonability without having either party reveal her true bottom line.

If you can't stop a party from telling you her bottom line, that bottom line almost requires the party who asserted it to walk away from the negotiation when that line in the sand is reached. At this point, you need to do your best people work, often helping the attorney and his party save face — the face (credibility and respect) they fear losing if their bottom line turns out to be posturing. For more about helping parties save face, see Chapter 14.

The claimant's most recent demand is $1.2 million, and the respondent's most recent offer is $650,000, representing a gap of $550,000. Neither party believes the other will compromise enough to justify further negotiations. I know from what each party has told me in separate caucus that the plaintiff would settle for $900,000 and the defendant is willing to pay $800,000. From my point of view, the parties are a hard $100,000 apart — a much more bridgeable gap.

The challenge is to let the parties know they have a smaller gap to bridge than they think they have without divulging each party's true bottom line. In this particular scenario, using the bracketing methods I describe previously, I could

- ✔ Ask the parties to suggest a bracket within which they'd be willing to negotiate.

- ✔ Tell the parties they're a hard $100,000 apart. They won't think the gap is $800,000 to $900,000. Instead, they'll think it means the plaintiff is willing to accept $1.1 million ($100,000 less than the plaintiff's last demand) or $750,000 ($100,000 more than defendant's last offer). Either way, the smaller gap encourages the parties, hopefully enough for one of them to make a more reasonable offer or demand.

- ✔ Tell the parties that although both are willing to make further compromises, because they're so far apart, neither is willing to put another number on the table that day.

- ✔ Suggest a hypothetical set of offers and counters by asking one or both parties, "If the plaintiff came down to $1 million and the defendant came up to $750,000, would you both be willing to negotiate in that range?" In response to a question like this, the parties always divide by 2 because they believe I'm suggesting that they split the difference to settle the case:

    $1,000,000 + $750,000 = $1,750,000 ÷ 2 = $875,000

    which is pretty close to what I know the defendant is willing to pay.

Nine times out of ten, bracketing breaks impasse and often settles the case. I highly recommend it.

Breaking hard impasse

Hard impasse occurs when the parties' walk-away numbers are outside the zone of potential agreement I discuss in Chapter 7. Suppose you want to pay $4 for a pair of sunglasses, but the vendor is asking $10. You're willing to go as high as $5 and he's willing to come down to $7. In this case, the zone of potential agreement is apparently missing because the walk-away prices don't overlap. A hard impasse of $2 separates them. To bridge the gap, you have two options:

- ✔ **Split the difference:** You buy the sunglasses for $6 — $1 more than you're willing to pay and $1 less than the vendor's willing to accept. You're both giving up $1, so it seems fair to both of you.

- ✔ **Give a reason:** You may tell the vendor you have only $5 on you. Or the vendor may explain to you that he purchased the sunglasses for $6 and needs to earn at least $1 a pair to make it worth his while. Assuming you believe the vendor and buy into the reasoning, the $2 may no longer seem like a huge difference to you, and you agree to his walk-away price of $7.

People skills also factor into negotiations, as I explain in Chapter 11. If, during the negotiation, either party loses trust in the other or simply doesn't like the other person's attitude or negotiating methods, that individual may become less flexible.

Don't let your disputants fall victim to distorted thinking and bad strategies. If they're negotiating in the nano- and stratospheres and you can't get them to negotiate close to the zone of potential agreement, let them know that he who makes the first reasonable offer typically gains the upper hand. The first offer exerts a strong pull on the other party throughout the negotiation. (See Chapter 7 for more about setting anchors and the strategic advantage of going first.)

Pitching a mediator's proposal

When the parties reach impasse because of exaggerated offers and nothing you do helps them see past their extreme positions, one option is to present a *mediator's proposal* — your professional, unbiased opinion of what you think both parties would likely accept to settle the case. Your proposal may go something like this:

I propose that the parties settle the case for $50,000, payable within 90 days. If both parties reject the proposal, I'll simply report back to them that there is no agreement. I'll also tell the parties that no agreement has been reached if one party accepts the offer and the other party rejects it. The parties will learn that the other has accepted the proposal only if both parties do so.

Before I make a mediator's proposal, I want both parties to understand how I've reached it. I don't make this proposal based on who I believe will "win" at the end of the day, nor even what I believe to be fair under the circumstances. No one has presented admissible evidence to me upon which I could base such a forecast. The number I choose is one I believe both parties will accept while at the same time believing it will be a stretch for both of them.

Don't show your proposal to either party. Meet with each party in a separate caucus, as I explain in Chapter 10, to test your assumptions about what each party will find acceptable. Without asking them to reveal their bottom lines, ask each one the question, "If your opponent came down to \$X, would you come up to \$Y?" When the numbers don't overlap, gauge how much pain each party will suffer to bridge the gap. Other purely subjective factors you may want to consider when crafting your proposal include the following:

- ✔ How invested each side is in walking away with a settlement on this day.

- ✔ How firm the sides are in their assertion that they wouldn't go below or above a certain number.

- ✔ Whether the attorneys needed help in bringing a little more reality to their clients before the parties would be ready to accept a mediator's proposal.

- ✔ How much street cred you've developed with the parties personally to make them more receptive to your settlement price-point, even if they wouldn't accept their own attorney's advice.

Assuming your proposal and follow-up efforts in caucuses are successful in getting the parties to agree, draw up a final agreement that both parties sign off on, as I discuss in Chapter 14.

Many master mediators have entirely given up on the mediator's proposal because they believe it's ineffective or runs counter to the mediation principle that resolution should be party-driven rather than recommended by the mediator. Too often, settlements reached by way of mediators' proposals are grudgingly accepted at best. When settlements are grudging, the deal isn't durable — you can't rely on it as a resolution. When buyer's remorse sets in, the more remorseful party may well fight the enforcement of the agreement, as demonstrated in the endless litigation between the Winklevoss twins and Mark Zuckerberg of Facebook.

Zuckerberg and the Winklevosses entered into a mediated settlement in 2008 and have been fighting to undo that settlement ever since. Their request to void that agreement was rejected by the federal Ninth Circuit Court of Appeals in April 2011. Their attorney has indicated that he'll seek a review by all the

Ninth Circuit's sitting judges. If the Winklevosses lose that petition, they're free to seek review from the U.S. Supreme Court. This is what people mean when they say "don't make a federal case about it." The Winklevosses have incurred millions of dollars in attorney's fees in their fight with Facebook. The mediator who helped them settle their case can't be at all happy about the work he did.

Some master mediators have turned against the practice of making mediators' proposals for other reasons. My good friend John DeGroote at Settlement Perspectives believes that a proposal for settlement by the mediator based on what she believes is possible has lost its utility. "Savvy negotiators," wrote John, "angle for an advantageous impasse rather than a settlement. Compromise is no longer the goal of the mediation exercise; instead it becomes a play to the 'neutral,' whose power to craft the mediation proposal will make her the real decision maker."

Mediation is always more effective when it's party driven — when both parties engage in collaborative problem-solving to arrive at a mutually beneficial arrangement. Because the parties have solved the problem together, both parties walk away satisfied that their interests have been addressed.

If the parties insist on a mediator's proposal, try a bracketed proposal first. If that doesn't move the parties closer and they still demand that you propose a solution, do so. People who insist they're incapable of resolving the dispute in the absence of an authoritative proposal from the mediator often have hidden interests to satisfy. One of the parties may need to tell her superiors that the mediator made a final proposal that she couldn't, in good faith, refuse. Not being the author of a difficult solution may also help a party save face not only with hidden stakeholders but also internally. Parties who see themselves as people who can't be pushed around and who will hold their ground under all circumstances often need an authoritative figure to all but *order* them to compromise. In this way, they can retain their preferred self-image while at the same time make a pragmatic decision that may otherwise make them feel weak, unmanned, or powerless.

Getting to Agreement via Concessions and Reciprocity

You may think your parties will never, ever agree. But consider this golden truth of human nature: When one person freely gives another something of value — time, information, goods, or, in negotiations, concessions — the recipient inevitably feels an obligation to reciprocate or, more commonly, over-reciprocate. Studies show that restaurant waiters who bring candy with the check receive dramatically larger tips, the difference being far greater than the candy's worth.

Your clients' satisfaction with the settlement and your performance depends on something other than the absolute dollar value. In fact, social scientists have discovered that people tend to be more satisfied with the outcome of negotiations in which the other side makes numerous concessions, even if they're small or inconsequential.

Tap the overwhelming human urge to reciprocate as a method of breaking through impasse. Whenever a party makes a concession, acknowledge it and stress how difficult it was for the conceding party to make it. Then, strongly suggest that the other party reciprocate. You may say something along the lines of, "If so-and-so is willing to make this concession, he's going to expect you to make similar concessions in return." Additionally, use the following two concession-centric techniques to break through impasse and leave everyone feeling like a winner.

Calling a bluff with a contingent concession

Negotiations will screech to a halt if one or both parties are bluffing, wildly exaggerating a claim, or overly concerned about how future events may affect their bottom line. Break through this kind of impasse by suggesting a contingent concession — one party promises something on the condition that a specific future event does or doesn't occur.

In an action between two partners over the value of the partnership, one party insisted that the inventory was worth "virtually nothing" while the other argued that it was worth $150,000. I asked the party who asserted the worthlessness of the inventory to include in his counteroffer an agreement to throw the inventory in *gratis* (free) in the event that a planned appraisal valued it at no more than half the value his soon-to-be former partner claimed it to have.

If the parties had agreed to such a contingency, the partner who valued the inventory at $150,000 would receive its full value as a reward for accurately appraising it. The other partner would have hedged his bet that the property was worthless, receiving a portion of its value only if it was worth $75,000 more than he predicted.

Neither party accepted my proposal. They backed down on their previous estimates of the inventory's value. After several more rounds of offers and counters, they agreed that the inventory was worth at least $100,000, adding that value to the buyout price they eventually negotiated to settle the litigation.

Had the parties stuck to their guns on their differing inventory valuations, the negotiation would have been ripe for logrolling, as I discuss in the next section.

Negotiating concessions with logrolling

Logrolling is a technique that takes advantage of differences between the parties, including differences in cost or valuation, predictions about the future, or the parties' appetite for risk. To logroll, ask diagnostic questions to reveal what's underneath each demand and the true cost of satisfying that demand. Ideally, you're looking for exchanges in which one party gives up something of low cost that has a high value for the other party.

Logrolling can come in handy on a daily basis. I've used it to negotiate dissatisfaction over a hotel stay. The hotel was new and the phone reception scratchy. Construction was going on outside my window, interfering with an important conference call I couldn't reschedule. Later, explaining my dissatisfaction to the desk clerk, I suggested that the hotel write off my bill those items that were low cost to them but a high price to me — a pay-per-view movie I'd watched, the telephone charges, and room service. The desk clerk was happy to do so, and we closed the deal right then and there.

Contingent concessions (see the section "Calling a bluff with a contingent concession") and logrolling play well together, so you may be able to use them in tandem to bring parties to agreement. If a party expresses fears about a future risk or possibility, look for trade-offs of low cost to one party and high value to the other.

In one patent case I mediated, we negotiated a license agreement between the plaintiff who claimed the defendants were selling car kits that infringed the plaintiff's patents. When I conveyed the defendant's offer to pay a 12 percent royalty on all sales over the next three years and a 7 percent royalty for the five years thereafter, the plaintiff resisted, predicting that the defendant was likely planning to increase sales after the third year.

I was already aware from the plaintiff that it planned to phase out the product within the initial three-year period. I suggested to the defense that it reverse the royalty schedule, so the plaintiff would pay 7 percent for the first three years and 12 percent for the five years thereafter. They readily agreed, as did the plaintiff, thereby using both a contingency provision and logrolling to satisfy all parties' fears and hopes about future unknowns.

Chapter 14

Closing and Memorializing the Parties' Agreement

In This Chapter
▶ Avoiding last-minute mistakes that can destroy a deal
▶ Making sure to get the agreement in writing
▶ Ensuring that agreements are durable and enforceable

*W*hen the parties achieve consensus, you should be ready to wrap up the negotiation and get them to sign off on their agreement. In this chapter, I help you fine-tune your endgame. You find out how to discourage the parties from engaging in deal-breaking activities such as nibbling, how to guide them in documenting their agreement to protect their interests, and how to establish an enforceable agreement without compromising the mediation's confidentiality.

Overcoming Last-Minute Missteps

How you end a negotiation can make or break a deal, even if everyone in the room believes the deal is done. So as you near the finish line, be careful of common mistakes that can weaken or undermine a deal. The biggest mistake you can make as a mediator is to try to split the baby as a last-ditch effort to salvage a deal. The biggest mistake a party can make is to *nibble* — to ask for something in addition to what's already been agreed to. The following sections describe these mistakes in greater detail and offer advice on how to avoid and overcome them.

Avoiding the urge to split the baby

Splitting the baby is a common but usually ineffective strategy for resolving a dispute. Instead of coming up with a creative solution that serves each party's interests, the parties decide to split the difference. For example, if the complainant demands $125,000 in damages and the defendant offers $75,000 (a difference of $50,000), they agree to settle for $100,000, splitting the difference in half. Unfortunately, both parties often walk away dissatisfied because neither party's interests have been served. Worse, the word about you on the street will be, "She always just splits the baby in half." Lawyers and clients alike are averse to resolutions that simply split the baby, for much the same reason that King Solomon originally suggested that two mothers fighting over parentage of an infant do so. Splitting the baby is unprincipled and suggests that one party or the other doesn't truly care about the item being negotiated. If you believe you're entitled to recover $100,000 from your adversary, why would anyone, particularly a so-called neutral mediator, ask you to take 50 percent of what you're owed? It feels random, without principle, *unjust*.

If you have the urge to split the baby, make sure you've exhausted all other avenues. Ask yourself whether you have

- ✔ Made a concerted effort to ascertain each party's interests (needs, desires, preferences, priorities, attitudes about risk, and the probability of future events) and to include them in the conversation.

- ✔ Helped the parties conduct a cost-benefit analysis, assigning probabilities to their likelihood of victory at each stage of the litigation or other dispute-resolution process and to the likely range of damages or recompense if they prevail at all those stages. (See Chapter 13 for guidance on how to perform a cost-benefit analysis.)

- ✔ Helped the parties articulate principled bases for their claims, as well as for their defenses to the other party's claims.

- ✔ Helped the parties reality-test the version of events upon which their claim or defense rests. To reality-test a party's version of events, ask diagnostic and follow-up questions, as explained in Chapter 7, and restate his answers in your own words to ensure that you understand what he said and that he can listen more objectively to what he's actually saying.

- ✔ Encouraged the parties to discuss their dispute directly with each other to identify hidden value, absent stakeholders, and hidden constraints and interests. In other words, have you engaged the parties in interest-based negotiation, as explained in Chapter 7? Have you probed for hidden interests, absent stakeholders, and secret constraints, as explained in Chapter 9?

✔ Assisted the parties in dealing with emotional obstacles to resolution such as the desire for revenge, the need to restore "face," the pressure to grieve the loss, and any other strong emotion that would prevent the parties from brainstorming a pragmatic resolution of a difficult dispute.

Mediators recommend 50 percent compromises when they run out of good ideas. By engaging in one or more of the activities in the preceding list, you can help the parties arrive at more positive and lasting resolutions, such as the following:

✔ When you make the effort to ascertain and discuss party interests, you may

- Uncover what new or different information one party needs in order to accept a proposal that's already on the table.

- Discover the source of a party's fear that some adverse consequence will follow resolution, so the parties can find a way to allay that fear.

- Find out that a party needs a certain amount of money today and is willing to accept partial payment with a promise to pay additional monies over time.

- Come to know that the parties have different priorities, both of which can be served at the same time.

✔ When you help the parties conduct a cost-benefit analysis, they often see the wisdom of paying more or accepting less than they were prepared to based on the dawning realization that prevailing in litigation or another dispute-resolution venue won't be as easy as they had believed.

✔ When you help the parties articulate a principled basis for their claims or defenses, their negotiation partner is often more willing to work toward a solution that satisfies the announced principle (fairness, for example) because it appeals to him as well.

✔ When you help the parties reality-test their version of events, you help them see how another person may view the fairness of their negotiation partner's requests or defenses.

✔ When the parties overcome their resistance to discussing potential solutions to their mutual problems, they often find hidden resources that permit the resolution of their dispute in a way that satisfies both of their interests.

✔ When you assist the parties in dealing with emotional obstacles to resolution, they're better able to recognize the needs and desires of their opponent as worthy. They may stop treating their opponent as an adversary, acknowledge their own fallibility, and recognize that much of their conflict rests on miscommunications rather than evil motives, all of which frees them up to work together to brainstorm mutually acceptable solutions.

Discouraging nibbling

Nibbling is a negotiation tactic that many negotiation "experts" recommend as a means to get a bigger slice of the pie just as the deal is closing. Although nibbling can be an effective technique for one party to get more of what he wants, it can also undermine progress and derail an otherwise successful mediation.

Here are a couple of examples of nibbling: "Oh, just one more thing. It's not much really. Could you pay that $100,000 over five years?" Or, as the deal points are being written up: "I'm fine with all this as I said an hour ago, but because your reluctance to close the deal yesterday required us to continue the mediation today, you should pay today's mediation fees."

In the way a rabbit nibbles at a lettuce leaf with small bites, so a negotiator nibbles at a done deal to have just one more bite of that leaf, and then another, and another one after that.

Those who recommend this style of play believe that the party being asked to give up a small additional item even after the parties have reached agreement will say "yes" because saying "no" seems miserly or because the party is exhausted and unwilling to fight over one last request that doesn't require him to give up very much. What those negotiation experts don't seem to understand is *face,* particularly as it relates to buyer's remorse. I've seen deals involving tens of millions of dollars blow up over a few thousand bucks while the parties are inking the agreement's deal points.

Here are just a few reasons why nibbling is a bad idea:

✔ Nibbling undermines what little trust the mediator has helped the parties develop with each other during the course of the mediation. That last-minute nibble comes across as dishonest and manipulative.

✔ Nibbling heightens buyer's remorse in parties who are already reluctant to accept the deal.

✔ The small request is almost always too insignificant to risk having it blow up a hard-won deal.

✔ The bad feeling nibbling creates may carry over into small acts of sabotage as the time comes for the parties to perform. The party who's been nibbled almost always seeks to save face by getting back at her bargaining partner for the humiliating final punch after the bell has rung on the last round of negotiations.

Discourage nibbling for all these reasons. By the time you're closing the deal, the parties have almost always come to see you as a trusted neutral authority. They respect you and the experience you bring to the table. Use that social capital to discourage nibbling. You can call the parties to their higher angels, talk to them about the pragmatics of future performance, or lightly shame them by expressing your disapproval. By the time the parties are ready to write up the deal, you'll know which of these techniques works best with the particular parties you're dealing with.

Don't confuse nibbling with instances when one party legitimately realizes that the agreement is missing a crucial element and asks to reopen negotiations. Clients may find inspiration in the waning moments of a mediation that transform a good agreement into a brilliant one.

Getting the Agreement in Writing

The parties often reach agreement very late in the day, sometimes not until early the next morning. By that time, the conference room is cluttered with the remains of morning croissants, bag lunches, pizza dinners, and candy wrappers from the nine-to-midnight shift. Everyone just wants to go home and draft the written agreement later.

What's so bad about that? After all, the parties have agreed to all the settlement terms — the total amount of money payable, the time over which it must be paid, the stipulated judgment in the event of default, and the stipulated judgment amount (higher than the settlement agreed upon because it contains a hammer clause).

What's so bad about waiting to ink the deal is that it can fall apart over any number of minor issues. Here are just a few of the kinds of provisions over which a deal can fall apart, even though the parties have agreed to what they believe are all the principal deal points:

- **The dismissal of ancillary proceedings:** If the parties are involved in more than one piece of litigation, or if administrative, family law, or criminal proceedings are pending or threatened, these issues need to be addressed.

- **Forbearance from inducing future actions by nonparties:** Where the parties have an extremely low level of trust and fear sabotage or retribution in the future, they can and should agree to refrain from engaging nonparties in acts of sabotage or retribution, such as encouraging a nonparty to break a contract with the adversary.

- **Liquidated damage clauses for the breach of certain critical deal points:** The parties should clarify the calculation of damages for any breach of the agreement when damages would be difficult or impossible to determine in the event of breach.

- **Attorneys' fees and arbitration clauses in the event of breach:** The mediation agreement is essentially a new contract, so it needs to state who pays the attorneys' fees and how arbitration will be handled if a party breaches the contract.

Each of these items can require separate negotiation and compromise. You need to guide these negotiations and keep the parties at the table by reminding them of the hard work they did to set aside their suspicions and hammer out a deal on the major points. In my own practice, I've found that the parties fail to come to agreement on these seemingly innocuous deal points unless I'm still there coaching and cheering them on.

In the following sections, I explain how to wrap up a mediation session that seems to be over so that the parties walk away with a durable, enforceable agreement . . . in writing.

Don't author the agreement or offer legal advice. Even if you're a lawyer, you're not *their* lawyer. And if you're not a lawyer, giving legal advice could land you in trouble for the unauthorized practice of law. If the parties are represented by legal counsel, they, not you, should draft the agreement, with you assisting them to make sure that the details won't blow up the deal. If the parties aren't represented by legal counsel, you may want to be the scrivener of the deal, but they should provide you with all its terms. You can help them clarify their desires while drafting the contract and ask them questions about items they may have overlooked, but you shouldn't be the author of the deal.

Making sure the deal is durable

A mediation agreement is durable when the parties are satisfied with the outcome. To ensure that the deal the parties reach is truly satisfactory to them:

- ✔ Talk to the parties to ascertain whether they have reservations about the proposed settlement. You'd be surprised how many deals are brokered by attorneys and then presented to the parties as a *fait accompli*. As a result, both parties usually have lingering reservations and disdain for each other. You don't want to get *between* the attorneys and their clients, so tell the attorneys you'd like to make sure everyone is on the same page before presuming to talk with their clients again about the deal points.

- ✔ Listen to the parties' story regardless of whether you believe it's relevant to the settlement. Parties who leave the mediation still feeling that they're the victims of a grinding injustice are highly likely to resist enforcement of the deal.

Parties typically honor agreements because they feel obligated to do what's right, not because they're threatened by the prospect of litigation. When parties feel as though they've been bullied into submission or presented with nothing better than a last and final offer, they can and often do find ways to initiate or prolong litigation.

Ensuring enforceability

Each jurisdiction has different laws that govern the enforceability of agreements reached in mediation. Because of the prevalence of postmediation buyer's remorse, it's not uncommon for one party to claim that the agreement reached isn't enforceable *and* that his adversary may not introduce written evidence or oral testimony to "prove up" the contract because everything said and done during a mediation is confidential.

However, the confidentiality rule usually has an important exception — that the parties have a right to prove, in writing, that they reached an enforceable agreement. Make sure you know what the requirements of that exception are.

Even in litigated cases, attorneys are often unfamiliar with the statutory requirements or the most recent appellate opinions interpreting those requirements. Let the attorneys know what you know, coupled with the warning that, as a mediator, you're not permitted to give legal advice, and you expect the attorneys to advise their clients of the law's requirements. If it appears to me that the attorneys are unfamiliar with the law, I suggest that they check it out before leaving the mediation with a written agreement I believe may well not be enforceable.

Dealing with the paperwork

Although oral agreements are enforceable, oral agreements in mediation can't be enforced in a court of law against the will of one of the parties, because the rules governing confidentiality prevent one party from introducing the terms of the deal into evidence. You should assume that the terms of an oral agreement reached in mediation can't be enforced in the absence of a *writing* (any written proof, not necessarily a formal contract) unless you're absolutely sure they can.

In California, most mediators provide the parties with a settlement agreement or term sheet template that complies with California law. That template usually looks something like this:

Date: _____

Settlement Agreement in _____ versus _____

The parties to the above-referenced case understand and agree that this Settlement Agreement is admissible in evidence to prove its terms, that it is enforceable against and binding between the parties, and that it may be disclosed for purposes of its enforcement, all in accordance with California Evidence Code section 1123. The parties further understand and agree that this Settlement Agreement is enforceable by motion of any party pursuant to California Code of Civil Procedure section 664.6.

After you provide an appropriate template, or simply paper and pen, the parties themselves should write up and sign the entire deal, which usually includes the following:

- ✔ **The settlement agreement:** At its most basic, the settlement agreement states in writing what both parties agree to give and give up in order to settle their dispute; when the exchange will take place; and, if the exchange occurs over time, the consequences of nonperformance.

  If one party has made representations to induce the other party to enter into the agreement, the parties should understand that the agreement gives them the opportunity to reiterate the substance of the representations, the parties' reliance on the truth and accuracy of those representations, and the parties' mutual understanding that the agreement is enforceable only if those representations are in fact true and accurate.

- ✔ **Mutual general releases:** Most settlement agreements contain mutual general releases that relieve both parties from any further claims by the other based on the subject matter of the complaint or dispute. Most states have laws that specify the wording that an effective mutual general release should include. The parties should seek legal advice about the enforceability of their general releases.

- ✔ **Terms:** Terms may include

  - Payment of attorneys' fees and costs in the event of breach

  - Submission of any breach to further mediation, followed by arbitration

  - Choice of law provisions, particularly when the parties live in different states or when questions are raised about whether the matter is controlled by state or federal law

  - Warranties of authority to enter into the agreement if corporate, partnership, or joint ventures are parties to the dispute

  - Indemnity clauses if necessary

  - Time is of the essence clauses

  - Agreement that the parties will take all action necessary to assure that the agreement is performed

If the parties agree on payment terms over time, they often want to draft the documents necessary to obtain a judgment in the event of default. In such instances, the parties usually prepare two additional documents:

- ✔ **The stipulation for the entry of judgment:** When the parties agree to exchange something of value at a later date, the party who risks nonperformance often requires the other to *stipulate to the entry of judgment* in the event of default. Sometimes these stipulations include *hammer clauses* specifying that the individual who promises to pay a certain sum of money over a specified period of time consents to the entry of judgment in a greater sum than the agreed-upon settlement if he fails to make payments according to the agreement. This provision gives the paying party a strong inducement to honor his agreement and gives the other party assurance that he'll either be paid in a timely manner or be entitled to more money.

✔ **The proposed stipulated judgment:** The proposed stipulated judgment is worded as a judgment for the court to sign and should contain a signature line for the court.

I carry sample agreements as well as sample stipulations for the entry of judgment and stipulated judgments on a thumb drive to assist the parties in drawing up their agreement. I always advise the parties that, though I'm a lawyer, I don't represent any of the parties, nor do I represent the agreement itself. I tell them that I don't provide legal advice and won't vouch for the legality or enforceability of any settlement agreement or legal document I provide to them for their consideration in drawing up their deal. I admonish them to seek out the advice of lawyers if they don't have lawyers present at the mediation. If they have lawyers present at the mediation, I tell the parties that their lawyers are charged with the responsibility of ensuring that the agreements drafted during the mediation are enforceable and contain all the terms necessary to resolve their dispute.

For sample mediation agreements and forms along with some additional bonus items, visit www.MediatorSuccess.com.

If the parties aren't represented by counsel during the mediation, you should advise them to consult an attorney in the jurisdiction in which the mediation takes place (or the jurisdiction in which the parties live or have chosen as the jurisdiction where the contract will be enforced). You might suggest that the agreement written up in the course of the mediation be made contingent on both parties notifying the other by X date that they have been given the right to consult with counsel, have chosen not to consult counsel, are satisfied with the agreement's terms and conditions, and will be bound by those terms despite the lack of legal advice; or that they have consulted with counsel and, having done so, agree to be bound by all the contract's terms.

You should also have these documents on a laptop or smart phone in case you forget your thumb drive when you're mediating. You can also access the documents remotely if you store them somewhere on the web — on Google Docs, for example.

You're the mediator, not the legal representative of the deal, and you may not be authorized to practice law. Therefore, whenever you suggest that the parties use your forms, tell them that you're not acting as an attorney (if you are one) or can't act as an attorney (if you aren't one). Tell the parties that their lawyers, if each party has a lawyer, should review the documents.

Part IV
Launching Your Own Mediation Practice

The 5th Wave   By Rich Tennant

JAY PELT
MEDIATION
AND
CONFLICT
RESOLUTION

"Mr. Pelt mediates business conflicts for $1000 and marital issues for $500, or for $50, he'll get your cat to lick your face."

In this part . . .

*H*elping people resolve their disputes and mend their relationships is very rewarding, but that in itself doesn't pay the bills. Success as a mediator also means earning a reasonable amount of money, and that requires some business acumen.

In this part, you shift roles from mediator to small-business owner. Here, I explain how to set up shop, market yourself and your services, and grow your business through networking and referrals. By increasing demand for your services, you can begin to maximize your earning potential.

Chapter 15

Building Your Business from the Ground Up

. . . .

In This Chapter

▶ Taking on mediation full time

▶ Putting together your business plan and budget

▶ Organizing your business essentials

▶ Figuring out how much to charge your clients

▶ Getting on a mediation panel

. . . .

As a mediator, you're a business — You, Inc. And you need to run your mediation career as a business, complete with a business plan, budget, forms, agreements, and even insurance. You need to know how much to charge your future clients, whether to charge by the hour or the day, and when to ask for your money. You may also want to explore the option of joining a mediation panel, which can take many of the management tasks off your plate so you can focus on your true passion — mediation.

This chapter explains how to go from point A to point B, from wherever you happen to be right now in your career to making a successful living as a full-time mediator.

Knowing When You're Ready to Embrace Mediation Full Time

Every mediator reaches a point when she feels ready to make the move from part- to full-time mediation. Doing so may mean shutting down a successful practice in another field or quitting a steady job. In any event, the leap from security into the unknown is usually scary. You may wonder, "Am I really prepared for this?"

Look for the following signs to guide you in your decision to leave the comfort and security of your current position and jump with both feet into mediation:

- ✔ You have no available time within the next three months to take on a new mediation case because your current caseload and marketing activities consume almost all your time.

- ✔ Your income from your mediation practice is at least half the compensation from your day job and has been trending upward for more than a year.

- ✔ The cost of running your practice is at least ten times less than your mediation income.

- ✔ You receive at least one request a week for your mediation services.

- ✔ You receive at least one referral a week from someone in your network.

When you notice these signs, or at least most of them, you're probably at a pretty good point to make the transition to full-time mediation.

When you're just getting started, particularly if you've never run a business, you're likely to experience some setbacks and disappointments. To get through these tough times, lean on your mediation community, as I explain in Chapter 17. You may be able to ride out the low points alone, but fellow community members can ease the strain and may offer valuable advice to help you clear the hurdles sooner. Most full-time mediators have to leave behind another career at some point, and these colleagues can provide the assurances you need when quitting your day job seems daunting.

Drafting a Business Plan and a Budget

Prior to ditching your day job to become a full-time mediator, you need two things to get started — a plan and a budget. This section helps you draft a solid mediation business plan and a realistic budget.

Planning your business

Entrepreneurs typically craft a business plan to persuade banks to lend them money. As a mediator, you too are an entrepreneur, but you probably don't need a lender or a venture capitalist to bankroll your business start-up, because overhead is so low. All you need is enough money to cover your living expenses and some incidental costs. When starting out as a mediator, a business plan enables you to reality-test your dream and envision how that dream is likely to play out in the real world.

Your mediation business plan is a summary of how you intend to launch your practice and stay in business. Start with an outline that contains the following section headings and then supply relevant details below each heading:

- **Vision/mission:** Your vision/mission statement may include what you plan on getting out of this venture, but even more important is what you plan to do for your clients; they must be satisfied for you to achieve your goals. For example, your mission may be to help parents with special needs children resolve disputes with their local school board without the costs, delays, and frustrations of doing so through litigation.

- **Market:** Are you working in the area of litigated or nonlitigated disputes? Private or public? Restorative justice? Diplomacy? See Chapter 2 for more about choosing a market.

- **Competition:** Identify the top competitors in your market and describe how you plan to compete against them. What makes you different and better?

- **Business objectives:** Describe what you hope to accomplish and how you'll know when you've accomplished it. List both short-term and long-term objectives. Following are a few examples to get you started:

  - **Long term:** To make mediation your day job and earn at least $60,000 net per year. Calculate the number of disputes you'd have to mediate to achieve that goal. The section "Setting Rates and Fees" later in this chapter helps you calculate that number.

  - **Long term:** To establish yourself as an expert in your field; for example, intellectual property disputes or disputes between teenagers and their parents. Jot down target measures of success, such as the number of times you're asked to speak in your area of expertise or are quoted in your local newspaper about the type of dispute you resolve.

  - **Short term:** To mediate X number of disputes per month.

  - **Short term:** To speak to your market at least four times a year or conduct communication training sessions for your market at least twice a year.

- **Income sources:** Mediators typically have more than one source of income, such as coaching, consulting, arbitration, fact finding, training, writing, and speaking; performing arbitration services for the American Arbitration Association or any number of similar organizations; and working on a panel. (See the section "Joining a Panel to Share Fees and Reduce Overhead" later in the chapter for more about panels.)

- **Projected expenditures:** Include the total here and then itemize expenses in your budget, as I explain in the next section.

✔ **Location:** Describe your center of operations, which may be your home, a separate office, or space at the county courthouse. Also jot down where you plan to conduct your mediations — perhaps in the courthouse, in attorneys' offices, or in executive suites. See the section "Choosing a name and location" later in the chapter for details.

✔ **Marketing:** List various ways you plan to market your business online and off, as I explain in Chapter 16. Bare basics include a website, a blog, Facebook and Twitter accounts, and business cards. Specify whether you're going to do your own marketing or outsource it.

If you're a rank beginner, you'll likely moonlight as an unpaid mediator first. Many mediators earn their first alternative dispute resolution (ADR) dollar when the parties to a court-annexed mediation program ask the "free" mediator to continue the session past the period the courts offer gratis. Although this period differs from state to federal courts and from state to state and city to city, court programs usually offer the first two to four hours to litigants free of charge, after which you're allowed to charge the parties your standard hourly fee.

Despite the seeming ease with which you can earn your first few hundred or few thousand dollars by going overtime, don't let yourself drift too long without a solid business plan. Your initial success builds hope, but hope isn't a plan. Your plan is the foundation on which you build your business.

For additional details on planning a business, check out *Business Plans Kit For Dummies* by Steven D. Peterson, Peter E. Jaret, and Barbara Findlay Schenck (published by Wiley).

Accounting for expenses

Few businesses have a lower overhead than mediation does. All you really need is a roof over your head, a vehicle to get you from point A to point B, a computer with Internet access, a telephone, and liability insurance. If you're planning to start out by moonlighting as a mediator, you may not even need a budget. When you're ready to launch a full-time mediation business, however, a budget is essential in ensuring that you have a sufficient cash flow to pay your bills and fuel your business venture.

When drafting your budget, be sure to include all expense categories, including the following monthly expenses:

✔ **State licensing/registration fees:** If you're licensed in another profession (for example, you're a psychologist or attorney), you'll need to budget for state licensing/registration fees if you want to retain your licensure in a profession other than mediation.

- ✔ **Living expenses:** Examine your personal finances to find out how much you need to draw from your business monthly to remain solvent. Be sure to include health and life insurance premiums, especially if you're currently working for an employer who provides coverage.

- ✔ **Office space:** If you're mediating cases in a court-annexed mediation program, you can often use court facilities for free. If you're not mediating with an organization that provides you with a place to hold your mediations, you may conduct sessions in a home or virtual office. (A *virtual office* provides a business address, phone number, support personnel, and access to meeting rooms and other facilities. It reduces the overhead of running your own office.) If you're mediating business disputes or disputes among professionals, you should feel free to suggest that the mediation take place in their offices. You have other choices, too; head to the section "Choosing a name and location" later in the chapter for more info.

- ✔ **Professional services:** You may want to hire a part-time bookkeeper and a certified public accountant (CPA) to keep records, balance the books, and make sure you fulfill your tax obligations and get all the tax deductions you qualify for. Find out from the bookkeeper and accountant how much to budget for these services.

- ✔ **Internet and communications:** List monthly Internet fees and telephone fees (if you have a separate telephone just for your business).

- ✔ **Office supplies:** Include paper, ink, file folders, staples, paper clips, and the like. Don't include one-time costs, such as for office equipment and furniture. You account for these costs later in this section.

- ✔ **Marketing:** The greatest marketing cost for mediators is measured in time and consists of networking face-to-face with the market. In addition to that sweat equity, budget for a website, a blog, business cards, brochures, letterhead, and a monthly newsletter (mail, e-mail, or both). You may also want to include additional funds depending on your marketing plan. See Chapter 16 for more about marketing.

- ✔ **Dues and fees:** Dues and fees for membership in organizations to which members of your market belong are also considered marketing expenses. For example, if you belong to the Writers Guild of America to keep in touch with members of that community, include those membership dues in your budget. Membership in some organizations is free, such as churches, PTAs, community watch groups, and the like. Membership in country clubs, bar associations, and industry groups may be quite costly. Some organizations, such as your local chamber of commerce, rotary group, or Toastmasters club, are mid-range expenses.

Budget enough money to belong to enough organizations that you attend at least one in-person event a month. Because those events are rarely free, add the cost of lunch and dinner meetings you attend during the year. The websites of most industry and bar association groups have calendars of events, the cost of those events, and, of course, the cost of membership.

✔ **Liability insurance:** Liability insurance is a must for any mediator. Fortunately, the cost is pretty low. See the section "Purchasing liability insurance" later in the chapter for details.

✔ **Property insurance:** Whether you rent or own office space, purchase property insurance to cover any slips and falls by visitors and damage to or theft of equipment or furniture.

If you rent offices or host mediations in your home office, make sure the premises meet the requirements of state and federal laws regarding the accommodation of people with disabilities. The federal government's Small Business Administration has an online guide to the ADA at www.ada.gov/smbustxt.htm. The Equal Opportunity Employment Commission (EEOC) also has a primer on its website advising small businesses how to comply with the ADA at www.eeoc.gov/eeoc/publications/adahandbook.cfm. States also have laws governing access to business premises. California's, for instance, can be found at www.disabilityaccessinfo.ca.gov/prvt_businesses.htm.

✔ **Taxes:** Federal and state income taxes are the two biggies. A good rule of thumb is to set aside about 35 percent of your gross income to cover these taxes, but check with your accountant to be sure. Also, most cities levy business taxes on any money-making enterprise, even if it's only part time or operated out of a home.

These are monthly fees. Also make sure you have enough money set aside to cover one-time start-up costs, including attorney fees (if you choose to incorporate), fees for registering your business with the proper authorities (the secretary of state in most states), and office equipment and furniture expenses for computers and accessories, desks, chairs, bookcases, filing cabinets, staplers, pencil sharpeners, and so on.

Include a prudent reserve of at least three months' worth of expenses to cover emergencies, such as unexpected vehicle repairs, a lull in business, or a sudden increase in dues, fees, taxes, or insurance premiums.

Keep your business and personal finances separate. Opening a separate checking account for your business and having a business-only credit card are two great ways to track business expenses. In addition, personal finance programs, such as Quicken, enable you to keep separate accounts.

Setting Up Shop

With a business plan and budget in hand, you're ready to set up shop — to put all the pieces in place that enable you to conduct business. Setting up shop requires that you choose a name and location for your business, incorporate (if you choose to do so), register your business, get all your paperwork in order, and purchase liability insurance. The following sections explain what to do and how to do it.

Naming my business

When I first started my ADR business, I named it *Settle It Now!* Dispute Resolution Services and I use the terms *ADR, alternative dispute resolution, mediation,* and *neutral* on my website for search engine optimization (SEO), so potential clients who Google those terms are likely to be presented with links to my site. I named it *Settle It Now!* because settling litigation early rather than late was part of my pitch, something I felt highly qualified to recommend given my 25 years of legal practice. Now that I mediate and arbitrate for ADR Services, Inc., an ADR panel with offices throughout the state of California, I have all but abandoned the "Settle It Now!" name.

Later, when I began to arbitrate, I added the term *arbitration* to my website. Now that I also teach negotiation, I use that term on my site as well. Because I have also started a separate small business to provide negotiation training and consulting services to women, I have aggregated all my activities under my own name, VictoriaPynchon. com. Whenever possible, you should make sure you obtain web addresses under your own name, including .com, .org, .us, and .biz addresses.

Choosing a name and location

The first steps I took when I began my mediation practice were to give it a name, register the business with the secretary of state, buy business cards, and build a website. I took these steps because I felt the need to create something more tangible than merely the idea that I was now in transition from litigator to mediator. Giving my business a name also allowed me to promote it without having to sing my own praises so much. For those who have no issues with shameless self-promotion, using your own name is probably best.

As for location, you probably don't need to rent office space. Your business address is your home address or a P.O. Box number. If your home has extra space, you may want to convert it into an office where you can consult with clients. You probably don't have enough space for a conference room and a separate room to conduct caucuses with each party, but you don't need that. You have other options:

- ✔ If you're mediating litigated cases, the attorneys have conference rooms and additional space to caucus separately with each party.

- ✔ If you serve on a court-annexed panel, the court invariably provides space in the courthouse. This is actually a very good venue for a beginning mediator because it lends you the authority of the court.

- ✔ If you're serving on a panel of mediators, as I discuss later in this chapter, the panel provides office space, conference rooms, and even administrative support.

✔ In the early days of your practice, consider conducting mediations in executive suites. For a relatively small monthly fee, you can usually contract with a motel or hotel that features executive suites to conduct one or two mediations per week.

✔ If you know any attorneys or other professionals who have office space complete with conference rooms, consider asking them if they wouldn't mind leasing their conference rooms.

Deciding whether to incorporate

Incorporating sounds like something reserved for big business, but it offers a couple of perks for small businesses too, both legally and financially:

✔ **Legally:** Incorporating establishes your business as a separate legal entity and provides some protection for you personally from any contract-based lawsuits filed against the business. Incorporation does not, however, protect you from personal liability for negligence in the performance of your services, because everyone is legally liable for his own conduct that constitutes a civil wrong (a tort) resulting in injury to other people, whether he's acting on behalf of a corporation or not.

✔ **Financially:** Setting up a corporation enables you to pay yourself as an employee of the corporation, which may significantly reduce your self-employment tax.

Now the bad news: Running the corporation adds to the paperwork and hassle of conducting business. You need to have an annual corporate meeting, complete with meeting minutes; to issue at least one share of stock; to file with the IRS for an employer identification number (EIN) so you can issue paychecks to yourself; and other such nonsense.

Consult your tax advisor and attorney to weigh the pros and cons of incorporating and to determine the best way to structure your business:

✔ **Sole proprietorship:** With a sole proprietorship, you don't incorporate. This is usually the most attractive option for consultants and freelancers who don't have employees working for them, because it is, by far, the easiest route. This option has two main drawbacks:

• You have to pay double the Federal Insurance Contributions Act (FICA) taxes. In other words, instead of paying about 7.5 percent in Social Security, Medicare, and Medicaid, which is what you'd pay as an employee (with your employer paying the other 7.5 percent), you pay the entire 15 percent as a self-employment tax, at least on the first $100,000 or so of income.

• A sole proprietorship offers no legal protection. If someone sues your business, they're suing you.

✔ **S corporation:** An S corporation is one of the most popular choices for individuals who choose to incorporate. Like a limited liability company (LLC), it provides some legal protection of the owner's personal assets. Perhaps more importantly, it reduces the amount of income that's subject to self-employment tax. Here's how that works:

You take half of your income as salary and half as distributions. On the half you receive as income, the corporation pays half of your FICA and you pay the other half. The half you receive as distributions is not subject to FICA, so you essentially pay self-employment tax on only half your total income. (You could take more than half as distributions, but if the IRS looks into it, it could make you reclassify some of those distributions as salary and make you pay back taxes and penalties on that amount.)

✔ **Limited liability company (LLC):** An LLC is sort of like an S corporation but in most cases is better for partnership-owned businesses. Potential benefits over other types of business structures include the following:

- An LLC provides some legal protection for your personal belongings; that is, if someone sues your business, theoretically they can go after only your business assets, not your personal assets, such as your home. In practice, however, most people who sue sue the business and its owners. Still, if managed properly, an LLC provides more legal protection than does a sole proprietorship. (A C corporation provides more legal protection.)

- Owners of an LLC may distribute profits as they see fit. With an S corporation, profits must be distributed according to the ratio of stock ownership, so if your partner put up 70 percent of the money to start the business, he gets 70 percent of the profit, even if you're doing 70 percent of the work and he's contributing only 30 percent of the work.

- Income passes through the LLC to the company's members, so the company doesn't pay taxes on it, which avoids the double-taxation issue that C corporations must deal with.

A major drawback of single-member LLCs as compared to an S corporation is that all of the money paid out by the LLC to its sole member is subject to self-employment tax. For multi-member LLCs, a major drawback consists of complications in dealing with tax issues. Multi-member LLCs have to file a return of partnership and make sure its members get a form K-1. The partners then file a Schedule E. If you go the multi-member LLC route, hire an accountant with experience in handling partnership tax issues.

If you establish a multi-member LLC, you should have an operating agreement in place that spells out everything from operation and management to distribution.

✔ **C corporation:** C corporations are primarily for large businesses or for startups that eventually may need to go public or attract venture capital. In other words, you probably don't want or need to structure your business as a C corporation.

✔ **Partnership:** A partnership is sort of like a sole proprietorship, except that the business is owned by two or more people. Like a sole proprietorship, a partnership offers the owners no legal protection. Although you can set up a partnership through a verbal agreement, I strongly recommend that you consult an attorney to have the partnership agreement written up in detail, including what happens in the event that you choose to dissolve the partnership.

However you choose to structure your business, you should consult with an attorney and an accountant who has experience with small businesses. Your attorney and accountant can help you choose the best way to structure your business, generate the necessary paperwork, and handle the details of processing payroll and distributions if you choose to form a corporation.

Some businesses, including The Company Corporation (www.incorporate. com), specialize structuring small businesses as corporations. They can help you obtain the required licenses and permits, write bylaws and operating agreements, register your business name, and obtain an Employer Identification Number (EIN), which the corporation needs to pay its employee — you. If you choose not to use one of these turnkey solutions and you're not an attorney, I strongly recommend that you consult an attorney to set up your corporation properly.

Registering a unique domain name

You may not have time right now to create a website and/or a blog, but take a few minutes to think up and register a domain name (such as www.your name.com) for your business. Be sure the name is relatively short, memorable, and easy to say and spell. Avoid using the underline character, but hyphens are okay. You may also want to include the word *mediator* or *mediation* in the name to help search engines find it and properly index it.

Before registering your domain name, consult other mediators or small business web masters to find out which hosting service they recommend. A *hosting service* is where your website ultimately lives. Choose a hosting service and then register your domain name through that hosting service so that your registration and service are through one provider, which, although not necessary, is convenient.

I highly recommend choosing a name with `.com` at the end. Using something like `.net` or `.biz` may confuse clients who are accustomed to typing `.com`. Potential clients may visit the `.com` site by mistake, driving traffic and potential business to a competitor! If the name you want to use is taken and the service prompts you to choose the same name with something other than `.com` at the end, try to come up with a different name.

Registering a domain name is just the beginning of building your online presence. For more about marketing via a website or blog, see Chapter 16.

Preparing the necessary paperwork

Like most businesses, the business of mediation involves some paperwork. Fortunately, it's fairly light, consisting of a couple letters and a contract. This section provides guidance on preparing the paperwork you need and avoiding what you don't need.

Create a boilerplate scheduling letter and contract that you can open and modify for specific clients and cases. If you're not an attorney, have your attorney review all boilerplate documents to ensure that you've covered everything required by law and anything that's useful to protect yourself against liability.

Writing a scheduling letter

A *scheduling letter* gives the parties everything they need to know leading up to mediation day. In your scheduling letter, include the following information or placeholders for inserting the following information:

- ✔ The date, time, and place of the mediation
- ✔ Instructions about the briefing requirements, as I discuss in Chapter 4
- ✔ A statement that all stakeholders must be present
- ✔ Your hourly or daily rate
- ✔ A request that the parties pay for the anticipated half day or full day in advance
- ✔ A statement regarding forfeiture of a portion of the fee if the mediation is cancelled within a certain number of days prior to the scheduled mediation
- ✔ A reference to the enclosed contract and instructions to sign the contract and return it by a certain date with the advance payment

Constructing a contract

Prior to any mediation, it's good practice to have signed contracts from all parties. When drafting your contract, be sure it includes the following:

- ✔ Your agreement to facilitate the settlement of the dispute on the date and at the time scheduled at the rate you charge

- ✔ A statement regarding forfeiture of a portion of the fee if the mediation is cancelled within a certain number of days prior to the mediation

- ✔ A choice of law provision that designates the jurisdiction in which any dispute that arises under the contract will be heard

- ✔ Signature lines for both parties and their counsel (if any), along with a space to write in the date

By the way, I *never* have signed contracts. I get paid in advance and I don't consider charging cancellation fees to be a great way to make friends in the community, but others disagree.

Some mediators include provisions in the agreement for confidentiality, a practice I don't recommend, as I explain next.

Writing a confidentiality agreement . . . or not

Though some mediators provide clients with confidentiality agreements, I strongly advise not to, especially if you're not a lawyer. If you tell the parties that their communications are confidential when they're really not, you become the target of a potential lawsuit. If the confidentiality agreement you draft doesn't hold up in court, either party may claim that certain disclosures during the mediation hurt their chances for success. In some states, like California, the statutory protection for mediation confidentiality is sufficient to impose it on the parties. Some states, however, require the parties to enter into signed agreements that reference the state's confidentiality provisions for confidentiality protection to arise. You must know the law in your own state and in your local federal trial court district.

Leave it to the parties' attorneys (if they have attorneys) to instruct them on the precise coverage of the confidentiality law in the state where the mediation is taking place. And remember that the law may vary based on disputes that could eventually be litigated in either a state or federal court. If you feel that you must present the parties with a confidentiality agreement, I encourage you to brush up on confidentiality basics in Chapter 7 and to draft the agreement only with qualified legal advice. If you're an attorney, make sure you follow the current confidentiality laws in the jurisdiction in which your clients' dispute is pending. The law is still in a state of flux and may always be.

What I tell parties about confidentiality

In California, where I practice, I tell the parties that the mediation of a dispute pending in the state court is protected by the statutory mediation confidentiality rule of law. That rule, which is contained in California's evidence code, prevents all parties and the mediator from submitting in evidence in a court or administrative proceeding anything any party said or did during the mediation. If the parties wish to have a written confidentiality agreement, I tell them that their attorneys should provide it.

I don't provide a confidentiality agreement of my own because I don't represent the parties and can't give them legal advice or properly present them with a document carrying legal consequences. In federal court matters, I tell the parties that no rule protects the confidentiality of their communications here in California and that they should look to their counsel for a written agreement if they wish to ensure that their confidences won't be disclosed. Whether it's New York or Constantinople, be aware of confidentiality laws wherever you practice mediation.

Avoiding the use of settlement agreements

A *settlement agreement* documents the understanding that the parties in a dispute agree on. Many mediation panels and community mediation centers have boilerplate settlement agreements. However, I strongly advise against such agreements, especially if you're not a lawyer. Why? Because if you draft a contract for the parties or provide them with a form that you or they fill in at the mediation's conclusion, you're setting yourself up for a malpractice claim if the agreement is found to be unenforceable. Drafting an agreement may also constitute the unauthorized practice of law and make you subject to fines or other penalties levied by the state board of bar overseers.

Attorneys spend one full year studying contract law. Furthermore, some attorneys spend their entire careers doing nothing but litigating the meaning of ambiguous terms contained in contracts. If you're not a lawyer and you present the parties with an unenforceable contract, you expose yourself to a lot of risk and gain nothing in return. The likelihood of being sued may be relatively low, but you're better off avoiding the possibility altogether.

That said, closing the deal reached by the parties requires *them* to put the terms of their agreement in writing, a process that mediators facilitate. The parties should never leave a successful mediation without a written document that lists all the terms of their agreement, but as the mediator, you shouldn't draft it. Flip to Chapter 14 for my complete how-to on closing a mediation.

Writing a follow-up letter

If the mediation ends in agreement, write the parties a follow-up letter that congratulates them on successfully resolving their dispute. If the mediation ends with no agreement, write the parties a follow-up letter that congratulates them on the progress they've made and suggest one or more additional mediation sessions if you believe they were sufficiently close to an agreement.

You may also use this letter to ask for the payment of any outstanding fees if, for instance, you charge an hourly rate and the advance payment for your time was insufficient to cover your full fee.

Purchasing liability insurance

As of the writing of this book, liability insurance for mediators is very affordable, probably because mediator lawsuits are rare. Nevertheless, before you open for business, you should purchase professional liability insurance.

Contact your insurance representative or search online for "liability insurance" to find companies that offer liability insurance. Choose a reputable company. You may find a company that offers reduced rates for members of mediation organizations; consult other mediators in your community for suggestions.

To calculate how much coverage you need, start with your *net worth* — the value of everything you own in excess of your debts to others — and add a reasonable amount to cover any attorney fees. Win or lose, the cost of defending against a malpractice suit can run into the tens of thousands of dollars, and you can't recover these fees, unless you have an agreement that permits you to recover them. That said, almost all liability insurance policies provide coverage for unlimited attorney fees. Policies rarely provide for the expenditure of attorney fees to reduce the policy limits, but you should be aware that such policies exist and make your cost/benefit decisions accordingly.

Setting Rates and Fees

Mediation rates and fees vary from as low as nothing for pro bono work to upward of $20,000 a day for commercial litigation. What you can expect depends a great deal on two factors: the arena in which you choose to mediate (community mediation at the low end and commercial litigation at the high end) and the level of demand for your services — the more prestigious the clients and the more prominent your background, the higher the rates and fees you can and should charge.

Because the legal market is so stratified, if you're an attorney or former judge entering the litigated-case ADR market, take a look at your location and market, and figure out what dollar amounts fit in each of these categories:

JAMS

JAMS (Judicial Arbitration and Mediation Service) is, by far, the best-known mediation panel in the world.

JAMS is top-heavy with retired judges. Its remaining mediators are retired attorneys who had very prestigious, high-flying careers litigating and trying high stakes commercial disputes. JAMS takes up to 50 percent of the fees charged by its mediators, which range from about $6,000 to $20,000 per day.

Other panels offer the same services as JAMS, often for far less money, including ADR Services, Inc. (my panel), Alternative Resolution Centers (ARC), and Judicate West (another panel on which I served) in California.

✔ **Low end:** What solo practitioners charge usually represents the rate for the low end of the free market.

✔ **Mid-range:** Check out what the mid-level panels charge.

✔ **High end:** Look at what the people at the Judicial Arbitration and Mediation Service (JAMS) charge. For more about JAMS, see the nearby sidebar and the organization's website: www.jamsadr.com. If you're not an attorney, set your fees according to your market's ability to pay you, what your fees were in the pre-mediation practice you were engaged in, or the value you provide to your market.

Typically, commercial litigation in specialty areas including antitrust, intellectual property, securities fraud, unfair competition, and all "bet the company" cases pay the highest rates, involve attorneys from the most prestigious AmLaw 200 law firms (the "Fortune 500" of the legal profession), and have the most dollar value in controversy. In my market, the commercial litigation numbers look like this:

✔ **Low range:** $200-$350 an hour

✔ **Mid-range:** Between $500 and $600 an hour

✔ **High range:** In the $10,000 to $20,000 per day stratosphere

Mediators who serve the general public often charge between $100 and $150 per hour, and I'd be loath to charge any less than that. Each party pays only half, so that's $50 to $75 per hour per party, assuming two parties are involved. If more parties are involved, the per-party cost is even less.

Keep in mind that these numbers represent rates in my market during the writing of this book. Use the numbers only to gauge the relative differences among low, mid, and high ranges. Do your own research to find out the going rates for your market, location, and type of mediation.

As you're getting established, aim for the average. If you price yourself too far below the average, you won't get your foot in the door, and if you price yourself too high, you'll have trouble attracting clientele. After a year or so, you have a much better read of the market segment you're actually serving. You know how much people can afford to pay and how much money you're saving them by ending their dispute.

Some mediators tack on to their rate a flat administrative fee to handle correspondence, parking, postage, and conference room expenses. Again, check your local market for the size of that fee. If everyone else is charging it, you should charge it too.

Don't try to compete on price by undercutting the competition. That's bad for the profession and could backfire. Many mediators discover that they must raise their fees to be a credible presence in their market, even when they're just starting out. If you set your rates and fees too low, prospective clients start to think that you must be a lousy mediator.

Joining a Panel to Share Fees and Reduce Overhead

When you're well-established as a high-flying and high-earning mediator, you may want to consider joining a panel. A panel functions sort of like a co-op, supplying office space, conference rooms, administrative support, and advertising for all its members and collecting a commission from members based on their earnings. Panels typically mediate only litigated civil disputes and usually not family law or cases in which the parties aren't represented by attorneys.

Joining a panel is a little like joining a club. Panels may not have a list of qualifications or a formal application process, but to join a private panel, you must earn or have the potential to earn in the six-figure range to be deemed worthy. You usually have to know somebody who knows somebody working on the panel and then parlay that connection into a meeting with the panel's owner or recruiter. Panel membership is based on the owner or recruiter's sense of your earning potential. The panel makes money only if you make money because the panel takes between 25 and 50 percent of the fee it charges for your services in addition to an administrative charge.

I'm affiliated with a panel called ADR Services, Inc., with offices in San Diego, Los Angeles, San Francisco, and San Jose. Approximately half of ADR's mediators are former judges, and the other half are retired attorneys. Fees at ADR Services range from $250 to $700 per hour. ADR negotiates a commission percentage separately with each of its mediators, but none, I believe, is as high as 50 percent.

Chapter 16

Marketing Yourself and Your Business Online and Off

*U*nless you go the mediation panel route, one of the roles you play as a mediator is a marketing specialist. Your goal is to promote your brand — You, Inc. — online and off, via a website, a blog, social media (Facebook, Twitter, and so on), press releases, business cards, public speaking, and press-the-flesh networking. This chapter shows you how to market like a pro.

Tuning In to Your Market

When you choose a niche, as I explain in Chapter 2, you choose a market, and that market becomes the community in which you practice. Your market/community may be special education, healthcare, human resources, assisted living, community mediation, or something else entirely. Your market also extends to your personal and professional contacts, especially attorneys who may secure your services and community organizations where you live and do business.

Whatever your market is, you must become involved in it as an active member of the community. The following sections explain where and how to get started. (For more about getting involved in your market, see Chapter 17.)

Immersing yourself in your market

To know where to invest your promotional efforts, make a list of all the organizations and groups of people you can think of that comprise your market. Start with the following:

✔ Attorneys

✔ Bar associations

✔ Colleagues

✔ Community and religious organizations

✔ Corporate counsel

✔ Educational networks, especially those related to mediation

✔ Friends and family members

✔ Law firms

✔ Trade organizations related to your area of expertise

Assuming that you focus on a specific niche market or industry, immerse yourself in that market by reading what your market reads and going where your market goes. In other words, read trade publications and attend relevant trade shows, conferences, and events. Immersing yourself in your market

✔ Sensitizes you to common concerns and areas of dispute.

✔ Brings you up to speed on essential terminology and concepts so that you can talk the talk.

✔ Gives you an inside perspective on how people in the community think, what they feel, and how they interact with one another.

✔ Provides valuable networking opportunities to connect with the movers and shakers in your market.

Tune in to the way community members talk, act, and dress, and do your best to fit in. Eventually, you want to stand out from the crowd, but do so by being better, not by breaking with tradition. Respect your market and its ways.

Building your marketing database

All the people you meet are potential clients, so keep track of them. Ask for business cards, and when you get back to your office, transfer the information on the cards to your database — typically a contact-management program such as Microsoft Outlook. But don't stop there. Keep detailed notes about each contact, including the following:

- Where and when you met
- What you discussed
- Where the person works and what she does
- Personal information, including marital status and children
- Whether the person has used your services
- Which marketing materials you've sent to the person and by what means
- Whether the person has referred business to you
- How the person found out about you, if she's seeking your services

Always ask new and returning clients who referred them to you or what brought you to mind when they needed a mediator. Write their responses in a notebook you carry with you for that purpose and then transfer them to your contact-management program when you return to your office.

Nobody likes to be sold, so avoid any hard-sell tactics or obvious business solicitations. Instead of selling yourself or your services, a better approach is to sell the mediation process. Talk it up as an attractive alternative to litigation and other less productive forms of "resolution," including breaking off relationships, resorting to online complaint boards, or keying someone's car. Discuss what you do and how you do it. Assuming you're a skilled and experienced mediator, as you discuss mediation, you accomplish two very important marketing goals:

- You sell the mediation process.
- You establish yourself as a credible authority, so if the person needs your services now or in the future, your name and face will take center stage.

Establishing an Online Presence

When most people are in the market for just about anything, including a mediator, they fire up their computers or their smart phones and search for it online. When people search for mediation services, you want your name to pop up at or near the top of the search results, and when people click your link, you want your site to send a clear message that you're the mediator they want to hire. The following sections explain how to create a respectable online presence.

Launching a website, blog, or both

The first order of business in establishing an online presence is to build a center of operations — a website, blog, or combination of the two. Having a site in place simplifies your other online efforts; for example, if you create a Facebook page later, you can feed content from your blog to your Facebook page to automate the process of keeping your page up to date. In addition, your website or blog gives you a destination to drive traffic to, so if you have a free business listing on Google Places, for example, you can drive traffic from that listing to your site.

Choosing a turnkey, do-it-yourself, or custom solution

When you're ready to set up shop on the web, you have some decisions to make, the first of which is related to how much of your own time, effort, and expertise you want to invest in building and maintaining your site. You have three choices here:

- ✔ **Turnkey:** With a turnkey solution, a service sets up your website and provides instructions and tools to populate it with the desired content. Mediate.com offers the most popular turnkey website solution for mediators — its Dynamic Web Site Package (see `www.mediate.com/products/pg41.cfm`).

  The most popular turnkey blog provider for lawyers is LexBlog (`www.lexblog.com`). The LexBlog package is pricey, but it comes with free webinars on how to best utilize social media to market your services. More important for the mediator in the litigated dispute market is LexBlog's placement of your blog entries on its many marketing portals, meaning that your blog is one of the few alternative dispute resolution (ADR) blogs in an online universe populated by your market — lawyers. For no additional fee, LexBlog tweets your interesting posts, includes them on subject matter pages on its own website, and displays your tweets on LexTweet, its legal community of members who use Twitter to discuss the law. That's a lot of marketing to a highly concentrated niche market.

- ✔ **Do-it-yourself:** You can create your own website or blog through a web hosting service, such as Bluehost (`www.Bluehost.com`), InMotion (`www.Inotionosting.com`), HostGator (`www.HostGator.com`), or iPage (`www.iPage.com`). These services enable you to register your own domain (such as yourname.com) and provide content management systems (CMSs), such as WordPress, that you can install and use to build and maintain your website or blog. This is the most affordable option, but it requires time and a certain amount of technical knowledge and talent.

- ✔ **Custom solution:** You can hire a web developer to set up a site for you according to your specifications. This may seem like the most costly option, but you can find plenty of highly skilled people willing to work inexpensively just to get their web design businesses off the ground.

Nothing's worse for your online marketing program than a poorly designed website; it's like wearing tattered jeans and dirty sandals to a business meeting.

Don't hire someone to build your site until you decide on a clear idea of what you want it to look like. Check out the websites used by the best, most professional, and most likely users of your services. Then look as much like that as possible (or better) without losing your own unique personality in the process.

Deciding on a website, blog, or combination website/blog

If you want a web presence without having to constantly post fresh content, a website is the ideal solution. A blog requires regular attention, typically at least two posts a week to keep visitors engaged. Perhaps even more important, a blog tells search directories that your site is constantly posting fresh content, which can significantly improve its search engine ranking.

If you want fresh content but don't have the time or inclination to develop it, hosting through Mediate.com is a very good option. Along with your website, Mediate.com provides fresh content in your area of practice once a week.

A third option is a combination website/blog. These sites typically consist of several pages of static content — including an about page, a contact page, and a page for each service you provide (mediation, training, consulting, speaking, and so on) — as well as a separate blog page, which can function as your home page. You can create and maintain a combination website/blog using a blogging platform such as WordPress. Check out my training and consulting site at `www.shenegotiates.com` for an example of a combination website/blog.

Include a biography and a professional-looking photo of yourself on your site. People want to know the person they're thinking about working with, and putting your bio and photograph out there in public helps build trust.

Blogging your way to opportunities

To be a thought leader in the field of mediation, I strongly encourage you to blog. You can set up a separate blog or have an integrated website/blog, but you really should be posting fresh content at least twice a week, along with contributing to online discussions in mediation groups, publishing press releases, and tweeting or retweeting.

Start by reading blogs, especially those in your area of specialty. You can add RSS feeds for the blogs that interest you to a news reader like Google Reader (`www.google.com/reader/view`) and skim through the headlines for intriguing stories. Reading what other people are learning and thinking about mediation, peace-building, and topics relevant to your industry provides inspiration for your own posts. In addition, you become more in tune with your community and what's considered acceptable both in content and tone.

Becoming a target for opportunities

I linked my way to blogging success when Forbes.com created a community of business and financial blogs on its website. Because I was a member of this community, I found good reasons to form relationships with Forbes managers and journalists. I pitched a couple of stories to Forbes editors and published my first article there in September 2009, three years after I launched my first negotiation blog. In short order, Forbes asked me to write for its legal blog, *On the Docket,* which I did between June and August of 2010.

Because I was starting a consulting and training business that same summer, I asked for and was given the opportunity to start my own blog, named after my business, at ForbesWoman. My first ForbesWoman *She Negotiates* blog post appeared on Forbes.com in December of 2010. In less than a year, that blog brought me to the attention of NPR's *All Things Considered, The New York Times, Toronto Star, Wall Street Journal,* CNN's *Headline News,* the *American Bar Association Journal, Minnesota Public Radio,* numerous journals and online blogs and websites, TV producers who wanted to produce a mediation reality show, and many Fortune 500, AmLaw 200, and professional and managerial organizations that wanted to book me for (paid) speaking engagements. A couple of years ago, Public Radio International called to ask me whether I'd come down to their studio and comment on negotiating retail. Not only was it fun, but several clients mentioned how pleased they were to hear me on their public radio station while driving to an appointment midday. Most recently, Minnesota Public Radio called me twice to opine on the legislative impasse that had recently shut down nonessential government services in that state. That increased my audience and also allowed me to bring the theory and practice of mediation into a venue not normally served by it.

Blogging also makes you known to the entire English-speaking world. And the one characteristic bloggers share is mutual respect for top-notch content and generosity. One of the largest, most sophisticated, and most lucrative mediations over which I presided came all the way to me from New Zealand via blogging. I have a good "blog friend" there who thought of me when a major Australian insurance carrier asked for the name of a U.S. mediator to resolve a lawsuit over the failure of a jet engine. That mediation was held in San Francisco and netted me $10,000 in fees for a two-day meeting.

All of this became possible because I became what you can become — a thought leader in the mediation blogging arena.

Blogging runs on the power of reciprocity — one of the most important tools of influence available to you as a mediator, as I discuss in Chapter 6. When you read something that piques your interest and spurs you to extend the conversation or challenge a claim, post about it. Include a brief excerpt from the source, cite it, and link to it. Soon, people with a natural affinity for what you're talking about will be citing you and excerpting your material.

Spreading the word via social media

Social media is content that's produced and distributed through social interaction on services like Facebook, Twitter, LinkedIn, and YouTube, as well as via e-mail. What's great about social media is that it has the potential to spread like wildfire, and all you need to do is set the spark. It's the ultimate in word-of-mouth advertising.

To maximize the return on investment for your social networking activities, participate actively in groups on several social networking sites — primarily LinkedIn (the most professional of the sites); Facebook (the most ubiquitous of the sites); Twitter (the most casual of the sites); and YouTube (the audio/video site). The following sections explain the basics of how to use these social venues to raise your profile and extend your reach.

Be willing to share your expertise, but be especially careful not to sell — this is called *social* media for a reason. Along the same lines, keep your social and business communications separate. Your friends and family are likely to tire of hearing shop talk very quickly, and your colleagues and clients probably don't want to hear about your personal life. On Facebook, you can accomplish this by creating a separate page for your business. On Twitter, you should have separate accounts.

Setting up shop on Facebook

Although Facebook is almost exclusively a social venue, most of its members expect businesses to have a presence there, and the service encourages businesses to do so. Facebook allows businesses, even freelancers like you, to set up a business page, claim your business listing, and even advertise where it's appropriate to do so. Although I can't possibly provide all the steps for establishing a business presence on Facebook, the following lists gives you the basics on what you need to do. For more detailed how-to information, check out *Facebook For Dummies,* 4th Edition, by Carolyn Abram and Leah Pearlman (Wiley), or consult Facebook's Help Center (click Account in the top menu bar and then click Help Center).

1. **Set up a Facebook page.**

   To get started, scroll to the bottom of any Facebook page and click Create a Page. Your page becomes your center of operations on Facebook. Be sure to include a link to your website on your page.

2. **Create an RSS feed to pull any entries you publish on your blog onto your Facebook page.**

   As long as you post fresh content to your blog, this ensures that your page always has fresh content.

3. **Get a vanity URL (such as `Facebook.com/montana-mediation`) for your page.**

   After your page has 25 "likes" (25 people indicate that they like your page), you can get a vanity URL. Go to `www.facebook.com/username`, click Set a User Name for Your Pages (below the box that allows you to set a user name for your profile), and follow the on-screen instructions.

4. **Claim your Facebook place.**

   Facebook Places is a feature that enables you to take advantage of *location marketing* — presenting content to customers and prospects that's relevant to their current geographical location. To claim your Facebook place, access the Facebook app from your smart phone or go to `http://touch.facebook.com` and click the Places tab. Or, if you're using Facebook on a computer, click in the Search box in the top menu and search for your business by name. If your business isn't listed as a place, add it, claim it, and then customize your listing.

5. **Add a *badge* to your website/blog that users can click to access your Facebook page.**

   See the section "Cross-promoting your website, blog, and social accounts," later in this chapter, for details.

Facebook provides *Insights* that display statistics about your page, including the number of visitors, number of people who interact with your page, number of comments posted, and so on. To access Insights, click View Insights (near the top of the right column when you're viewing your page).

Tweeting on Twitter

Twitter is another popular social venue where you can and should be active. With Twitter, you send *tweets,* short messages that consist of no more than 140 characters, including spaces. Though these tweets enable you to distribute only snippets of content, you can use them in the following ways to generate business and open doors to new opportunities:

✔ **Drive traffic to your website or blog.** Whenever you publish a blog post, tweet about it and include a link to that post. If the link is too long, you can get an abbreviated version of it at `www.bitly.com`.

✔ **Find out when someone needs a mediator.** People who are actively involved in a lawsuit or dispute are likely to tweet about it, and if they do, you'll be one of the first to hear about it.

✔ **Demonstrate your mediation skills.** Play the peacemaker with people who are engaged in passionate, heated, or even explosive disputes. If you can keep your head and level the discussion's tone, folks in the "Twitterverse" will think of you whenever they need an intermediary.

✔ **Network.** Use Twitter as a cocktail party or industry event, chatting with people about their business, legal practice, interests, and the challenges they face. It's cheap, it's easy, and you don't have to wear a suit.

To quickly build a network on Twitter, follow the market leaders and their followers. Kevin O'Keefe, LexBlog's founder and owner, has the same market I do — lawyers in the AmLaw 200. When I began tweeting two years ago, he had about a thousand followers, so I clicked on Kevin's followers and followed them. Because it's customary on Twitter to reciprocate following by following back, I had an instantaneous network.

Use hash tags (#) to flag keywords and hot topics in your market, such as #adr, #mediator, and #mediate. A hash tag appears as a link in your tweet that Twitter users can click to see tweets by others that pertain to that topic. Lots of people tweeting about the same topic and hash-tagging the term can increase your exposure in the community. (If you need to hash tag a phrase, just run the words together; for example, #basketballmediation.)

Be patient. Your followers and the people you follow on Twitter may not need your services for several years. When they do, however, they'll know your name and handle and where to find you.

To find out more about Twitter, including how to get started, visit `http://support.twitter.com`. For more about using Twitter for marketing and sales, check out *Twitter Marketing For Dummies,* 2nd Edition, by Kyle Lacy (Wiley).

Getting connected on LinkedIn

LinkedIn is more for business than social networking, which makes it a great place to network with fellow mediators and the people who are likely to be in the market for mediators, especially attorneys, corporate executives, and small-business owners. In addition, LinkedIn gives you another opportunity to link back to your website and blog.

To get started, create a free account on LinkedIn at `www.linkedin.com` and follow the on-screen instructions to flesh out your profile.

After you create your profile, customize your profile URL (web address) to make it more descriptive. For example, you may want to use your name as part of your LinkedIn profile address. To customize your profile URL, log in to LinkedIn, click Profile, Edit Profile, and Edit (next to Public Profile). Scroll down to the Your Public Profile URL section (bottom right), click Customize Your Public Profile URL, enter the last part of the URL in the text box, and click Set Custom URL.

Don't use LinkedIn simply as an online résumé or a fishing pole dangling lazily and unattended in your market's waters. You need to join or form groups and ask and answer questions. Following are just a few of the groups I belong to, two of which I created:

✔ Networking with Colleagues Who Will Refer ADR Business to Me and Who Will Mentor and Sponsor Me and I Them

✔ Networking with Colleagues Who Will Refer Consulting and Training Business to My "She Negotiates" Business

✔ My Litigated Case Market

These LinkedIn groups are the equivalent of professional and business organizations that you'd be going to in order to get to know your market and how to serve it better. You can network here free in your jammies with no rubber-chicken dinners! How much better does networking get than that?

Answering and asking questions are also great ways to engage with the mediation community and your market, establish your expertise, and get new ideas for blog posts. Asking questions can serve as subversive marketing. For example, you may ask an industry group what it looks for in a mediator. Doing so places you in immediate contact with members of your market who are interested enough in mediation to answer your question, and it provides valuable feedback on how to better meet your market's needs. You may even want to highlight those qualities in your promotional materials.

Consider sharing your blog posts in LinkedIn groups to drive traffic to your site. You may also want to add a question to the end of your blog post to elicit feedback from colleagues and people in your market while establishing yourself as an authority among those who are most likely to use your services.

For additional details on how to use LinkedIn, check out *LinkedIn For Dummies,* 2nd Edition, by Joel Elad (Wiley).

Posting video on YouTube

If you have any video you can use to help promote yourself — video of interviews, speaking engagements, mediation training sessions, and so on — consider creating a YouTube account (at www.youtube.com) and uploading the video. If you want to upload video of a TV interview or some other footage you don't have the rights to, be sure to obtain permission first.

YouTube is great for two main reasons. First, it's the place people go when they're looking for video on just about any topic imaginable. Second, YouTube video is very easy to share on your site. All you do is pull up the video on YouTube, copy the embed code, and paste it on a web page or in a blog post.

Don't post any obviously commercial ads on YouTube. They'll likely drive away more clients than they can possibly attract. Instead, consider posting the following types of video:

✔ Educational videos that show people how to mediate.

✔ Entertaining videos that show the lighter side of mediation.

✔ Taped interviews or speaking engagements that establish you as a credible authority on mediation.

Encouraging users to share your web content via social media venues

One of the best ways to disseminate the content you post on your website or blog is to have other people do it for you. Add share buttons to appropriate content on your web pages and to every blog entry you post. Users can click a share button to "like" the content on Facebook, retweet it on Twitter, or share it on other social venues. If you're using a content management system, such as WordPress, to manage your site, adding share buttons is easy — all you do is install a plugin that adds the share buttons for you.

Cross-promoting your website, blog, and social accounts

You have a website and/or blog and social media properties on Facebook, Twitter, LinkedIn, and YouTube. Now you want to pull them all together and use them to cross-promote one another. You've already accomplished half of this by adding your website and blog addresses to your social accounts. All that's left to do is link your website/blog to your social properties. Here's how:

✔ On Facebook, you can create different types of *badges* to add to your website or blog that people can click to access your Facebook page. Facebook provides the HTML source code to paste on your site for displaying the badge. To get a badge, visit `www.facebook.com/badges`.

✔ On Twitter, you can create a Follow button to add to your site. After logging in, scroll to the bottom of the right pane and click Resources. This takes you to a page where you can create a Follow button, Tweet button, or Widget to add to your website or blog.

✔ On LinkedIn, log on to your account, click Profile, Edit Profile, and Edit (next to Public Profile). Scroll down to the section called Your Public Profile URL (lower right), click Create a Profile Badge, and follow the on-screen instructions to create your badge.

✔ To link your site to your YouTube account, head to YouTube's Creator's Corner at `www.youtube.com/t/creators_downloads`, where you can find YouTube buttons and Banners.

✔ To link your Twitter and Facebook accounts, log in to both accounts in separate browser windows or tabs, go to `http://apps.facebook.com/twitter`, and when asked, "Would you like to connect your Twitter and Facebook accounts?" click Allow.

Poke around on the various social media sites to find out more about linking your social accounts.

Rounding out your online presence

Maintaining a website, blog, and various social media properties is an excellent foundation for your online marketing efforts, but you should attend to a few additional items, including the following:

- **Adding an e-mail signature:** Whenever you send e-mail, you have the opportunity to promote your online properties — your website, blog, Facebook page, Twitter account, and so on. The easiest way to promote your properties via e-mail is to add a *signature* to all outgoing messages. A signature includes your name, contact information, and anything else you want to include, such as your e-mail and website addresses. The steps for adding a signature to outgoing messages varies among e-mail clients. Check the client's help system for details.

- **Claiming your business listings:** Google Places, Yahoo! Local, Yelp, and Facebook Places are like online Yellow Pages, providing listings for businesses. If your mediation practice is an established business, you may already have listings on these services. As the proprietor of the business, you can claim these listings and then customize them with additional text, photos, and links. If your business isn't listed, you can and should add it.

- **Posting press releases:** Although your readers will naturally distribute your content, you may be able to increase the speed at which they disseminate your content by posting a press release. Press releases are especially useful for announcing special events, such as the launch of a new business or service; for example, if you decide to enter the public speaking arena, you may want to announce your availability to the world. One of the best ways to get started is to set up an account on PRWeb (at www.prweb.com). PRWeb provides information and tools for composing and posting press releases, and it distributes releases to all the major search engines and news sites, including Yahoo!, Google, Bing, Google News, Yahoo! News, and Topix, as well as to subscribers, including websites, bloggers, and journalists.

- **Sending newsletters:** Some people believe that the newsletter is the best marketing tool ever. As a lawyer who used mediators and other legal services providers, however, I personally steer clear of e-mail marketing because it's incredibly annoying and often diverted by spam catchers. When I wake up in the morning to 50 e-mails, 95 percent of which are marketing materials, I sit at my computer and press *Delete, Delete, Delete, Delete.* Word on the street, however, is that you should stay in contact with everyone on your mailing list at least four times a year. More often is irritating; less often and they won't recall who the heck you are. Short, punchy, get-to-the-point advice is most appreciated.

- **Sending strategic communication:** A *strategic communication* is one that delivers information that's relevant and valuable to a specific market segment. If, for instance, your referral sources are matrimonial lawyers, you might send a newsletter or e-mail that contains updates on laws that affect the settlement of family law disputes.

The most popular program among mediators for managing e-mail marketing is Constant Contact. You can check it out and obtain a free trial at www. constantcontact.com.

Make sure the information you send is relevant and of value. Sending something merely to remind people that you exist could backfire. They may remember you but for all the wrong reasons.

Pressing the Flesh

Although online marketing is an absolute necessity in this day and age, mediation marketing is still primarily a flesh-pressing business, and the people whose flesh you need to press consist of clients, potential clients, and referral sources. To be successful with this face-to-face networking, you need to know what your contacts value most in a mediator, prepare yourself with business cards and brochures, and know the best places to go to get connected.

When parties seek to resolve their dispute through litigation and mediation, they usually consider the problem they're facing right now one of the most difficult challenges they've ever had to deal with. And no matter how much the dispute seems to be "only about money," personal issues of worthiness, fairness, trust, and reliability are so close to the surface you can see their periscopes. Both parties want someone they can count on to resolve the dispute in a fair and equitable manner. They want the King Solomon of mediators — a highly competent individual with character and integrity.

Of course, to qualify for the job, you have to be that person. This isn't something you can fake. Moreover, you must project those qualities in everything you do and through your marketing. The following sections provide the guidance you need to allow your character to shine through in your marketing efforts.

Producing business cards and brochures

Even in this age of paperless publishing, business cards and brochures are essential. When you meet someone, you need to be able to hand her something to remember you by that contains your contact information.

At the bare minimum, you should have a business card. You can create business cards yourself using a desktop publishing program and business card stock from your local business supply store, have them professionally designed and printed at your local copy shop, or order them online — check out www.moo.com. Make sure the front of your business card contains the following details:

✔ Your business name, if any, and your name

✔ A professional photo of yourself so people can recognize you

✔ Your title or what you offer, such as "Mediator," "ADR Services," "Mediation, Training, and Consulting," and so on

✔ Your phone number, fax number, and e-mail address

✔ Your website and/or blog address

Use the back of the business card to add details about your education and experience. A brief bulleted list of your education and training along with three or four major accomplishments as a mediator should do the trick.

Give the people you meet a few business cards so they can hand them out without giving away the only card they have.

Brochures are a great tool for giving people even more information about what you do. Include the same information on your brochure as you have on your business card but add information about your education, experience, specializations, and the services you offer. Brochures should also include testimonials from satisfied clients. Don't be afraid to ask for these. Most people whom you help resolve a dispute are pretty darn grateful, and if you ask, they'll gladly provide you with a blushingly flattering snippet of praise.

Striking up conversations

Regardless of how you meet people, you eventually need to talk with them. If you're at an event or conference, I recommend picking out someone who's clearly uncomfortable wading into the crowd. She hangs out in the corners with a drink in her hand, looking a little like a middle school kid at her first dance. Walk up to her, extend your hand, and say, "Hi, I'm so-and-so, and I'm feeling a little uncomfortable about plunging into the crowd right away myself. What do you do?" or "What brings you here?"

Just as you don't walk into someone's home and pull out your sample case of jewelry or nutritional supplements, don't start selling when you're networking at an "on the ground" event. My market (lawyers) is tired of being sold to by mediators. A good rule of thumb is to make the beginning and middle of the conversations about *them*, *their* business, and *their* concerns. Start with the usual small talk — traffic, weather, whatever — and then transition to an open-ended question like, "How's business?" If they're shy, draw them out by sharing your own concerns. "It's been a tough year; I've been awfully surprised at how deep and long this recession has been and how much it has affected the legal market. How about you?" People like people who like them. And to genuinely like another person, you have to get to know them. Be inquisitive and let your curiosity drive the conversation.

Don't talk about your profession until the person asks about what you do. Because I begin problem solving as soon as a potential client reveals his greatest business challenges, eventually he'll look at me quizzically and ask, "What do *you* do?" and I say, "I solve problems . . . by helping litigators settle disputes with difficult clients or issues that seem to require the decision of a judge or jury." Then we're off to the races.

Make striking up conversations with people profitable to you. Whether you host networking events, provide in-house training, or speak at industry events, always have sign-up sheets available to capture the attendees' names, addresses, telephone numbers, and e-mail addresses. In addition to including these people in your database and tracking any business that comes your way as a result of these events, communicate regularly with your new contacts by way of your online or printed marketing materials. Just be sure to follow my previous recommendations related to any direct-marketing efforts.

If you speak or train, provide attendees with evaluation forms to get their feedback on your presentations. Improving your presentations is one of the best ways to improve your marketing.

In my database, I note the issues that former clients and networking contacts are interested in. If I run across something in my own reading, I send it in the mail along with my business card and a brochure if it seems relevant, or I simply send them a link. This is casual yet professional, and most important, it counts as doing a favor for a potential client — once again using the powerful principle of reciprocity in your marketing efforts.

Attending trade shows

If you specialize in a certain area, such as franchisee-franchisor disputes or the travel, recreation, automobile, or garment industries, attend trade shows to get better acquainted with your market and allow your market to become better acquainted with you and what you offer. When you hear about a trade show in your area of expertise, head to its registration website, research it, and, if it sounds interesting, register.

Don't waste your money on a booth or table. You need to be as mobile as possible. I tend to hang out in the exhibitor room or by the coffee/sweet stand and simply start up conversations with attendees, as I explain in the preceding section. Have plenty of business cards and brochures to hand out, but keep in mind that giving is better than receiving — you can't stay in touch with someone unless you have *his* contact information.

Avoiding the most common faux pas

Networking is a two-way street. That is, you have to give to get. If you want referrals, give referrals. If you want someone to keep your card and pass it along to others, keep their cards and pass them along to your contacts. Avoid these two most common faux pas:

- ✔ **Call us, but don't expect us to call you.** Keep track of the people who call you the most and refer business to you, and think of ways to return the favor. If you can't refer business back to them, think of other ways to show your appreciation.

- ✔ **Take our cards even though we'll throw yours away.** Save everyone's business card and ask for additional copies to pass along to your clients and colleagues, and then be sure to distribute those cards. When you hand someone's card to someone else, ask the recipient to please mention your name to the person who gave you the card so that person knows where the referral came from.

Although you have to give to get, don't focus on the get part. Give for the sake of giving and the get will naturally follow. If you're constantly expecting favors in return, you're likely to become disappointed and perhaps even resentful when you don't receive referral business from certain individuals.

Constantly strive to improve your marketing efforts and build on what works. The best way to find out what's working is to ask and keep track of how clients found you. Did they stumble upon your website, wander past your booth at a trade show, hear about you from their attorney, or read an article or blog post that you published? Whatever it is, jot it down and keep tally of where your clients are coming from.

Busting a few common marketing myths

Being a successful mediator isn't just about being good at your job; it also means being able to make a good living at it. As you venture into the business end of mediation, however, you're likely to encounter some common myths that deflate your marketing enthusiasm. The most effective way to deal with these downers is to confront the myths head on and bust them:

Myth: *I have to get my skills down before I build my market.*

Fact: Business development and skills development go hand in hand. You need a network of fans and allies to help you build your reputation, as well as a client base to hone your skills.

Myth: *If I join an ADR firm, it will market for me.*

Fact: The business of building your professional reputation is *your* responsibility and should be done both inside and outside your ADR panel, should you manage to get on one.

Myth: *I'm not good at singing my own praises.*

Fact: Welcome to the club. Business development is a practice, and like mediation, you get better over time by committing to consistent habits that leverage your strengths and your market at the same time.

Chapter 17

Growing Your Business through Client Retention and Community

*B*uilding a business requires more than hanging your shingle and marketing like mad. To grow your mediation business and maximize your earning potential, you have to accomplish two goals:

✔ Keep your best clients.

✔ Get more great clients through marketing and referrals within your community.

In this chapter, I show you how to accomplish these goals through client retention and referrals. (Chapter 16 covers the marketing component.)

Getting Repeat Business

One of the best sources for new business is the clients you've already served, so keep in touch with them. You want to show your clients that you care about them and that you're more concerned about what you can do for them than what they can do for you. The following sections explain how to identify your best clients and show your appreciation.

Identifying your best clients

Your best clients are your most dollar-productive clients. To identify them, look for clients who

- ✔ **Pay you what you're worth:** The best clients recognize that your time is valuable and pay you accordingly without trying to haggle.

- ✔ **Honor your boundaries:** You want clients who contact you when they need your services and are willing to hire you to provide those services. Clients who contact you only for free advice or ask you to mediate their cases for free are time wasters, unless they're an entryway into a particular niche in your market, such as upscale law firms or corporate legal or HR departments.

- ✔ **Provide referrals:** You want clients who not only need your services but also refer others who need your services to you.

- ✔ **Expose you to new opportunities:** Certain clients may serve as a doorway to markets or other opportunities you want to explore.

- ✔ **Challenge you:** Great clients demand excellence and let you know what you can do to improve.

Gathering and using contact information

Retaining quality clients requires that you stay in touch with them, and staying in touch necessitates having their contact information. Following are great resources for gathering contact information:

- ✔ E-mail
- ✔ Business cards
- ✔ Member lists from professional associations and organizations to which you belong
- ✔ Online networking communities
- ✔ Member lists or directories for teams, clubs, schools, hobby groups, churches, volunteer organizations, and so on

After collecting the contact information, organize it. You have a few options here:

- ✔ **E-mail program:** Nearly every e-mail program enables you to store information and keep notes about your contacts. Free programs, such as Windows Live Mail and Mozilla Thunderbird, are fine. Microsoft Outlook and Mac Address Book are more robust.

✔ **LinkedIn:** LinkedIn (www.linkedin.com) is a great way to keep track of clients, assuming that most of them have LinkedIn accounts, because whenever they add or update information about themselves, you immediately have access to the new information.

✔ **Upload to a cloud:** *Cloud computing* is the practice of using web-based applications to perform tasks and access data. You can upload your contacts to a service like Plaxo (www.plaxo.com) or Mac.com and manage them in the cloud with a bit more sophistication and ease. One of the major benefits of cloud computing is that you don't have to copy files or sync devices; you can easily access contacts from your desktop or laptop computer, your smart phone, or any other electronic device wherever you happen to be. All you need is an Internet connection.

✔ **E-mail marketing program:** Bring all your contacts into an e-mail marketing program like iContact or Constant Contact. In addition to functioning as a database, these programs enable you to launch and manage your own marketing campaigns, typically via e-mail and social networking. For example, you can design a professional newsletter with your company logo and use it to regularly deliver articles, updates, information, offers, and the like to everyone or to a select group of your contacts.

Take precautions to protect your clients' information. If you store contact information online, choose a user name and password that are easy for you to remember but difficult for others to guess, and change your password every few months. You may also want to password-protect any portable electronic devices and encrypt files that contain your clients' contact information.

After choosing your contact management preference, enter information for all your contacts. (This is a great job for a high school or college student who wants to earn some money.)

If all you're doing is managing contacts, you're done. If you're using your contacts for online marketing, you have to complete a few additional steps:

1. **Ask permission to add your clients to your e-mail list.**

   You can ask permission in one of the following ways:

   • E-mail clients and request their permission.

   • Provide an opt-in form on your website or blog.

Always allow clients to opt in to receive information, and always provide a quick and obvious way, in every automated e-mail communication, for them to opt out at any time. In addition to giving your clients a choice, allowing clients to opt in or out motivates you to provide content that's valuable enough to keep them engaged.

2. **Develop your marketing campaign.**

   Online marketing programs have instructions or wizards to lead you through the process. Your program may even help you with the preceding step of requesting clients to opt in.

3. **Launch your marketing campaign.**

   After you set up your campaign, launching it is simply a matter of clicking a button to give your okay.

4. **Track the success of each campaign and make adjustments to improve it.**

   Online marketing programs include their own analytics to help you measure the success of campaigns based on client response.

As you focus on keeping track of your clients, provide them with the information they need to keep track of you. Create and attach an e-mail signature to all outgoing e-mail messages that links to your website, blog, and any social networking services you're a member of. (Check your e-mail program's help function to find out more about creating and attaching a signature to outgoing messages.)

Following up with clients postmediation

One of the best ways to retain clients and generate referrals is to follow up with clients after the mediation has concluded. Checking in with clients about a recent mediation, whether or not they've successfully resolved their dispute, gives you the perfect excuse to contact someone.

Keep a journal (or spreadsheet) of every mediation that includes the names of the parties and their attorneys (if any), personal information you learned during the mediation (names of children, important occasions, and the like), a summary of the dispute, the party interests revealed during that dispute, and how the parties resolved the dispute or why you believe the matter went unresolved.

Sometime during the two weeks following the mediation, call the disputants (or their attorneys if they were represented by counsel) to check in and see how everything is going. If the parties settled, has everyone performed as promised? If the dispute remains unresolved, how has it evolved since the mediation? If the parties are still struggling with certain issues, let them know that you're available to help.

Don't treat these as sales calls! Talk to the parties the same way you'd inquire about the well-being of a friend. For example, you can say something like, "I'm always available if you need me." That should be the extent of your promotional efforts.

While you have a party on the phone, request feedback. If the matter wasn't resolved, ask whether you could have done anything better or differently to resolve it. If the parties resolved their dispute, ask whether you could have done anything better or differently to resolve it to their greater satisfaction.

Asking for feedback is difficult, or at least it was difficult for me for a number of years, because no one wants to hear criticism, especially people who shame easily. Still, if you don't ask, you'll never really learn how to improve your performance. Sometimes, the parties haven't even formed an opinion regarding your performance. They're grateful you've called because it gives them another opportunity to celebrate the end of a bad experience or rethink their position and find a way to come back to the negotiating table without losing face.

Asking for feedback is one of the best and easiest ways for you to learn the good, the bad, and the ugly of your own practice; to demonstrate to your market how dedicated you are to your job and how much you care about your clients; and to increase your good reputation in your market.

Remaining in constant contact

After the mediation and follow-up call, remain in regular contact with clients through your soft-sell e-mail and social marketing efforts. A major challenge you face, however, is in coming up with something to say — something that's relevant and valuable for your target market.

If you're involved in a group with shared interests, such as a trade organization, coming up with ideas is often a matter of simply keeping track of ongoing discussions and hot topics. Every question and every problem, for example, is an idea for a blog post or an article in your newsletter. If you're having trouble coming up with ideas, consider the following:

- ✔ Let people know what you're doing, such as

  - Events you're attending or hosting

  - Classes you're taking or teaching

  - Books you're reading

  - Insights you've had during recent mediations, while still retaining confidentiality

  - New services you're offering

- ✔ Refer your contacts to blogs you think they'll find useful.

- ✔ Cite articles and stories that are relevant to your market and link to articles if they're online.

- ✔ Review resources and tools that may help your market solve a common problem or fulfill a desire.

Know your audience. If you're writing for lawyers, for example, demonstrating your substantive knowledge in their area of practice is key. If you're writing for other mediators, insider language may be acceptable. But if you're writing for consumers, establish a more conversational tone and avoid industry-related jargon, unless your market *is* an industry, such as construction or tech. If you're not sure what your audience wants and needs, ask, and then give it to them.

Your goal is to establish yourself as an authority by writing about the issues, concerns, wants, and needs of your niche market.

Growing Your Client Base through Referrals

The mediation business is first and foremost a relationship business. Mediation training and experience, and the diplomas, certificates, and awards hanging on your walls, don't prove that you're a top-notch mediator. Only recommendations within your market do.

To harness the power of the people, you need to work on building and expanding your referral network so that great clients will come your way.

Sizing up your market

When you decide to grow your client base, one of the first steps is to target your niche, so you need to know specifically what that niche is. If you're unclear what your niche is, ask who, what, when, where, and why questions, as explained in the following sections.

Who?

Your niche market typically is defined by the people you serve. Who are they? Do they work in the same industry? Are they all in the school system? Are they business owners or employees? Are they married couples? Are they mediators who can benefit from your experience and expertise?

What?

What exactly do you do? At the very least, you help parties resolve their disputes and mend their relationships, but try to get more specific than that. Perhaps you specialize in corporate mediation, in a specific industry, or in a certain type of mediation such as family or community mediation or personal injury claims. Maybe you provide mediation training and speak at conferences.

When?

Another way to define what you do is to ask yourself when people typically need your services. Do they usually contact you when they're dealing with personal injury claims, divorce, labor disputes, or child custody?

Where?

Location is everything in mediation, just as it is in real estate. You may shine in a certain area of your town and be an apparition in another. To find your place, ask the following questions:

> Where do you consistently find kindred spirits?
>
> Where are you most credible?
>
> Where is the greatest need coupled with the greatest appreciation for your work?
>
> Where do the people in the greatest need of your services live or work? Are they in small business, communities, schools, corporations, government offices, online, offline?

Why?

When identifying and serving a specific market, the people in that market usually want to know why. Think of it in terms of a mission statement, 50 words or fewer. Knowing your *Big Deal Why* helps you get outside of yourself and focus on the needs of the people you're serving and the results you're committed to producing.

Develop an authentic elevator pitch for each service you provide. Your elevator pitch must accomplish the following:

- ✔ Demonstrate your understanding of the challenges the parties face
- ✔ Express your vision of the ultimate outcome — the parties being empowered to resolve their own disputes

For example, if you're presenting to a troubled homeowner's association, you might say, "I help communities like yours preserve your standards while seeking to adapt to the changing needs of the people invested in it." This example demonstrates a general understanding of the challenges the parties face — the association must uphold standards while the homeowners themselves have needs that must be met. It also expresses a hope that the community will ultimately develop a system for resolving its differences.

Finding recruits for your referral network

Expanding your client base is often easiest when you approach it as a team sport. Join forces with an elite squad of like-minded professionals and associates in your niche market and work together as business partners to generate clients for one another. To find recruits for your referral network, look to the communities you're already a member of, including

- ✔ Local attorneys in your area of expertise
- ✔ Professional associations and networking groups
- ✔ Social networking circles, including those on Facebook, Twitter, and LinkedIn
- ✔ Legal and mediation bloggers and journalists

Be selective. Finding recruits is about quality, not quantity. Invest time and energy networking only with people or groups who are likely ideal clients or are able and willing to refer you to potential clients that meet your criteria.

To expand your search, draw up a list of organizations, associations, and communities in your target market or niche. Place the ones that have the most potential for generating business at the top.

After you identify your short list, join a group and provide leadership. A visible leadership position in the right kind of business organization can be the cornerstone of your referral network. Too often a mediator simply attends the meetings and is just one more face in the crowd. When you take a leadership position, you immediately raise your profile, and members become more motivated to get to know you.

Mingling with prospective clients and referral network recruits

Although your primary networking goal may be to generate referrals to garner some business, that's the worst way to approach it. The best way is to become a servant; that is, focus on meeting the needs of others. Do that and the people you serve will reward you. They'll hire you when they need a mediator and refer clients to you when they meet someone who needs your services.

If you go to an association meeting, be prepared and have a clear idea of what you want to accomplish. Go with the intention of meeting one or two new people. If possible, target specific people in advance and introduce yourself to them.

As you meet new people, work on perfecting your networking skills. Following are some networking do's and don'ts:

- ✔ **Be curious.** Transfer your mediation skills to the networking arena by engaging in small talk and asking diagnostic questions to gather information about what people do for a living, where they live, what challenges they face, and details regarding their family and interests. Then, move toward questions about their profession or their business and the function they serve in that business.

- ✔ **Listen actively.** Make sure you understand what your conversational partners say by restating your understanding of any communication that seems important to them or that you *genuinely* don't quite get. Ask follow-up questions to clarify your understanding.

- ✔ **Don't make it all about you.** If you're networking at a cocktail party, concentrate on your conversation partner instead of yourself. Ask her how her day is going, how business is, and what her greatest challenges are.

- ✔ **Be a problem solver.** If the person mentions that he's struggling with a certain problem, recommend professionals you know who may be able to provide assistance.

- ✔ **Be open-minded.** If people stray into those forbidden topics of politics or religion, remain tolerant, open-minded, and able to see the flaws in your own thinking.

- ✔ **Don't sell.** Engage and inspire. If asked about yourself, be ready to say how you help people. Deliver your elevator pitch in a way that frames your services as a benefit to your conversation partner.

- ✔ **Ask for the person's business card.** Getting a person's contact information is essential for following up. If the person has no business card, ask for a phone number and e-mail address.

- ✔ **Close with an invitation.** Ask your conversation partner to take the next logical step with you — coffee, lunch, an e-mail follow-up, a complimentary consultation, or whatever you feel is suitable.

Focus more on giving than getting. Be of service and provide something of value in every interaction, including connections to people who can help your conversation partners achieve their goals; tips, tools, strategies, articles, and links; or invitations to upcoming events, workshops, or speaking engagements.

Thanking your referral sources

Whenever a prospective client contacts you, ask how the person heard about you. If someone's sending clients your way, you need to know who that someone is so you can show your appreciation (and, hopefully, so he continues his referrals). If you don't know the person, ask some follow-up questions to find out who the person is and to gather details to help you find him. Your conversation might go something like this:

So, how did you hear about me?

Jill Martin told me about you.

Really, Jill Martin? Hmmm, I'm not sure I know a Jill Martin. What does she do? (or Where does she work? or How do you know her?)

I don't know her very well either; my business partner told me that Jill Martin recommended you.

[If you feel too much like a private investigator trying to track down a murder suspect, preface your next inquiry with a statement of your intention.]

I'm in the habit of sending thank-you notes to referral sources. Would you mind telling me who your partner is?

Jane Kelly.

[If you don't know who Jane Kelly is, continue your interrogation.]

Initially, you'll tend to get referrals from friends and colleagues or former colleagues. Keep a list of referral sources and be sure to send a note of thanks to each one. (I prefer to send a handwritten note because it's much more personal than an e-mail.)

As your marketing activities expand, you'll tend to get referrals from people who read your blog, people on your mailing list, and people in organizations and companies to which you've spoken or whose networking or training events you've attended.

Branding may not lead to referrals

Some of the promotional work you do, such as blogging, publishing articles, and speaking at conferences, generates referrals because it's *branding* work — marketing activities that make you recognizable in your market.

When parties in dispute or their attorneys hire mediators, they often exchange lists of people they believe would do a good job. The parties take a look at their dispute partner's list and ask around for recommendations or criticism of any of the people whose names they don't recognize.

Rarely does a party say yes to an unknown mediator. Branding ensures that you're a known entity so that when your name is mentioned as a potential choice, people recognize it and presume that you're a well-established and trusted mediator.

When people tell you that they don't know how they know you or who recommended you but that they're aware you have a good reputation, you can ascribe that return-on-investment to your general, high-level, community-wide marketing materials.

Joining Mediation Associations, Formal and Informal

Fellow mediators are often a great source for referrals, as well as support and guidance, so I strongly encourage you to join one or more mediation associations and get involved, as I explain in the following sections.

Joining, participating, and leading

If you don't yet belong to a local mediation or dispute-resolution association, your first step is to find and join the largest and most active group of mediators in your area. Ask experienced mediators in your area for recommendations or search online for "mediation association" in the state or jurisdiction in which you work. The Southern California Mediation Association, for example, provides a wide array of opportunities for growing a practice, sharpening skills, keeping current with new laws and best practices, marketing services, engaging with peers, speaking, writing, and training.

Don't merely join and pay your dues. Attend the association's meetings, introduce yourself to its movers and shakers, and let people know that you're eager to serve. As soon as people know that you're willing to work, you'll have as many opportunities as you're willing and able to handle. One day you'll be picking up speakers for the annual conference at the airport, and the next day you'll be editor of the organization's newsletter. These extra duties demand your time and energy, but they pay dividends in raising your profile and building trust.

Only one thing is in short supply in all professional organizations — people willing to do the hard work of keeping the organization going and growing. Here's a short list of opportunities that are almost always available when you join a professional organization:

- ✔ Participate in and eventually lead organizational sections such as community mediation, litigated case mediation, professional development, annual conference planning, newsletter publication, speaker's bureau, website management, and on and on.

- ✔ Create an organizational section that meets your own needs as well as your market's. If you're engaged in parental custody mediation, for instance, and your local mediation organization doesn't have a section devoted to that topic, create and lead it yourself.

- ✔ Write articles for the organization's newsletter.

✔ Serve as a liaison to organizations where your market gathers, such as bar associations, the church community, organized youth sports, animal lover organizations, and the like. If your local organization doesn't have liaison positions, create them yourself.

✔ Begin marketing yourself by speaking on topics important to your market niche either at monthly section meetings or at the organization's annual meeting.

✔ Run for office. Most organizations have several officers — including president, vice president, secretary, and treasurer — and few candidates to serve in those positions.

✔ Form study groups for new mediators.

✔ Offer seminars about dispute resolution, negotiation, or peace work under the auspices of your local mediation organization to legal groups, local business leaders, and community organizations.

Getting involved in a trusted professional organization is a great way to lend credibility to your own platform as you promote your services. Offering seminars to the community under the auspices of an established mediation association is much more effective in garnering interest than merely promoting the seminars under your own name. Serve a professional organization and it'll serve you.

Engaging in networking activities

Whether or not you belong to a mediation organization, you need to make a literal or figurative appearance in your marketplace at least twice a month — one online promotional activity every month along with either a speech, an organizational meeting, an article, or a personal meeting (lunch or coffee with someone in your market who can send you business, for instance).

If you're having trouble coming up with ideas for networking activities, consider the following suggestions:

✔ Participate in at least one activity every month for one of the organizations you belong to, even if it's only attending a cocktail party, committee meeting, or training session.

✔ When you attend a networking event, introduce yourself and converse with at least one fellow attendee with the goal of finding out as much as you possibly can about the person. See Chapter 17 for guidance on how to network productively.

✔ Take as many mediation classes that interest you as you can afford to in respect to both time and budget.

✔ Volunteer your time as a mediator in a local court-annexed or community mediation panel.

✔ Talk passionately about mediation whenever someone asks you about it.

✔ Write an article about mediation for a journal your market reads, addressing an issue of concern to your market.

✔ Ask a seasoned mediator if you can observe her in action or ask for tips on commencing a mediation practice.

✔ Speak about mediation and negotiation skills to a business, law firm, or community group for free.

✔ Attend a business, law, community, or mediation conference or workshop.

✔ Take someone in your market to lunch or coffee.

Pace yourself. You don't want to burn yourself out. Two activities per month are two more than most mediators in your market are doing.

Getting the Most out of Mediation Conferences

Mediation conferences are a great place to mingle with colleagues, expand your network, and generate business. These conferences generally have one or two well-known keynote speakers and numerous break-out sessions where you can learn additional techniques and skills and find out more about hot topics in your field. Attending these sessions can help you hone your skills and connect you to people you want to know.

Hang out in the exhibitor hall, where the people who sell their products and services hang out. My ROI (return on investment) in exhibitor hall networking has been so high that I now do almost nothing but hang out there during conferences where my market gathers. You'd be surprised how many people are bored and looking for someone to talk to and how easy it is to make new friends in an amazingly short period.

Exhibitors *want* to talk to you, so if you're shy about networking, this is the best place to practice. They'll always greet you with a smile because they want to sell you something.

As you chat amiably with the exhibitors, other conference attendees will join you. These people are often prospective clients. If you specialize in mediation for litigated cases, for instance, and you're attending a bar association convention, you'll meet many potential clients hanging out in the exhibitor hall.

After exchanging small talk, you can ask your conversation partner what she does, even if you already have a pretty good idea based on the conference focus. If the person is a lawyer, for instance, you can ask about her practice and introduce yourself as a mediator. If you don't specialize in her area, let her know that you're able to recommend other mediators who practice in her field. Ask for her business card and follow up, providing her with a list of recommended mediators.

If you're fortunate to be chatting with someone who's in the heart of your own market, you'll have plenty of subjects to discuss in your area of shared interest. Ask your new acquaintance who he uses when he needs a mediator and how satisfied he is with the mediation services. You need not hard sell your own services. You can, however, empathize when he shares stories of mediations gone bad and provide your insight about better or best practices. Get his business card and follow up, providing him with your résumé and any information you have that may be of interest to your new potential client.

Speaking with and Training Fellow Mediators

As soon as you have an opportunity to speak publicly about mediation you should do so. Speaking and training others to mediate makes you a mediator's mediator. Not only do speaking and training engagements lend you credibility and authority (and thus, probably score you some future mediation opportunities) but you also learn much more by teaching and training than you learn by being taught or trained.

Here are a few good places where it's easy to start:

✔ Mediation conferences

✔ Trade association conferences for businesses in your niche

✔ Church and other community groups, if you're marketing yourself as a community mediator

✔ Youth groups and parent teacher organizations, if you're specializing in parent-child, family, or custody disputes

✔ Law firms, if you're mediating litigated cases

✔ Bar conferences such as local, state, and national bar associations, particularly those that concentrate on your specialty, such as family law, personal injury, or commercial disputes

✔ Affinity groups, if you're specializing in family or employment disputes

If you're already a seasoned public speaker, you have all you need to get started. Otherwise, try to get some training and experience before taking the stage. You can join a group like Toastmasters International to get training, experience, and more networking opportunities. You may also want to check out *Public Speaking For Dummies* by Malcolm Kushner (published by Wiley).

Part V
The Part of Tens

The 5th Wave   By Rich Tennant

"Or, we could just agree to disagree."

In this part . . .

Want a quick rundown of the top do's and don'ts for your mediation practice? What about an expert's checklist for how to break through impasse? Welcome to the Part of Tens. This particular part reveals ten practices of the super mediator, ten big mediation no-no's, and ten tips for impasse-busting.

Whether you're just starting out or you've guided folks through hundreds of mediations, your mediation practice will soar if you incorporate the concise, important advice in these three chapters.

Chapter 18

Ten Practices of the Super Mediator

*Y*ou're not content with just being a mediator. You're determined to excel in the field and become a super mediator. In this chapter, I present ten tips that'll take you from average to excellent.

Exhibit Faith in Your Mediation Model

No matter what mediation theory or practice you follow — transformative, facilitative, evaluative, faith-based, directive, separate caucus, joint session, or a medley of several of them depending on the circumstances — exhibit faith in the chosen process. (See Chapter 6 for info on different mediation styles.)

Active disputes make people fearful, defensive, self-concerned, and tone-deaf to the other party's suffering. To brainstorm solutions, reframe issues, and replace demonization with trust, the parties need to feel that you're the secure center of the process and be certain of your ability to guide them through these perilous waters.

I once rafted Class V rapids through the Costa Rica rain forest in the driving rain. We amateurs could smell the fear on our river guide as we prepared to meet the day's challenge. When he finally sat before us, our guide became the calm center of the storm. "Keep your oar in the water," he said, "and paddle through your fear."

One of our rafts flipped that day because one rafter pulled his oar out of the water and froze in fear. That single act unbalanced the raft and caused it to flip. One person very nearly drowned.

Think of the conference table around which the parties sit as a raft in treacherous waters. Your job is to be steady and trust in your own competence to get the parties safely to the end of the river. You must keep your own rational, safe, and hopeful oar in the water while assuring the parties that if they do the same, you'll all emerge intact and possibly happily exhilarated.

Be Confident and Persistent

Even if you have little experience, as a trained mediator and negotiator, you know more than the parties do about the best way to settle their dispute. You're the expert, and you must act like one. And if you're not completely confident, then *fake it till you make it.*

Turn inexperience into strength. Experienced mediators err on believing they know just what to do. Inexperienced mediators don't know what doesn't work, so they try anything, and often it's anything rather than a single thing that works.

Just remember that saving face isn't always possible while you're doing your job. If you make a fool of yourself, that's okay. The parties will give you multiple opportunities to fail if you continue to radiate hope that they'll succeed. If you want to be a super mediator, doing your job well must trump fear, embarrassment, and the desire not to look foolish.

Remain Humble

A great mediator is humble. She knows she plays a key role as an intermediary, but she also knows that the outcome, to a great extent, is out of her hands. If you start to feel despair, repeat this Zen mantra to yourself:

I can't take credit for the victories or blame for the defeats.

You enter the parties' conflict at a particular point in time. It's a timeout from the naming, blaming, shaming, claiming contest in which gray has been turned into black and white and blurry lines sharpened into hard boundaries.

You hold the space in which the parties can, for the first time, let down their guard a little and acknowledge the weaknesses in their opinions or positions. They may even admit that they've omitted facts that undermine their position. If you're persistent in your pursuit of a peaceful resolution, you give the parties the greatest opportunity to acknowledge the humanity of the opponent they've demonized as well as the touch of malice within themselves.

Feel the Parties' Pain

Think for a moment about how desperately you want to disengage from any argument you have with a loved one. You do so by going silent, slamming doors, or intimidating your partner with wild accusations. You go to your room or leave the house for a while — anything to get a little relief.

Think about that discomfort every time you mediate a case. I want you to be aware of the pain the disputants are suffering so that you're hyper-alert to their desire to give up, give in, or begin to shout. I want you to acknowledge their courage.

Whenever you feel hope fly out the window and safety begin to crumble, suggest a separate caucus where the parties can vent their feelings of frustration without damaging the chances that the dispute can be resolved. Listen actively to their complaints and help them reframe rage, fear, or grief in a way that makes it possible for them to address the issues without acting them out. See the next section for more about active listening.

Listen Actively; Respond Reflectively

People with a long-brewing dispute don't simply want to tell their side of the story. They want to know that the other party has heard it. You know you need to do more active listening if you hear any of the following complaints:

- ✔ She's not listening to me.

- ✔ I've explained that 100 times, and no matter what I say, he has a comeback that disparages and dismisses all my concerns.

- ✔ You're buying her story without having seen any evidence to support it. I feel as if you've discounted everything I've said and credited everything she's said.

- ✔ You're not working hard enough for me/you're not stating my case clearly enough/you're not helping me achieve my goal.

Don't get defensive when a party tells you why the mediation's not working for him, especially if that reason is *you.* Employ active listening, like this:

- ✔ I hear you saying that she's not hearing you. What in particular are you trying to communicate that she doesn't appear to understand?

✔ The one thing you've explained 100 times to him is what again? I know his resistance to hearing is frustrating. Do you think together we can find a way to communicate it in a way he's able to hear it? No? I think we can. Let's do a little brainstorming before we go back into joint session.

✔ I hear you saying that I believe her story and that I'm ignoring yours. I apologize for that. Tell me again what it is she's saying that I'm buying into, and then let's talk about a strategy for better communication among all three of us.

Never waste an opportunity to increase or correct communication. You won't screw this up as long as you're willing to be accountable for your own human inability to meet the parties' needs and to work with them to get the job done better.

Ask for Feedback and Use It to Improve

You won't improve your performance in any task that requires feedback unless you ask for it from your clients *and* from your mentors. All the research on mediation processes and outcomes confirms this.

When talking to your mentors, don't sugarcoat your performance. Focus on what you believe you may have done that caused the negotiation to break down or that left one of the parties visibly frustrated or angry. You'll be tempted to paint your performance in the most favorable light, but you won't get any better if you're not rigorously honest with yourself and your advisors.

Whatever you think about the disputants' behavior, your place is not to judge. It is to help. Remember, *you* don't resolve the dispute. The parties resolve it with your assistance. When you stop taking credit or blame, you'll likely achieve master mediator status.

To know how you're doing, you must call the parties several days after every mediation to ask them what they think went well and what they think went poorly. Tell them that you're attempting to improve your own practice. Don't discourage them from telling you what you did right (you need to know this too), but you're most interested in what they believe you could have done better.

As a side benefit, your phone call gives you a second opportunity to show your clients that you're a professional with integrity. They're usually impressed with that. They don't expect perfection, but they do expect and respect effort.

Be Respectful and Predictable

Do what you say you'll do. If you assure the parties that you won't reveal their confidences, don't risk disclosure in any communications with anyone else except your mentors, and then disguise both the story and the parties. If you ask the parties to bind themselves to certain rules of behavior, follow those rules yourself. If you make an agenda, stick to it, and if you deviate from it, explain why. If you tell one side that you'll be gone for only ten minutes, return ten minutes later, even if it's only to tell the party that you'll be away longer than you anticipated.

Adjust to the Parties' Preferences, Hopes, and Characteristics

Adjusting to the parties' preferences, hopes, and characteristics doesn't mean that you should pander or be inauthentic. Rather, you want to take seriously what the parties believe is serious, align yourself with their deepest hopes, and make enough of an effort to understand the culture in which the dispute arose so you can speak their language.

For example, I live in a cosmopolitan city teeming with immigrants from widely diverse cultures. When I'm conducting a mediation, I've learned not to extend my hand to a man who appears to be an Orthodox Jew. I don't make an assumption, but I raise the issue by saying, "I'd shake your hand but I sense that you may live in a culture in which it's inappropriate for a man to touch a woman who is not his wife."

When I'm wrong, laughter and appreciation follow. When I'm right, I receive gratitude and appreciation in return. I've begun the mediation respectful of cultural customs that aren't my own. I've adjusted my behavior to the other party's beliefs out of respect. The party returns my respect, and the trust necessary to conduct a successful mediation begins to build.

Expect and Elicit the Best in People

To be a great mediator, you must find something unique, valuable, and even lovable in every client you serve. If you expect people to be sly and duplicitous, they'll reward you by exhibiting those characteristics. If you expect them to be honest, speak frankly, and work hard on the task before them, they'll reward you by exhibiting those attitudes and behaving in that manner.

Nobody can give you step-by-step instructions on how to be yourself, give up pretense, accept your own fallibility, and humbly approach every task as both a great challenge and a problem that you're certain is resolvable. Nor can anyone teach you how to listen for the cry for help under every accusation or how to find the pain seeking relief inside the most bitter contest. I can, however, provide a few suggestions on how to get to that centered place inside yourself:

- ✔ **Meditation:** Imagine a place where others can freely come and go without threatening your sense of identity or disrupting your sense of well-being.

- ✔ **Prayer:** Some people center themselves through prayer, relinquishing control and judgment to a higher power and asking for the grace to become more sensitive to the needs of others.

- ✔ **Commitment:** I make an effort to empty myself of judgment by making a fresh commitment before every mediation to treat each person as the most valuable, irreplaceable, and honorable human being on the planet. I vow to hold my judgments, to stay curious, and to continue seeking the truth of each person's subjective experience no matter how many layers of defense the person has built around it.

I also forgive myself my failures each time I blunder. I acknowledge those missteps aloud and let the parties know that I'm going to try again. In this sense, mediation is as much spiritual practice and discipline as it is knowledge, strategy, tactics, and technique.

Develop an Attitude of Ubuntu

Mediators are models of Ubuntu. Archbishop Desmond Tutu described *Ubuntu* as the ability to be open, available, and affirming of others. A person with Ubuntu doesn't feel threatened when others are good and doesn't judge when he perceives others to be bad. He believes that whatever diminishes another also diminishes him. Those who possess the qualities of Ubuntu are naturally generous because they feel themselves to be a part of the whole, so that in giving to others, they also give to themselves.

Chapter 19

Ten Major Mediating Mistakes and How to Avoid Them

In This Chapter

▶ Remaining calm, nonjudgmental, and positive

▶ Respecting the parties and focusing on justice issues

▶ Maintaining confidentiality

*I*n the heat of battle, keeping your cool and doing everything right is often very challenging. You're going to make mistakes — everyone does. Hopefully, however, you can learn from other people's mistakes instead of repeating them. That's what this chapter is all about. Here I point out ten of the worst mistakes you can possibly make as a mediator so that you're less likely to step on these mines yourself.

Arguing and Judging

The worst trap any mediator can fall into is making a judgment about the truth or falsity of either party's recitation of the facts or about the bona fides of either party's legal position. This is particularly true of litigated disputes. Arguing with an attorney is like raising your voice to communicate with someone who's deaf. No matter how hard you try, you're never on the same channel, particularly because the attorney always knows far more about the facts and laws of his own case than you do.

Rather than drawing judgments or arguing, be curious about how the parties are going to prove their facts to a judge or jury or how they expect their negotiating partner to adopt their version of the facts or share their opinions. The parties are often more able than you are to identify the holes in their own narratives and the weaknesses of their own opinions or positions. After they do so, you can brainstorm ways to communicate something the parties don't want to hear in a way they can understand it.

Delaying the Opening Offer

Some mediators spend so much time talking with the parties about their opinions and positions that they don't leave enough time to start and complete the negotiation "dance." The purpose of a distributive negotiation — to distribute the deal's value between the parties — is to help the parties believe that they received the best deal possible.

Research has demonstrated that party satisfaction with a negotiated resolution depends more on the number of concessions the other party makes than on the resolution reached. This is partially due to the parties' need to reevaluate their positions, grieve their losses, and find a way to save face. The exchange of concessions also helps people feel that they worked as hard as possible to get as good a deal for themselves as may reasonably be available. Parties also need assurances that their negotiating partner gave up as much or more than they did to restore their injured pride or serve their justice issues.

Wallowing in Pessimism

The mediator's job is to remain hopeful and encouraging throughout the mediation. The parties need you to be a coach and a cheerleader to help them move through the negotiation without giving in to the hopelessness that brought them to your door. You also help them not to demonize their bargaining partner; rarely is one party completely evil and the other completely good.

Remain upbeat, hopeful, and respectful of both parties. Reframe as much of the dispute as possible as arising from miscommunication or carelessness rather than sinister intent and purposefully harmful activity.

Sidelining the Parties

Mediators who are judges and lawyers aren't often used to dealing with the emotions raised by people in conflict. The process of litigation and trial is designed to take as much emotion out of the dispute as possible. The rules of evidence permit a party to exclude information that may cause jury members to become emotionally involved in the matter they're being asked to decide. The parties in court proceedings don't talk to each other and often don't even look at each other. They address the judge or the jury, and their behavior is constrained by rules of the court that keep emotion out of the proceedings.

When lawyers and judges first start mediating, they're often far more comfortable pulling the lawyers away from their clients and conducting all the negotiating outside the disputants' presence. This approach not only leads the parties to feel that their justice issues were never addressed but also doesn't make available to the mediator all the interests that are driving the dispute or creating impasse.

Ignoring the Justice Issues

Fifty million years ago, the human species separated from the species that gave rise to both modern-day humans and today's capuchin monkeys. When Yale scientists created a "monkey economy" to study the way primates think, they found that the capuchin refused to work if it observed a nonworking monkey nearby getting five times the "pay" (in cucumbers and grapes). The monkeys would scream, jump up and down in their cages, throw all their food back at their captors, and go hungry rather than work under such unjust conditions.

That's how deep the desire for justice is in the human species — 50 million years deep. People don't bring lawsuits or stop speaking to their siblings for 20 years over money. They bring lawsuits and stop speaking to their relatives because they've experienced an injustice. Whether they're right or wrong about their rights and obligations under the legal system, they *feel* as though they've been *screwed*. And no amount of money will restore their need for fairness unless the money itself speaks justice or the disputants' justice issues are aired, respected, addressed, and resolved. Remember the capuchin and never ignore justice issues.

Bargaining in the Nano- and Stratospheres

When the parties make ridiculously high demands or miniscule offers, the conflict between them escalates and creates an even greater degree of bitterness and distrust than already existed. The parties and their attorneys have many reasons for bargaining in the nano- and stratospheres. The case won't likely settle in either of those ranges, thereby protecting all parties from making a negotiation error. In other cases, the parties want to express their anger by making offers or demands that they know are insulting.

You can soften insulting offers or demands by explaining, before bargaining begins, the negotiation process and the emotions so often expressed in monetary terms. You can also probe the parties for the idiosyncratic reasons that they're stuck on outside of a reasonable bargaining range, helping them to understand that not much will be accomplished until both sides enter the range of reason. This is often the point at which suggesting a bracket is useful. For more about bracketing, see Chapter 13.

Cutting the Baby in Half

I've heard more than one party to a dispute say, "Any moron can subtract $X from $Y and divide that number in half. I need a principled reason to settle, not an arbitrary one." That pretty well sums up the entire reason the parties resist settling their dispute by dividing the delta between them. This is also why the parties often refuse to make a concession, even when they agree to settle on the suggested number; they're afraid they're moving into territory where the mediator will suggest that the parties split the baby.

Assure the parties that you're no baby splitter and that the parties' ability to move closer to each other won't lead you to suggest that at some point the parties simply split the difference (although they often will).

Telling the Parties That Their Concerns Aren't Relevant to the Resolution

Nothing a party to a dispute says is irrelevant to its settlement. If a disputant says the moon is made of green cheese, he's trying to express a feeling or state a fact that stands in the way of his reaching resolution. When lawyers and judges become mediators, they often tell the parties that their concerns are irrelevant because the law doesn't consider them pertinent to the legal resolution of a legal claim. But mediation is outside the legal process. You're involved in a negotiation where the law, while informative, doesn't restrict the resolution options available to the parties.

If Party A wants to tell you about his experience being abducted by aliens, listen for the cry for help contained in that narrative and explore that experience in all its dimensions until you find what it is he's trying to say.

Failing to Master Your Own Emotional Responses to Conflict

People don't want to sit across a conference table from someone they consider their nemesis, because doing so opens them to the possibility of being shamed — the most powerful constellation of emotions known to humankind. In the midst of all the emotion — anger, fear, shame, and even rage — one person is required to hold the center, maintain a calm demeanor, and help the parties withstand the powerful emotional responses they feel and are subjected to from the other party. That person, of course, is you.

Many mediators meditate or simply make sure they get plenty of sleep and lots of exercise so that they don't get swept up in the parties' strong emotions the way one might get physically carried away by a crowd of people in a public square. The best way to master your own emotional responses to conflict is to be mindful, nonjudgmental, curious, and compassionate.

Breaching Confidentiality with a Wink and a Nod

The parties, who don't care a bit about your obligation to maintain confidentiality, will do everything in their power to wring confidential information out of you. Often the questions seem innocent enough:

- ✔ Is that really his bottom line or is he just posturing?
- ✔ What's the mood in the other room?
- ✔ Is this an issue that's genuinely important to her or do you believe she'd drop it if I can pay her $X within Y amount of time?
- ✔ Who's the strongest party in the other room?
- ✔ Is that his attorney talking or does the party also feel that way?
- ✔ Do you think she'd accept $X if we put it on the table?
- ✔ Does he really want to spend two weeks with the children this summer or is he just angry at me?
- ✔ Does she genuinely want an apology or is this just a ploy to get us in the same room together so she can vent?
- ✔ If you make a mediator's proposal of $Y, do you believe he'll accept it?
- ✔ Has she shown you any evidence to support her claim?

Don't fall for these traps. Even if you're conducting the mediation in separate caucuses, the parties do talk to each other, and if you breach confidentiality, one party may disclose your breach to the other while they're in court together a few weeks hence. That's the punishment angle to convince you to maintain confidentiality. There's also the ethical angle that every mediator must observe confidentiality or the profession itself will be weakened as being corrupt. You've pledged to maintain confidentiality and promised it to the parties to encourage them to be more open about their negotiation strategy than they would otherwise be. If you betray them, you betray yourself and your profession. For everyone's sake, please don't do it.

Chapter 20

Ten Tips for Busting Impasse

*U*ltimately, mediation is an exercise in breaking through *impasse* — a period during which the parties have lost hope that they can resolve the matter on that day and in that place. Impasse isn't the end of negotiation; it's actually the beginning of the end, the starting point for the negotiation process. Your job is to keep the parties at the table and get them to start talking again. This chapter offers ten tips to accomplish this goal.

Harnessing the Power of Bracketing

Bracketing allows the parties to test the waters without dropping an anchor there. Without asking the parties to reveal their bottom lines, ask each party the question, "If your opponent came down to $X, would you come up to $Y?" Bracketing enables the parties to play with hypothetical numbers in order to narrow the distance separating their positions without having to make a concession. Narrowing the gap with hypothetical offers and counteroffers allows the parties greater room to maneuver and also permits them to save face if their "last and final" offer or counteroffer is just another bargaining position.

Although bracketing, per se, applies only to disputes over money, you can use the concept of hypothetical offers and counteroffers to similar beneficial effect when the parties are fighting over something less material, like a barking dog in one apartment and noise from hardwood floors in the other. A hypothetical proposal in that situation would go something like this: "If Mr. Dog Owner is able to ensure the dog's silence after 10 p.m. and before 7 a.m., would you be willing to take off your own shoes and ask guests to take theirs off during the same hours?"

Using or Avoiding Mediator's Proposals

Mediators are often called upon to act as judge and jury by presenting a *mediator's proposal* — an objective, third-party opinion of what would be a fair solution or what the mediator believes each party would accept, however reluctantly. A mediator's proposal is often useful in the following scenarios:

- ✔ The parties insist on a mediator's proposal.

- ✔ A party needs to answer to a hidden stakeholder and is more inclined to agree to a deal if he can explain that the mediator made a final proposal that he couldn't, in good faith, refuse.

- ✔ A party needs an authority figure to all but order him to compromise.

Try bracketing first. If that doesn't work, then draft your proposal without showing it to either party. Meet with each party in separate caucus to try to gauge how well the parties will receive your proposal. You can then tweak it, if necessary, to make it more acceptable before presenting it to the parties. I personally don't make mediator's proposals without already knowing that the parties will accept them.

Making the Agreement Contingent upon Future Conditions

Making an agreement contingent upon future conditions is often useful if impasse is due to one of the following:

- ✔ A party exaggerates the future value or cost of something to gain an advantage in negotiation.

- ✔ One party believes the future will be more profitable than the other party believes it will be and wants to use the higher projection to calculate the settlement.

With a contingent agreement, you can call a party's bluff. For example, if a party demands an unreasonably high price for her half of the business based on an inflated estimate of future profits, you can ask whether the party is willing to accept far less for, say, 10 percent of the future profits over the next five years. If the party knows her estimate of future profits is high, she may back down into reasonable territory when you call her bluff.

✔ One party doesn't trust the other to honor the agreement, such as making payments over time. In this circumstance, you can suggest that the parties build in consequences for failures to pay.

✔ A party is afraid that a future event or condition may turn what seems to be a good agreement into a bad deal. In this circumstance, you can suggest that the parties make the effectiveness of their agreement contingent upon the future event or condition.

You can use a contingent agreement to remove the reason a party declines a solution. For example, if one party doesn't trust the other party to make scheduled payments, you can include in the agreement that in the event of a missed payment, the total amount is due immediately.

Drafting a High-Low Agreement

A *high-low agreement* is a form of settlement agreement in which the case continues toward traditional resolution through trial or arbitration but the parties agree that, whatever the outcome of the proceedings, the plaintiff will recover at least $X and the defendant will pay no more than $Y. Under this arrangement, the plaintiff is certain to recover at least the number at the low end of the range, and the defendant caps his losses at a number he can deal with. A high-low agreement makes sense when the plaintiff, the defendant, or both need to avoid an extreme verdict. Some situations where this approach may be useful include:

✔ The defendant is simply not comfortable with the runaway downside risk the case presents.

✔ The defendant needs to cap his liability to satisfy some of his stakeholders (such as insurers, lenders, or the CFO).

✔ The plaintiff in a case with significant damages faces a real possibility of a defense verdict and needs to cover some expenses, such as medical costs.

✔ The plaintiff needs some money in the short term and agrees to limit his potential recovery in exchange for an agreed-upon "low" where the low is paid immediately.

✔ The plaintiff or his lawyer needs to ensure that litigation costs are covered.

✔ The defendant needs to settle within the limits of his insurance policy to protect his assets, but his carrier would rather take the lawsuit to trial.

✔ Either party wants to narrow the dispute as a first step toward settlement.

Engaging in Baseball Arbitration

In *baseball arbitration,* each party submits a proposed settlement that she deems is fair, and the parties agree in advance that they'll abide by whichever proposal the mediator chooses. Then, the mediator does one of the following:

- ✔ Chooses the proposal she thinks is fairest.

- ✔ Without looking at the parties' proposals, presents her own proposal and then chooses the party's proposal that's closest to hers. (This is sometimes referred to as *nighttime baseball arbitration.*)

Baseball arbitration, often referred to as *either/or arbitration,* avoids the problem of merely splitting the baby and encourages the parties to submit what they sincerely believe is a fair resolution. Major league baseball has used this type of arbitration for several years to resolve contract disputes between owners and players.

Calming Future Fears with Stipulated Judgments and Hammer Clauses

A party who doesn't trust the other party to follow through on the mediated agreement is often reluctant to sign off on it. In situations like these, a stipulated judgment with a hammer clause may provide the assurance the person needs to commit to the deal:

- ✔ **Stipulated judgment:** A stipulated judgment is based on the parties' agreement that a judgment can be entered against the defendant if he fails to deliver on his end of the deal. In other words, if the defendant defaults, all the plaintiff has to do is prove nonpayment. He doesn't have to haggle in court over the amount because the party in default has already agreed to the entry of judgment. A judgment is enforceable by means such as the garnishment of wages, judgment liens on real property, writs of attachment against bank accounts, and the like.

- ✔ **Hammer clause:** A hammer clause applies a penalty for default. For example, if a party fails to deliver on a promise to pay a certain sum of money over a specified period, he must pay a certain amount more than the agreed-upon total settlement amount.

Stipulated judgments and hammer clauses motivate parties to honor their agreement and provide each party with the assurance that the other party will deliver on his promises.

Transforming a Dispute into a Business Opportunity

Parties in dispute often have more than just money to bargain with. They have opportunities, skills, connections, possessions, and other assets. During a mediation, get to know the parties personally and professionally and encourage them to get to know each other better. Engage them in small talk to identify their needs and everything of value they can bring to the table. Then look for ways to match the assets of one party with the needs of the other. In doing so, you're likely to find numerous trade and business opportunities. Generating such options can melt impasse over hard, bottom-line, dollar and legal-position conflicts and transform a distributive negotiation session ("what I lose, you win, and what you lose, I win") into a business opportunity that leaves both parties better off than they'd be if they were to win at trial.

The most efficient deals are those in which the parties trade an item that's of low cost to one party but of high value to the other — a technique called *logrolling*. Party A may have a better distribution network but a less reliable product than Party B. Party A could profitably trade access to its distribution network (low cost to Party A but high value to Party B) for the technological information required to make its product more reliable (low cost to Party B but high value to Party A).

Making Money Talk

Dollar values that appear to be objective carry subjective meanings that are useful in helping the parties understand each other's position. When you ask the parties what they intend to do with the money or why paying it is so painful, you identify practical and emotional reasons that the parties have reached impasse. Some people see a money payout as an apology or a way to exact revenge. Others have specific uses for the money, such as getting job training and education, buying something they've always wanted but could never afford, or providing security for the future. Knowing that the plaintiff's monetary demand has a rational basis can often break impasse, as can suggestions to achieve the same goal with nonmonetary means.

Resolving Justice Issues

Beneath every monetary demand for a perceived wrong is a *justice issue* — a reason why the party believes she has been treated unfairly. A dispute is rarely just about the money. In fact, if you don't help the parties identify the underlying justice issues, no amount of money may be able to resolve the dispute.

Ask the parties about the unfairness they believe they've suffered. The plaintiff usually identifies the act leading to her injury or damage as the unfair treatment she has been subjected to. The defendant usually identifies the claim or lawsuit itself as the injustice she's suffered. When the parties are able to acknowledge each other's grievances as being made in good faith, that communication alone often breaks impasse when no sum of money could.

Lawyers and their clients often fail to realize that they're working in the justice system, not the financial reward system. Sometimes, the parties haven't yet identified these justice issues even to themselves. Often, the parties know what justice issues they're attempting to serve but have never discussed them with their attorneys. The parties' own lawyers often believe that their clients are in it just for the money, which is rarely true.

Strategically Using Apologies

Many disputes can be resolved with a sincere apology. If you feel that one party is stuck because he really needs and probably deserves an apology from the other party, consider raising the issue in separate caucus and coaching the party who needs to apologize on how to apologize effectively. A sincere apology requires the following:

✔ **Acknowledgement of accountability:** "I am responsible for my actions."

If an apology doesn't come with an acknowledgement of accountability, don't encourage it. Some attorneys forbid their clients from acknowledging accountability. These attorneys fear that any acknowledgement of civil wrongdoing may come back to bite them in court or some other civil proceeding, even though confidentiality provisions and laws would prohibit the disclosure of such an admission.

✔ **Acknowledgement of the harm caused:** "I am also responsible for the loss you suffered as a result."

Apologies that don't acknowledge responsibility for harm done are of little use. They're often insincere and made for the sole purpose of getting one's opponent to accept less or pay more than he wants to.

✔ **Offer of redress:** "I can offer to do the following things or pay you $X to partially compensate for your loss."

✔ **Offer of reconciliation:** "I hope that this can restore good relations between us or at least allow us to set aside our resentment or bitterness."

Don't try to coerce an apology. Offering or demanding an apology as a concession almost always makes it seem insincere and inauthentic, wasting the opportunity to use the apology as a means of breaking impasse.

Index